LARRIKINS

A HISTORY

MELISSA BELLANTA

UQP

First published 2012 by University of Queensland Press
PO Box 6042, St Lucia, Queensland 4067 Australia

www.uqp.com.au
uqp@uqp.uq.edu.au

Typeset in 12/16 pt Bembo by Post Pre-press Group, Brisbane
Printed in Australia by McPherson's Printing Group

Cataloguing-in-Publication entry is available from the National Library of Australia
http://catalogue.nla.gov.au

Larrikins : a history / by Melissa Bellanta.

ISBN (pbk) 9780702239120
ISBN (PDF) 9780702247743
ISBN (ePub) 9780702247750
ISBN (Kindle) 9780702247767

Youth – Australia – History.
Youth – Australia – Social life and customs.
Subculture – Australia – 19th century – History.
Subculture – Australia – 20th century – History.

305.2350994

Cover image credits: Mug shot of Frank McGowan, Robert McFarlane and John
Dennis McFarlane, 23 May 1921, Central Police Station, Sydney, photographer
unknown, New South Wales Police Forensic Photography Archive, Justice & Police
Museum, Historic Houses Trust DES_COS102

University of Queensland Press uses papers that are natural, renewable and recyclable
products made from wood grown in sustainable forests. The logging and manufacturing
processes conform to the environmental regulations of the country of origin.

Melissa Bellanta is a Brisbane-based historian who writes about popular theatre, masculinity, and class. Her work has been published in journals such as *Australasian Drama Studies*, *Australian Historical Studies*, *Labour History*, and the *Journal of Social History*. She currently has an ARC postdoctoral fellowship and teaches history at the University of Queensland.

CONTENTS

LIST OF ILLUSTRATIONS

Figure 1. *Melbourne's 'larrikin belt', Whitehead's Map of Melbourne and Suburbs 1893*

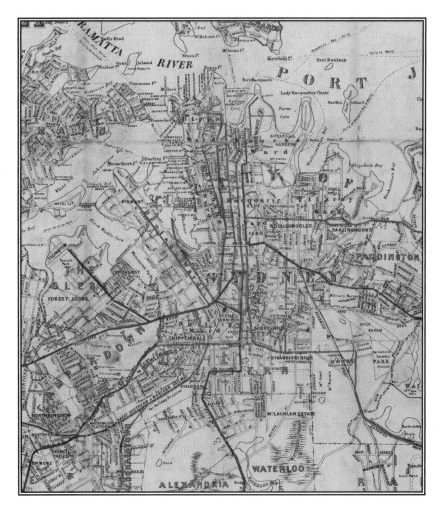

Figure 2. *Sydney's 'larrikin belt', Sands' Directory of Sydney 1887*
City of Sydney Archives

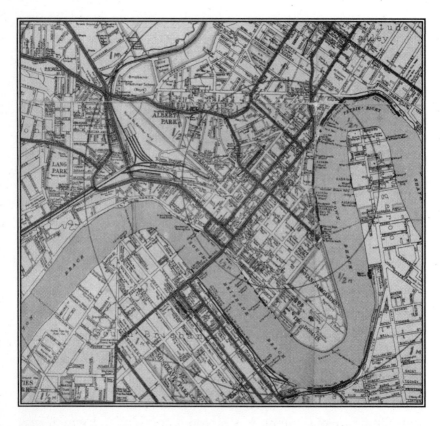

Figure 3. *Brisbane's 'larrikin belt', Map of Brisbane and surrounding suburbs, 1924*

Introduction

The true blue Aussie larrikin

When Steve ('the Crocodile Hunter') Irwin died in September 2006, pierced by the poisonous barb of a stingray at Port Douglas, the valedictions came as thick and fast as a northern Australian monsoon. Among the deluge of sorrowful comments and obituaries, one phrase was repeated continually. Irwin, it was said, was a 'true blue Aussie larrikin'.

In May 2006, a few months before Irwin's sudden demise, two miners at Beaconsfield, Tasmania, were described in the same way. They had been trapped underground for 14 nail-biting days after their mine collapsed. During this period and in the glowing weeks after their rescue, Brant Webb and Todd Russell were praised for their ability to joke in the face of adversity. The moment they had emerged above ground the pair had mugged for the waiting scrum of cameras, pretending to log off their shift for the day. It was that 'laconic Australian style' that summed up what was great about the country, the then prime minister John Howard said. One of Webb's friends also lauded his humour over celebratory drinks that night. Brant Webb was 'a true blue full-blown Aussie larrikin', he told journalists. He was a born joker, always 'cracking up' his mates.[1]

For a little less than a century now, larrikinism has played a key role in myths about what it means to be Australian. Few immigrants or visitors to the country arrive having heard the word. When they do, they are made to understand that it unlocks the secret to Australian national identity. It is because of their 'larrikin streak' that Australians refuse to stand on ceremony, they are told. To be a larrikin is to be sceptical and irreverent, to knock authority and mock pomposity, engaging in a practice known as 'taking the mickey' – or more often, 'taking the piss'. To call someone a larrikin is also to excuse their bad behaviour, offering an affectionate slant on their disrespect for social niceties and raucous drunkenness with mates. Often, too, it is a reference to someone's ockerness: the broadness of their Australian accent and facility with crude slang.

If the titles of numerous recent biographies are anything to go by, knowing what 'larrikin' means now operates as a sign of initiation into Australian ways, like passing a citizenship test. How else to make sense of recent works such as *Larrikin Angel, The Literary Larrikin* and *Larrikin and Saint* – quite apart from older titles such as *Memoirs of a Larrikin, Confessions of a Larrikin, Larrikin Days* and *Larrikin Crook*? What, too, about the prime ministers hailed as larrikins: Bob Hawke, with his cockatoo-like coif and beer-swilling record, and 'Jolly John' Gorton before him? Back in 1971, not long before he sacked himself, Gorton was described as a larrikin by an American journalist who was unfamiliar with the affectionate nuances of the term. 'John Grey Gorton is what Australia calls a larrikin', this journalist wrote in *Time* that March, 'a rough-hewn fellow who often embarrasses his colleagues'.[2]

In mid-2009 the decidedly unlarrikin-like Labor prime minister, Kevin Rudd, tried to ape the rascal blokiness that Hawke and Gorton had once exuded so effortlessly. 'Fair shake of the sauce bottle, mate', he said in an interview on women's under-representation in the ALP. Rudd was lambasted by supporters and adversaries alike for this botched effort at ocker colloquialism. ('It sounded . . . like one of those phrases that you feed into Babelfish to translate into German and then back into English again', wrote the political commentator Annabel Crabb).[3] This was an ironic testament to Australia's larrikin mystique: the fact that a prime minister might embarrass his colleagues by trying unsuccessfully to appear rough-hewn rather than because he could genuinely be described that way.

One of the classic images of twentieth-century larrikins in Australian popular culture was the result of a sophisticated middle-class writer trying on a rough vernacular for size. First appearing in the *Bulletin* in 1908 and later in a book of collected verse in 1915, CJ Dennis' Bill, the Sentimental Bloke, was a coarse Melbourne fellow in love with a pickle-factory girl. 'Oh strike me pink! She is a peach!' he said of this 'tart', Doreen, in *The Songs of a Sentimental Bloke*. Bill's friend Ginger Mick was a rabbit-oh with rapscallion wit and callused knuckles, a *habitué* of Melbourne's Little Lonsdale Street. In the follow-up volume, *The Moods of Ginger Mick* (1916), he was depicted donning khaki and dying on an Egyptian battlefield.

Though Dennis had grown up far from the hard-bitten *milieu* he wrote about, coddled by maiden aunts and developing extravagant tastes in suburban Adelaide, his excursion into an imagined larrikin idiom was vastly more successful than Rudd's. Australian audiences were immediately enamoured of his tough protagonists, Bill and Mick. The pair would go on to become staples on Australian vaudeville stages, the stars of musicals and no less than three films in the interwar years. 'Ginger Mick' also became a moniker for any rough-and-ready fellow given to roguish japery, no doubt influencing the popularity of Ginger Meggs, the mischievous star of a children's comic strip begun in 1921.[4]

The second decade of the twentieth century, the decade in which Dennis published *The Songs of a Sentimental Bloke,* really marked the beginnings of positive public attitudes to larrikinism and its relationship to Australian national identity. Before that, no reputable Australian would have called themselves a larrikin. Nor would they have celebrated the concept as a sign of their Australianness. Until the 1910s, 'larrikin' was overwhelmingly a term of abuse or defiant self-identification, a synonym for 'hoodlum' or 'young scoundrel'. Less often it was used mockingly, not unlike 'bogan', mostly by caricaturists who portrayed larrikins as the epitome of boorish manners and taste. In none of these instances, however, was 'larrikin' a term that members of the broader community would have wanted to have applied to themselves.

When one considers the people who either called themselves larrikins or were labelled as such in the late 1800s, it is little wonder that the general public shunned association with the term. To be a larrikin then was not only to be young, aged between one's early teens and early twenties, but also poor, engaged in factory labour or attempting to earn a living on the street. The term first came into use in late 1860s Melbourne as a way for these poor youths to boast of their 'leariness' or flamboyant street-credibility. By the 1880s, it was caught up in a moral panic about out-of-control adolescents who gathered in loosely-composed street gangs known as 'pushes', 'talents' or 'forties'. Larrikinism, it was said at this time, was the scourge of urban colonial society.

Some of the members of larrikin 'pushes' were involved in sensationally violent incidents in the years between the 1880s and early 1900s: gang rapes, attacks on Chinese immigrants, revenge bashings, battles with other push-ites and riots against police. All were also part of what had become a larrikin subculture by then: a loose cluster of relationships, styles and practices in which self-consciously rowdy youth engaged around the city markets, on street corners, in cheap entertainment venues, parks and empty inner-suburban lots.[5] It was only immediately before and during the First World War, especially when Australian soldiers branded themselves 'diggers' and began celebrating their affinity with larrikins, that the term started to detach itself from this connection to an unruly street subculture and acquire the positive inflection it still possesses today.

Figure 4. *David Barker's now-famous larrikin-soldier image* The Anzac Book, *Cassell, London, 1916, p. 22.*

One of the most famous images of what would later be known as the larrikin-like 'digger' was drawn by David Barker, an Anzac serviceman at Gallipoli. Reproduced in the *Anzac Book* of 1916, it portrayed the typical Australian soldier as a grubby-faced gap-toothed fellow, a Norman Gunston-esque cut to his chin and a mischievous glint to his eye. By that time, there were plenty of larrikin figures on Australian vaudeville stages who were portrayed in a similarly shambolic way. Some of these characters even starred in 'ragtime army'-style skits during the war which drew a connection between larrikins and soldiers. After the armistice, these larrikin digger characters were increasingly celebrated as quintessentially Australian. It was at this point that the idea that the real Australian was a bit of a larrikin crystallised; the idea that to be 'true blue' one had to be a Ginger Mick, quick with one's fists, given to salty language and tomfoolery, but with a heart of gold underneath it all.

Given how much the idea of larrikinism now resonates in the culture, it is surprising how little is known of its pre-First World War history. Try to find about the first larrikins and one immediately enters a wilderness of hoax articles, quotes from fiction and hearsay cleansed of all traceable origins. In *The Companion Guide to Sydney* (1973), for example, the author Ruth Park claimed to have interviewed an old-timer from The Rocks who told her his father had been the member of a larrikin push – but she almost certainly made up his comments from a 1950s newspaper article itself based on nostalgic anecdotes. In the 1960s, the biographer of the bare-knuckle pugilist, Larry Foley, claimed that Foley was the captain of a push that fought others around the Rocks from the late 1860s – but his account seems to have been more influenced by Henry Lawson's 1892 poem, 'The Captain of the Push', than sources from the day. More egregiously, many historians have relied on a 1901 article by the Sydney lawyer-turned-novelist, Ambrose Pratt, as evidence of nineteenth-century larrikin gangs. Pratt styled the article as an *exposé* based on firsthand knowledge of a push from The Rocks. In actual fact he had concocted his allegations to foment publicity for his second novel, *The Great 'Push' Experiment* (1902).[6]

The mythic character of larrikinism being what it is in Australia today, it might be considered fitting that its early history is so much the subject of scam *exposés*, fabricated interviews, and literary lore. This book has been written, however, to present a more rigorous account. Though its afterword deals with the rampant growth of the larrikin mystique since the Anzac era, its key concern is with the lives of the first larrikins, beginning in the late 1860s and ending in the late 1920s. For the most part, it tells the story of the rough adolescent subculture that thrived in the largest places of population, particularly the east-coast capitals of Melbourne, Sydney and Brisbane. It follows the members of this subculture, the first larrikins, into cheap dance saloons near Paddy's Market, past fairground attractions near Melbourne's Eastern Market, through sweaty crowds at Brisbane boxing shows and into vacant lots where they 'ran the rabbit' with bottles of beer from the pub down the road.

Telling the story of Australia's early larrikins is important because of how little has been said about poor urban youth in this period, about their everyday lives and sensibilities, in spite of the influence they have since had on Australian youth cultures and notions of national identity. This book shows that the practices and identities of these self-consciously rough youth changed along with wider historical developments between the late 1860s and the late 1920s. It starts in the late 1860s when 'young blackguards of both sexes' hung about together in roadways and pub-singing rooms, adopting a hedonistic and colourfully street-smart style as a way of proving themselves a cut above others from humble backgrounds. It then moves on to chart their formation of loosely composed all-male 'pushes' and growing antipathy towards authorities during the law-and-order crackdown that took place in the 1880s. It ends in the aftermath of the First World War, a time in which less outwardly hostile pushes were engaging in internecine fights over football and inner-suburban territory.

Considering the pre-war history of larrikinism is also important because it challenges us to think about what is new and what is old about any moment in history. The world in which the early larrikins lived was one in which poor adolescents were tossed into prisons with adults, where primary schooling had only just become

compulsory but not yet treated as such, and secondary schooling was simply not an option for lower working-class families. At
the same time, however, it was a world in which concerns about
adolescent smoking, drinking, gang-fights, racist attacks, what we
would now call 'raunch culture' among girls and sexual violence
among boys strike a surprisingly contemporary note. Even the sartorial style affected by larrikins at the height of their disorderly
leariness in the 1880s – a style sometimes called 'fly' and inspired
by their favourite singers and comedians – has unexpected resonances with attention-seeking 'bogan' youth today.

Yet another reason the history of early larrikinism is significant
is that it provides us with new perspectives on the larrikin mystique in current-day Australia. It shows that young women were
energetic participants in early larrikinism, something that flies
in the face of the arrant blokishness we now associate with the
term. It also shows that far from being 'true blue', early larrikin
humour was shaped by interactions with Cockney music-hall,
burlesque and American blackface-minstrel acts. Not only that:
the late nineteenth-century larrikin subculture disavowed a connection to the working class. While larrikinism is often linked to
working-class egalitarianism today, the first larrikins hankered after
small-time capitalist enterprise and tried to distinguish themselves
from the other poor urbanites around them in a far from egalitarian way. Finally, too, this history challenges us to re-think the extent
to which Australian national identity was produced through a love
affair with the bush. The early larrikin subculture was profoundly
urban in its location and focus, which is perhaps why Russel Ward
neglected to discuss it in his famous work on the influence of the
bush on the Australian legend.[7]

Along with the lack of reliable evidence underpinning existing
accounts, the very word 'larrikin' has attracted a luxuriance of DIY

etymology over the years. From time to time, it has been said to have derived from *leprechaun* or *larron,* the French verb 'to steal', flimsy speculations that are easy to knock down. Others tell us that the term came into being via a mispronunciation of 'larking' by a Melbourne policeman. The most common version of this anecdote concerns a Sergeant Dalton in the 1860s, said to have routinely described the misdemeanours of young ruffians as 'larking, Your Worship' when appearing in court. Another version features Jack Staunton, a policeman working the city beat in the 1850s, who was also said to have regularly talked to magistrates of larking juveniles. Either because of a speech impediment or an Irish accent, the phrase was supposed to have come out as 'larra-kin, Your Worship', prompting others to take up the word as a noun. Apt as this story might seem, we have it on the authority of several august lexicographers that it was an urban myth. 'Larrikin' in fact came to Australia like so much else: that is, in a ship from England. It was a dialect word from around Warwick or Worcester which meant 'mischievous or frolicsome youth', and was also related to a Yorkshire verb 'to larrack', meaning 'to lark about'.[8]

However enjoyable it might be to speculate on how words came into being, trying to establish a singular origin for 'larrikin' misses the point. Regardless of where it came from, the term was taken up in the colonies around 1870 because it evoked the qualities of 'larking about', 'leariness' or 'lairiness', both of which meant 'streetwise', although the latter bore the extra connotation of rowdiness. The more interesting question is thus not where larrikin came from, but why it attained acquired broad circulation in the colonies when it did. Why was it thought necessary to find a new word for urban youngsters given to rowdy insolence on the eve of the 1870s?

To contemplate what is in a name and why things acquire their names is always a tricky business. Not only can it lead you through intricate thickets of etymology, it can also mean that you become lost in labyrinthine arguments over the nature of words to things. Does an object exist before it is named? Would larrikinism have been a different thing if it had been given a different name? Does a social phenomenon have any existence outside the terms we use to describe it? These are serious questions, with broad-reaching implications for the way we understand the role of language in the world. Thinking through them could take a lifetime if you allowed it to, however – and if you fell amid that dense forest of debate, rendered dizzy by its vastness and complexity, would anyone hear or care?

The questions some scholars have asked themselves about larrikins are slightly less abstract than the ones just mentioned. In a nutshell, the key quandary has been: did the appearance of the word 'larrikin' sometime around 1870 reflect something new about colonial street culture – the emergence of a new kind of young 'rowdy class' – such that people needed a new word to describe it? Or to the contrary, did it only reflect something new about attitudes to frolicsome street youths and new policing strategies to deal with them? To put it another way: should we see larrikinism as a concept which came about from the top down, as a category imposed on boisterous lower-class youth by authorities and public opinion? Or should we see it as something which emerged from the bottom up, as a movement or a subculture elaborated by unruly youngsters themselves?

The best answer to this question will no doubt irritate those who would seek a categorical response. Well, it was a bit of both, actually. The term 'larrikin' was used as a handy way for journalists and the authorities to label any apparently lowborn young person who spent time in the streets and engaged in uncouth behaviour. Young people once called 'street Arabs' or 'low youths' now began to be branded as larrikins and thus seen as part of a dreaded scourge of larrikinism plaguing the larger cities. Much like the labelling of certain youth as Aborigines or Muslims or simply 'hoons' today, this branding of poor juveniles as larrikins contributed to a spike in police prosecutions in the 1870s. Most of these prosecutions were for offences against good order – drunkenness, obscene language, riotous behaviour and the like. The apparent increase in the numbers of such offences being committed was then key to the public perception of a rising larrikin menace in colonial society.[9]

While it was definitely the case that the extent of larrikinism was exaggerated in late nineteenth-century courts and newspapers, the phenomenon was never simply about a label being imposed on young ones from above. The term had originated on the street rather than among journalists or police officers. The public hype concerning larrikinism also had a self-fulfilling effect. Youths of both sexes increasingly took on a larrikin identity over time, proudly mixing in pushes and daring onlookers to brand them as bad 'uns. As with the creation of youth subcultures today, there was a push-me pull-you relationship between what was publicly said about larrikins and those who took it on as a defiant marker of identity.

This account essentially explores how this reciprocal relationship worked in late nineteenth- and early twentieth-century Australia. It shows that to understand the early larrikin phenomenon you cannot just look at what was being said about larrikins in popular culture and public life. Nor can you solely focus on authorities' treatment of unruly youth. To really explore early larrikinism, you also have to look at the interplay between these things and how the unruly youth called larrikins acted and presented themselves. Doing this requires going beyond an analysis of public discourse towards callow juveniles to find evidence of larrikins' dress, lingo, pursuits and cultural influences from a diverse range of sources produced in the day.

★

Almost before Steve Irwin's body had grown cold in 2006, Germaine Greer published an article in the *Guardian* in which she criticised his crash-tackle-the-beauties approach to wildlife. Called 'That sort of delusion is what it takes to be a real Aussie larrikin', Greer's piece was one in a long line of critiques of the true blue larrikin. In discussing the confronting features of early larrikinism – not least flagrant racism and sexual violence towards women – this book arguably belongs to this line of critique. Yet it is not my intention to simply take potshots at the tradition *à la* Greer. There are plenty of good things about the way larrikinism now operates so far as I am concerned. There is ample sly pleasure to be had from acting the ocker buffoon like the Anzac diggers in London or exhibiting the 'scepticism in the face of bombast' that we now associate with a larrikin sensibility. Pleasure may also be had from the fact that non Anglo-Celtic Australians have provided their own versions of larrikinism in recent decades: among them, the Indigenous artists Mun Mun Larrikin and Larrikin Sturt.[10]

Even if one dislikes the mugging jokesters known as larrikins today, there is still plenty to learn from the first larrikins' history. Whether it is exploring their eclectic cultural influences or contemporary resonances, whether reflecting on their efforts to create their own identities and what this says about inner-suburban Australian communities, there is more to this history than either reviling the 'larrikin streak' or shouting the colonial equivalent of 'crikey!' among the gum trees.

Chapter One

The leary bloke

The noise made by rowdies at the Granites used to annoy the good citizens of Gertrude Street, Fitzroy. At almost any hour of the night, youths described as 'larrikins' could be found on this inner-Melbourne lot. The young ones were attracted to the mass of rocks dumped on the site from a nearby development. Flung about like a squalling toddler's toys, these offered ready-made nooks, clambering surfaces, inviting pathways, even a makeshift stage. When youngsters weren't guzzling brandy or holding prize fights at the Granites, weren't step-dancing or drunkenly skittering from rock to rock, they could be found performing scenes from Theatre Royal melodramas on this improvised stage. The scenes they chose included hiss-at-the-villain moments from thumping plays such as *Luke the Labourer*; perhaps, too, they included comic vignettes in which Cockney pranksters traded heckles with the crowd. Songs were also performed on that granite platform. These were drawn either from music-hall songbooks imported from London or from acts in local singing rooms. According to a Melbourne journalist in 1869, rough youth reigned supreme at the city's singing rooms.

They shrieked madly for an encore when they liked an act, and at the same time kept up a hectic presence in cheap theatre seats and sideshows in town.

We know about the Granites today from letters by outraged residents in its vicinity. They sent missives to the *Argus* in the early 1870s, published under headings such as 'The Larrikin Nuisance'. We also know about the Granites from an anonymous man who later claimed to have been one of the rowdies at the site. Calling himself 'Fitzroy Boy', he wrote his own letter to the *Argus* in the 1890s. Back in the 1860s, he declared, he and his friends coined the term 'larrikin'. Performed for each other on that long-ago 'stage', their favourite act was a London music-hall number called something like 'The Leary Cove' or 'The Leary Bloke'. This song appealed to them because it smacked of streetwise panache, full of back slang and *braggadocio*. So appealing was it that 'leary' became the word of the moment among the youths of Fitzroy and Collingwood who socialised at the Granites. They used the term for anyone they approved of, so that over time any youth who 'ran out o'nights' became known as 'learykins'.[1]

Fitzroy Boy and his fellows did not in fact coin the term 'larrikin'. We now know that it was a dialect word from around Warwick or Worcester in England, from which it was imported to the colonies. It is still possible, however, that one of the reasons the term took off in Australia was because it sounded like 'learykin' and thus brought the quality of leariness to mind. The word 'leary' itself was an old cant word meaning sharp, savvy, not easily duped or 'fly', all synonyms for streetwise. The concept of acting leary and the occupations to which it was linked played a vital role in the larrikin story as it unfolded from the late 1860s. It helps us now to account for the allure of the larrikin identity to the youngsters who hung around disused lots, 'low singing rooms' and other cheap amusement venues. According to the *Argus* in 1882, in fact,

Australia's criminal population did not pronounce the word 'lar-a-kin', 'but always "learykin"'. The phrase 'leary kinchin', too, was a cant term for a 'knowing lad' and was in circulation in Australia when 'larrikin' came into use.[2]

Since words in the vernacular are living things, they are invariably difficult to pin down. They shift in meaning not only over time, but according to who uses them and their demeanour when uttering the word. Once a colloquialism leaves a trace in the written record, however, it becomes easier to deal with. We can now be reasonably sure that 'larrikin' first appeared in the Australian press in an article for the Melbourne *Age* on 7 February 1870. Entitled 'A Night at the Lock-up', this article detailed its author's trip to the Little Collins Street lock-up the previous Saturday night. The usual suspects were led into the lock-up at first, this author wrote. These included an amiable drunk singing the music-hall hit 'Champagne Charlie', a sailor whose pockets yielded a songbook and 'jew harp', a young woman who had smashed a glass in her partner's face at a music hall, and a young man arrested for shouting 'smash the peelers!' to a crowd. Later on, however, a constable entered with a couple of youngsters belonging to the 'rowdy class': the sort 'commonly termed "larrikins"'. These so-called larrikins had been 'amusing themselves with some twenty others of similar taste', congregating on a footpath and insulting passers-by.

According to the *Age* reporter, the larrikins led into the lock-up had probably been models of bravado while in the street with their friends. Now they were arrested they made a pitiful spectacle: two scrawny teens of obviously low parentage being hauled ashen-faced to the cells.[3] As this suggests, 'larrikin' was used for quite young adolescents when it first appeared. It did not yet denote rowdies in their late teens or early twenties who went about in gangs and made their own efforts to smash the peelers (a slang word for police taken from Robert Peel, creator of London's police force in 1829). Back in the summer of 1870, 'larrikin' was a word for ruffians-in-training rather than the genuine article. It described callow youth in their mid-teens or younger, some of whom were perhaps on their first Saturday night in the city and who aspired to be considered leary. Larrikins were 'young hopefuls', as one of Gertrude Street's residents would later put it. They were youngsters who attempted to big-note themselves with a show of bluster for their pals.[4]

In using the term 'larrikin' in his article on the city lock-up, the *Age* journalist was doing what investigative reporters on criminals or youth culture still do: strive to appear in-the-know. Since the word on the street for these proto-roughs was 'larrikins', he included it in his article as proof that he was abreast of the latest vocabulary. Almost immediately the term caught on among other writers for the press who were similarly anxious to appear up to date. On 19 March 1870, the bohemian writer Marcus Clarke published a sketch in the *Australasian* in which he hailed the larrikin as an obnoxious new breed. Two days later, the *Argus* complained that police charge-sheets were filled with 'fresh accounts of "larrikin" exploits and "colonial cad" outrages'. By April 1870, the *Argus* was drawing attention to 'three youngsters, of the species now known as "larrikins"'. Aged between 13 and 16 years, they had been caught stealing a bottle of perfume from a Collingwood shop. Other reports of larrikins at police courts or kicking up a ruckus in the Theatre Royal made a showing over the following months. Before long the word 'larrikin' was making headlines: '"Larrikins" in the Botanical Gardens', 'More of the Larrikin', 'The Larrikins Again'.[5]

In the first years of the 1870s, almost all talk of larrikins was focused on Melbourne. In December 1870, in fact, Sydney readers were congratulated that their city had far fewer 'assemblages of unruly youths on street corners' than its southerly rival. Brisbane readers received the same assurance in August 1871. 'We are not so troubled with the "larrikin" element as they are in Melbourne', the *Brisbane Courier* declared. After a series of violent offences committed by rough youths in the 1880s, however, Sydney's residents could no longer afford to be smug. With the death of a youth in a city street fight in 1891, Brisbanites became similarly conscious of a 'larrikin menace' in their midst. A worrying upsurge in youthful rowdyism was taking place across the civilised world, Australian readers were being told at this time. Over and again, it was said that a new species of street-lout had emerged: not just in the colonies, but 'in London, in the pupils of Fagin; crossing the Atlantic, in the youthful rowdy of the Five Points and the Bowery', and again, 'over river and prairie and mountain' in the hoodlum on San Francisco's mean streets.[6]

When one starts looking at the rise of the word larrikin in print, what one is really charting is a trend in journalistic reportage and public rhetoric about rough youth. The late-Victorian era witnessed a spike in this rhetoric, prompted by fears about the corrupting effects of cities and unease about where to draw the line between childhood and adult maturity. A spike in arrests for crimes against good order also took place: arrests for vagrancy, public drunkenness, obscene language, riotous behaviour, prize fighting, and the like. Some commentators have thus argued that the appearance of the word 'larrikin' only represented a shift in public anxieties about lowborn youth rather than anything novel among those youth themselves. The fact that the word came into being and was adopted with such alacrity was because of newspaper accounts and the nerve they struck in the populace – it was 'not due to a change in the behaviour of working-class youths'.[7]

Those who argue that 'larrikin' was simply a new word for an old phenomenon raise a number of points worth considering. The idea of acting leary was in circulation in eighteenth-century London, and had thrived in the streets of convict-era Sydney. In 1840s Sydney, for example, there were plenty of insolent youth who loitered about the entrance to the Royal Victoria Theatre, offering bloody noses and 'the crimsonest of adjectives' to passers-by. These youths were known as the cabbage-tree mob because they wore low-crowned hats woven from the leaves of the cabbage palm tree. One of their favourite pastimes was to attack the hats of other men deemed too full of themselves. This 'bonneting' trick, as it was called, involved bashing one's fist on the top of the man's hat in the hope that it would fall over his eyes. Bonneting was also carried out in England among the 'pupils of Fagin', and continued among the Australian youths called larrikins after 1870.[8] Since those latter youths also went about in packs and loafed in pimply impudence outside theatres, can it really be said that they were different from the rowdies of earlier years?

While it is obvious that youths called larrikins had much in common with earlier street mobs, the word 'larrikin' was used by young people themselves before it was taken up in Australian public life. It also continued to have its own street life in the ensuing years. Rather than just acting as a label that public commentators imposed on disorderly youth, it was a way for certain youth to describe themselves. Rather than simply functioning, too, as a new word for an old phenomenon, it was also a word for young people to describe others among their peers. Consider, for example, the 16-year-old girl, Frances 'Cocky' Danby, who gave evidence in a court case about seeing a lot of 'larrikins' – friends of hers, most of them – hanging out on a street corner in Woolloomooloo. Consider, too, Richard Turvey, a 17 year old who worked for a bootmaker and chalked up arrests for street gambling and assault in the late 1860s and early 1870s. He was touting himself the 'King of the Richmond larrikins' in 1871. The same boast was made by

20-year-old George Howe, inmate of Pentridge prison in 1874–5, although he called himself 'King of the Collingwood larrikins'. Ned Kelly would certainly have met youths like Howe during his term at Pentridge in the early 1870s. No doubt he had them in mind when he compared himself to the 'half-starved larrakin' in his Jerilderie letter of 1879.[9]

Since some young people thought of themselves or those in their circle as larrikins, it is a moot point to show that youthful delinquents such as the cabbage-tree mob were in existence before the word larrikin was used. Once the word entered the Australian lexicon it allowed subtly new forms of street-identities to appear which then increased in defiance and visibility after 'larrikin' was taken up in the press. Terms such as 'punk', 'bikie', 'goth' and 'emo' have come in and out of currency in the same way in more recent years. Like 'larrikin', they have been adopted by young people as well as being the subject of anxious public commentary. They have also referred to new subcultural identities which nonetheless have obvious connections to others in existence before them.

It is no accident that 'larrikin' first took off in Melbourne. With the colony of Victoria attracting immigrant masses during the gold rushes in the 1850s, Melbourne was by far Australia's largest city in 1870. Historian AR Hall has spoken of a 'kinked age distribution' throughout the colony as a result of the gold rushes. By this he means that the Victorian population had a distorted age structure as a result of the numbers of gold-era immigrants who had married and had children. This kinked age distribution ensured that there was an astonishing proportion of Melbourne's population in the early to mid-teen age group by the census of 1871. In South Melbourne, a locality that would later become renowned for its larrikinism, about 40 per cent of the inhabitants were less than 15 years old in that year.[10] A yawning gap had opened up across the city between the older generations, many of which had been

born in the United Kingdom, and the gaggles of colonial-born
youngsters who sought each other's company in the consciousness
of being a new breed.

The period between 1860 and 1890 has often been described
as the eastern Australian colonies' 'long boom'. The population
explosion that took place is one reason for this. Melbourne's population mushroomed from 125,000 to 473,000 between 1861 and
1891. Sydney's population ballooned from 86,000 to 400,000 over
the same period; Brisbane's from a puny 6000 to 94,000. Though
still only a small part of the overall Australian economy, manufacturing also grew in all three capitals. Back in the 1850s, colonial
manufacturing had been focused on the production of boots,
clothes and basic furniture. By the 1880s, it ran to the production of carriages with upholstered seats, wrought-iron railings and
other metal-work, a cornucopia of canned fruit, crockery, cutlery
and fancy-goods for *bourgeois* homes. Small factories were beginning to develop from the cities' network of tiny workshops, a
modest number of which were powered by steam.[11] It would be
ludicrous, given this, to suggest that there were no significant differences between the cabbage-tree mob of the 1840s and larrikins
of the 1870s. The former belonged to a pre-industrial society in
which urban life had not yet acquired any intensity; the latter to a
time of growing urbanisation and industrial change.

When the larrikin phenomenon first came into being, *subur-
banisation* was not yet a feature of life in the colonial capitals. Most
people either lived within the bounds of the cities or in districts
in easy walking distance from them. By the 1880s, however, networks of tram and train routes were snaking out from the city
centres in Melbourne and Sydney. Roads around Brisbane were
also much improved. This infrastructure allowed development to
sprawl out across flats and gullies, enticing those who could afford
it into suburbs built on newly cleared fields. Over the 1870–80

period, steep rises in rents were also pushing workers into more overcrowded housing within the cities. Either that or they were inducing them to look for cheaper accommodation nearby. Small workers' cottages began encroaching on areas previously dominated by a fashionable constituency: in Sydney's Surry Hills, for example, or Melbourne's Fitzroy and Brisbane's Spring Hill. The population of rather less fashionable suburbs such as Collingwood and Waterloo also swelled. This was another aspect to the development of the larrikin subculture: a greater concentration of workers in city-fringe districts and inner suburbs, and worsening conditions for residents within the cities themselves.[12]

It is possible to envisage a kind of 'larrikin belt' around the edges of all three capitals between 1870 and the 1890s. The districts in which most larrikins lived included port districts which offered jobs for carters, coal lumpers, packers and general hands on the wharves. They also included suburbs devoted to the old trades (clothing-, footwear- and furniture-making) and noxious enterprises such as soapworks, full of the boiling of animal fat in stinking vats and deliveries of seeping entrails. In Melbourne terms, this meant that the 'larrikin belt' ran from South Melbourne (then Emerald Hill) to Richmond, Abbotsford, Collingwood, parts of Fitzroy and Carlton through to North Melbourne (then known as Hotham)(Figure 1). Larrikins also lived within the city itself, especially in the vicinity of Little Bourke and Little Lonsdale Streets where cabinet-makers and cookshops abounded and cheap housing lined back lanes.[13]

Along with its own inner-city lanes, Sydney's 'larrikin belt' comprised the waterfront districts from Woolloomooloo through Miller's Point to Pyrmont, streets on either side of Blackwattle Bay in Glebe and Balmain, and the industrialising suburbs running from Chippendale, parts of Surry Hills, Redfern, St Peters, Alexandria and soupy-when-wet Waterloo (Figure 2). In Brisbane, the larrikin districts were Woolloongabba, West End, South Brisbane, Fortitude Valley, the area within the city known as 'Frog's Hollow', Spring Hill, Petrie Terrace, the low-lying parts of Red Hill, and their immediate environs (Figure 3).[14]

At all times larrikinism had a profound connection to unskilled labour. Any notion that quantities of larrikins were from white-collar families or apprentices to the skilled trades (an idea sometimes voiced by contemporaries) simply doesn't bear up against the over-whelming numbers of larrikins who were among the colonies' least fortunate citizens. This link between larrikinism and unskilled labour was sometimes made explicit in the names larrikin groups called themselves. One such group in mid-1880s Sydney called itself 'the livers' because most of its members worked at the Glebe Island abattoir. Another called themselves the 'red blacks' because most worked the kilns at an inner-suburban brickworks. An even closer link existed between larrikinism and entry-level jobs in the clothing and footwear trades. This was recognised by a Brisbane magistrate when sentencing a misbehaving youth in 1884. Noting that the miscreant worked for a bootmaker, he expressed surprise at how many larrikins 'claimed fraternity with that particular class of tradesman'. As the centre of Melbourne's boot and clothing trades, Collingwood was widely considered a larrikin heartland. The many youths from that suburb arrested for stoning Chinese immigrants or 'insulting behaviour' often turned out to work at places such as Wallis' or Auld's Boot Factories.[15]

The clothing and boot trades were intimately connected to lar-rikinism because they were experiencing processes of 'de-skilling' and casualisation in the last decades of the nineteenth century. While others were enjoying the fruits of the boom, these trades were in the midst of sour times. The labour-intensive nature of the work and constant fluctuations in demand meant that their mainly small-time players were cutting costs at every opportunity. Between 1870 and 1890, employers increasingly outsourced aspects of their production to sub-contractors and women working from home. They also offered greater numbers of casual jobs to juveniles who were taught only one aspect of production rather than the whole trade. Permanent jobs or apprenticeships for up-and-coming young men were thus becoming hard to find in these trades. The same applied to furniture-making, once a source of zealously-kept craft traditions and male working-class pride.[16] Yet although the experience of 'de-skilled' labour was patently relevant to the emergence of larrikinism, an admiration for streetwise enterprise also played a huge role.

To wander Sydney and Melbourne in the 1870s was to come across any number of people engaged in enterprise on the streets. Every thoroughfare was frequented by roving boot-blacks, pickpockets, busking acrobats, men called costermongers pushing fruit-barrows, and others selling an astonishing miscellany of items: brooms, Turkish delight, patent medicines, flowers, oysters, toys, cigars and melancholy cockatoos. By the 1880s one would also have encountered itinerant types in central Brisbane and 'larrikin belt' suburbs in the larger cities. The travelling lecturer Helen Hart discovered this when she visited Fitzroy in 1885 after a couple of years away. In her absence, this inner-Melbourne suburb had become a 'tremendous market for street hawkers and criers', she wrote to the local press. 'There is scarcely an hour in the day but the noise of men and boys . . . is filling the air with . . . roars of "oysters – 3d per dozen".' By the early 1890s, the numbers of youthful newspaper sellers in Brisbane was attracting the ire of some citizens, especially since many of those who congregated in Albert Street were self-described larrikins.[17]

Along with streetsellers and criers, visitors to the east-coast capitals during the boom could find juveniles of both sexes 'wheeling small handcarts containing assortments of what were termed "marine stores"': bottles, rags and bric-a-brac, which they sold to older dealers in secondhand goods. Children eager to mind horses for payment or carters offering to lug goods were another common sight. Young people offering sexual turns for coin were less common, particularly if they were male – but certainly by the early twentieth century there were some of the latter operating clandestinely in city by-ways and abandoned buildings.[18] As the case of 11-year-old Sydney boy, Henry 'Dutchy' Keogh intimates, there were also people attempting to supplement their incomes through sub-contracting of some kind. All of these endeavours were alternatives to wage labour; some, too, were surrounded by a sort of nimbus of leary allure.

At the start of the 1890s, 'Dutchy' Keogh was living in McEvoy Street, Waterloo, and attending Mount Carmel school on weekday mornings. Each afternoon, he travelled into the city to sell newspapers and remained there until after dark. Keogh employed two younger boys under him to do the same, paying them a shilling and a tram ride home every evening. Some nights he also added to his small income by turning tumbling tricks in bars. 'I can touch my hand with my feet and bend my back and pick up 3d', he told social investigators in 1891.[19] At only 11, few would have considered Keogh a larrikin, although they may have done so in time. As the son of a coal lumper living with his family in a busy Waterloo street, however, he was very much from the social fraction to which most larrikins belonged. Combining street work with freelance performance and small-scale sub-contracting, he was also engaged in the tilt for independence that most larrikins longed for themselves.

Growing up in Cumberland Street at The Rocks in the 1870s and 1880s, Albert 'Griffo' Griffiths was another youth who made his own way rather than spending his life in grubbing labour. He worked variously as a newspaper boy, carter and as a hand for a boilermaking company in his teens. Disenchanted with these jobs, he made the decision to become a professional prize-fighter in the late 1880s. It is unclear whether Griffo had regarded himself as a larrikin before he became a famous boxer hailed in America as well as Australia. His colleagues and biographers would give mixed reports on this, although some commentators have claimed confidently that he was a member of a larrikin 'push' or gang in his youth. Whether or not this was the case, he certainly became a larrikin icon after stacking up victories in the ring.[20] This was in part because of admiration for his aggression and canny muscularity as a boxer, but also because he made a living through his own enterprise.

Though not a prize-fighter, the Waterloo larrikin Michael Mangan was attempting to make his own living in the mid-1880s. A member of the 'Waterloo push', he had his own cart and pony and hired himself out as a carter of building materials around Sydney's inner suburbs. His friend, 17-year-old William Newman, worked three mornings a week at Paddy's Market with his grandfather, a dealer in fruit and vegetables. The rest of the time Newman tramped the streets in search of what work or money-making opportunities he could find. Other acquaintances of Mangan's and Newman's were similarly engaged in activities that blurred the boundaries between working for a wage and self-employment, even though this meant periods of unemployment along the way. Leslie Douglas was another carter-for-hire, while Thomas Oscroft found occasional employment delivering vegetables for a Redfern greengrocer.[21]

When upwards of 40 larrikins were arrested over a fight with Sydney police at Chowder Bay in October 1890, a good many listed 'carter' or 'dealer' when describing themselves. This led the *Sydney Morning Herald* to observe that larrikins typically came either from the class of carters or dealers or were 'labourers of no fixed trade'. The notorious Valentine Keating, a North Melbourne larrikin who walked on crutches and belonged to the Crutchy

Push, was a dealer in secondhand goods with a pony and cart at the turn of the century. Bottle-gathering was also seen as a larrikin pursuit. This was Banjo Paterson's choice of occupation for his larrikin character in 'The Bottle-Oh Man', published in 1899. Paterson's bottle-oh emphatically preferred the vagaries of a footloose life to the certainties of wage servitude:

> I ain't the kind of bloke as takes to any steady job;
> I drives me bottle cart around the town;
> A bloke what keeps 'is eyes about can always make a bob –
> I couldn't bear to graft for every brown.[22]

The possibility of actually being able to earn a living as a prize-fighter, performer, independent carter or bottle-gatherer was of course little more than a pipe dream for most underprivileged youth. In reality, far more larrikins were 'labourers of no fixed trade' than penny capitalists, a word sometimes used for those involved in small-scale entrepreneurialism or self-employment. Most of those who tried their hand at freelance endeavours from time to time also had to work at local factories or brickworks to survive. The Collingwood larrikin John Finnegan, for example, sometimes busked on the street with his brother Frank in the 1880s. Possibly he imagined making a living through his musical abilities at such moments, but he still had to work at a local cigar factory to get by. The Brisbane larrikin George Howard was a thief who stole items of clothing and the like, but he still worked for a boot factory in Fortitude Valley the rest of the time.[23] The point here, however, is that the dream of an independent life, especially one that exuded a streetwise glamour, provides the key to the larrikin sensibility. The dream was what mattered when it came to determining which unskilled youth became larrikins and which chose to move in different company.

Figure 5. *Mugshot of George Howard, 1889*
Queensland State Archives[24]

Along with the dream of independence for larrikin youth came
a desire to think of themselves as a cut above other unskilled
labourers. With his slicked hair, snowy-white shirt and wine-dark
neckerchief, the Brisbane youth George Howard certainly longed
to big-note himself in this way. Making trouble at working-class
events was another way that groups of larrikins distinguished themselves. In 1882 one such group descended like the vengeful fairy
at the royal christening on the Sydney Journeymen Tailors' annual
picnic by the harbour. They seized a football being used by some
of the picnickers and began hurling it at some of those seated,
scattering them to every side. Another group turned up to a wharf
and coal labourers' picnic at Chowder Bay in the late 1880s. Some
of these larrikin interlopers ran along the dance pavilion with a
stretched rope, felling dancers like nine-pins. Still others turned
up to union parades, strike pickets, workplace socials and friendly
society picnics to deride their avowedly working-class peers.[25]

The dream of being something other than an unskilled labourer fuelled the practice of constantly shifting between jobs among rough youngsters. During the long boom, young colonial workers of both sexes were notorious for their tendency to run 'from one factory to another and from one class of work to another instead of remaining and thoroughly learning a trade'. 'They want to run away . . . The generality of them do not like to be bound' was an oft-heard refrain. Job-hopping and itinerant work were also a way for these youngsters to disclaim interest in the values espoused by prominent members of the Victorian-era working class. Rather than trying to gain working-class respect through earnest industry, loyalty to an employer, sober habits and thrift, larrikin youth directed their efforts at uncertain and sometimes shady endeavours aimed at marking themselves out from the masses.

The blustering style exhibited by Richard Turvey, self-titled King of the Richmond larrikins, was the quintessential mode of larrikin self-presentation in the late nineteenth century. The sources of inspiration for this style came from the sort of leary 'penny capitalists' that larrikins admired: sideshow operators, boastful costermongers, prize-fighters, swaggering freelance performers and the characters they embodied on stage. The role played by popular performance and showman traditions in helping to shape the larrikin persona is another reason why the experience of social disadvantage and 'de-skilled' work cannot tell us the whole story about the emergence of larrikins. To tell that story we have to visit not only abattoirs and boot-making factories pungent with rawhide in the inner suburbs, not only the often-insalubrious streets in which larrikins lived, but also colourful entertainment districts such as the noisy blocks between Melbourne's Eastern Market and its Theatre Royal.

Theatres sprang up like gaudy mushrooms in the humid soil of eastern Australia's long boom. With their rococo façades or state-of-the-art roll-back ceilings, they were some of the most overt signs of the colonies' aspirations to culture and modernity at that time. When the Theatres Royal in both Sydney and Melbourne burned down in 1872, for example, each was immediately and lavishly rebuilt. The central chandelier of Sydney's new Theatre Royal was bright as a Guy Fawkes' bonfire, replete with 376 gas burners – an ambitious inclusion since the old venue had just gone up in flames. A rash of still more brilliant theatres appeared in the capitals during the 1880s: among them Melbourne's Alexandra Theatre and Princess Theatre, Sydney's Her Majesty's Theatre, and Brisbane's Opera House and Theatre Royal.[26]

The splashiest theatres of the boom were obviously targeted at an elegant clientele. Their proprietors hoped to entice patrons who could afford the dress circle, their necks swathed in jewels or cravats. Even the cheapest seats in these theatres were aimed at decent hard-working patrons and largely succeeded in attracting them. Families of Anglo and Chinese descent, groups of shop-workers, young women, children and the elderly were among the crowds packed tight as cloves in a garlic crusher in the galleries high above the stage. Nonetheless, most galleries still included a callow knot of boys and adolescent men who made a habit of noisily – sometimes uproariously – enjoying the show. This was particularly the case at Melbourne's Theatre Royal. With a sixpence admission fee in the 1860s and 1870s, half what other venues of equivalent stature charged, it had a reputation for attracting 'unsavoury costermongers and foul-mouthed roughlings' to its performances.[27]

Though some critics exaggerated the extent to which larrikins attended the theatres, there are enough reports of rough youths making a rush at the gallery entrance of the Royal, or trying to pass in with forged tickets, or spitting onto patrons seated below the gallery, to suggest that there was a keen interest in the theatre among the 'rowdy class'. Fitzroy Boy's recollections of scenes re-enacted at the Granites also suggest this was the case. So do indications that self-described larrikins were present at certain plays. When George Coppin appeared at Melbourne's Royal in the early 1870s, for example, loud hisses emanated from the gallery when his low-comic character Billy Barlow joked about 'educating larrikins with the lash'.[28]

In the late 1960s the Brisbane historian Ronald Lawson interviewed a couple of men who told him they had been larrikins in the 1890s. Neither of these men knew each other. Each, however, said that they had often gone to the theatre to see vaudeville, and sometimes also melodrama, while being the member of a larrikin mob in his teens. Lawson interviewed another man who told him that he 'went wild' as an adolescent in the 1890s, prompted by his father's death. This man shifted fecklessly from job to job throughout his youth; now working as a tailor's assistant, now getting a job driving trams, most likely with stretches of unemployment in between. He still managed to get to the theatre most Saturdays, even if it meant going other nights without food.[29]

Occasional nights out at swank theatres no doubt contributed to larrikins' aspirations: to the value these youth placed on dash and hedonistic display. But such youngsters were far more likely to attend downscale entertainments than blockbuster dramas. In Sydney, most of these could be found around Haymarket and Paddy's Market, not far from where Central Station now stands. Over the last four decades of the century, the streets in this district were taken over by a slew of theatres, pubs with singing rooms, billiard halls, dance saloons, sideshows, occasional circuses and pugilistic displays. The same thing happened in the eastern part of Melbourne's Bourke Street, where cheap amusement venues stood cheek-by-jowl with the larger theatres. Though on a much smaller scale, billiard halls and pubs showing live entertainment similarly proliferated in Brisbane alongside the fancy theatres in Albert and Edward Streets.

Dancing in cheap saloons was a much-loved larrikin pastime in the late-colonial years. There were many such saloons in Melbourne's Bourke Street. One of these was Jennie Donigan's Hanover Dance Hall, located on the ground floor of the Eastern Arcade. Squeezed against a wine saloon and drinking booths selling threepence pints, it was a place where youth could go for what was described then as a 'rorty' (meaning uproarious) night in town. Upstairs was the thousand-seat Apollo Hall, reeking with the sweat of stage pugilists and grease-faced minstrel companies. In Sydney, too, larrikins of both sexes from Waterloo and Alexandria used to frequent a dance saloon in Harris Street at the start of the 1890s. Lower Castlereagh Street near Haymarket was another favoured location for small-time dance halls:

> Well, that winter we all joined a dancing establishment,
> known as the 'Sixpenny Hop'.
> The place has changed hands, I was past t'other day,
> and it's now a confectioner's shop.
> There are several such dens near the very same spot,
> I'm alluding to Castlereagh street;
> We had plenty of fun, with occasional rows,
> soon suppressed by the cops on the beat.[30]

Being light of funds did not prevent disadvantaged youngsters from enjoying themselves in entertainment precincts such as Brisbane's Albert Street or Melbourne's Bourke Street east. Plenty of amusements costing sixpence or less were to be found in this latter district. With its live freaks and waxen celebrities, Kreitmeyer's Waxworks was one of these. So was the Ghost Show, offering magical illusions and black-comic stunts. For those unable to raise sixpence for this show, promotional excerpts of the evening's fun were performed *gratis* on the pavement outside. Brass bands and

Figure 6. *Lower Pitt Street, Sydney, not far from Haymarket and Paddy's Market. This shot was taken in 1908 when cheap vaudeville shows were sometimes performed at the Masonic Hall, visible top right. Though taken long after the first larrikins appeared on Sydney's streets, it gives a sense of the kind of streetscape in which most larrikins would have attended entertainments by night. It also shows a youth employed as a street sweeper and another with his handcart slightly to the right of centre.*
City of Sydney Archives

noisy spruikers were similarly to be found outside the sideshows in the Eastern Market on the corner of Bourke and Stephen (now Exhibition) Streets. Though these spruikers were there to drum up business for the sideshows' displays – snake charming, wire walking, optical illusions and human freaks – they constituted an entertainment in themselves.

From the mid-1890s a gang of South Melbourne larrikins began calling themselves the 'Flying Angels'. Since the Flying Angel was an amusement ride (the kind we would describe as a 'flying fox' today), this suggests their familiarity with the market-cum-fairground scene. A Flying Angel was in operation at the Hippodrome across the road from the Eastern Market at the turn of the century, described by the *Argus* as 'highly popular among young people'. In earlier decades, the Eastern Market was disparaged by police as a site of male-larrikin fights by night and unruliness among adolescent girls. An 1883 report drew attention to the 'horrid sketches and obscene writings' left by factory girls on the walls of the public toilets.[31]

Figure 7. *Inset entitled 'Sketches in the Crowd' from a newspaper image called Saturday Night at the Eastern Market, 1881. It shows a larrikin youth eyeing off a flirtatious young woman.*
State Library of Victoria

In Sydney, Paddy's Market was as much a magnet for larrikins as the Eastern Market in Melbourne. In the early to mid-1880s, a group of male larrikins calling themselves 'the bummer gang' hung around the Haymarket and Paddy's Market. One of these went by the name of James 'Rorty' Grey. In 1887, too, an unruly Waterloo girl went walking through Paddy's by herself one Saturday night. Out for amusement, she ended up meeting male larrikins from her neighbourhood on their way home. Among these was 'one of the Mangans' – either the Michael Mangan who drove his own cart and pony or one of his siblings. These Waterloo youngsters had perhaps been joining in the hubbub around the hoopla or other amusements at Paddy's. They may even have seen a performance in a colonial equivalent of an English 'penny gaff': a tent in one corner of the market in which plays and tumbling displays were offered at rock-bottom prices. Though Brisbane had no under-cover market like Paddy's, its Queen Street night market was also criticised as a larrikin drawcard in the 1870s.[32]

Music-hall routines were even more significant for larrikins than dance halls and sideshows. Full of slangy catchphrases and with choruses meant to be shouted by their audiences, they were the forerunners of both Top 40 hits and stand-up comedy today. Put-ting on costumes and accents and gender at will, their performers were the Sacha Baron Cohens and Barry Humphries of the late-Victorian age. These routines were usually performed in rented halls or singing rooms attached to pubs rather than in purpose-built music halls as in London.

Colonial attempts to start up stand-alone music halls were com-promised by lack of capital on the part of their backers, resulting in unsafe fittings. They were also compromised by the unruliness of their clientele. In June 1890 a fight broke out in the gallery of the Haymarket Music Hall. Part of the gallery collapsed, six of the young male combatants were hospitalised and the venue was never heard of again. Known variously as the Variety Hall and the Oxford Music Hall, a venue on the corner of Brisbane's George and Turbot Streets lost its licence in similarly rorty style. It offered a cocktail of music-hall acts, blackface minstrelsy, male impersona-tion, boxing displays and amateur clog-dancing from early 1888 until May 1889, when a violent rumpus broke out among a baying Saturday night crowd.

More than ten years before the demise of Brisbane's Oxford Music Hall, the Melbourne journalist calling himself the Vaga-bond went to a 'low concert hall' in Bourke Street. In the early part of the evening, he said, the 'usual low music-hall acts' were performed, full of 'gross' comedy and tawdry dancing – including one act by an adolescent girl. These were watched by a gallery containing large numbers of male larrikins and girls 'of the very lowest class'. Other journalists commented on the quantities of lower-class youths who flocked to 'low singing rooms'. In the early seventies, a Sydney reformer claimed such youth were addicted to 'low places of amusement'. Comedians calling themselves 'star-*comiques*' strutted the stage of these places, he said. As in the case of Fitzroy Boy & co., patrons paid homage to these *comiques* by bearing away 'villainous songbooks' containing lyrics to their acts.[33]

The characters to be found on the stage of 'low places of amusement' whet rough youths' desires for leary competence. One of the acts performed at Ellis' London Music Hall in 1869, a singing room attached to the Tattersall's Hotel in Bourke Street, was an act known as 'The Chickaleary Cove' or 'The Chickaleary Bloke'. Made famous in London by the music-hall celebrity and so-called 'lion-*comique*', Alfred Vance, it was a perfect example of acting 'fly'. In Australia, it was performed by Barry O'Neil, a man who billed himself a 'champion clog-dancer'. No doubt he accompanied the act with snappy shoe-tapping when he appeared at Ellis' London Music Hall. Possibly he also included some of the acrobatic flips that Vance had brought to the original routine. It was this style of vaingloriously *macho* act that appealed to the first larrikins. The Chickaleary Bloke was a show-pony thief with a devil-may-care attitude to life. He had a 'rorty gal, also a knowing pal', he told the audience in his act, 'and merrily together we jog on':

> And I doesn't care a flatch
> So long as I've my tach,
> Some pannum in my chest – and a tog on.

The heaviness of the slang in 'The Chickaleary Bloke' was clearly a big part of its appeal. There was something seductively exotic about it (for the record, a *flatch* was a coin; a *tach*, a hat; *pannum*, food; and *tog*, an outfit of clothes). It drew certain members of the audience, at least, into a sense of conspiracy with the Bloke. It was as if in sharing in his thievish argot they were being invited to be the friends of this fellow with his self-confidence and quick-stepping moves. The end of his song, with its hailing of the audience as 'pals', reinforced this view:

> Now my pals, I'm going to slope, see you soon again I hope,
> My young woman is awaiting, so be quick,
> Now join in a chyike, the jolly we all like,
> I'm off with a party to the 'Vic'.[34]

It is impossible to know whether 'The Chickaleary Bloke' was the actual song that caught the fancy of Fitzroy Boy and his friends at the Granites in Gertrude Street. Even if they had been enamoured of another song, however, other rowdies would have seen 'The Chickaleary Bloke' performed. After first offering it at Ellis's London Music Hall, Barry O'Neil was indeed still performing it two years later when he head-lined at the Café Chantant in the thick of the lodging-house district in Sydney's York Street. 'The Chickaleary Bloke' then continued to be offered on Australian stages and in the community for years. In 1888 a journalist for the *Sydney Morning Herald* tried to remind his readers of an old song called 'It's sad to say farewell'. Most people probably wouldn't remember it, he lamented, because '"They've got "em on" and "Chickaleary" have long since secured undisputed possession of the public ear'.[35]

A swatch of songs whose characters exhibited Chickaleary-like qualities was circulating in Australia when the word 'larrikin' emerged. Those featuring the barrow-pushing hawkers known

as costermongers, or simply costers, became even more popular in the early 1870s. Songs with titles such as 'Costermonger
Joe', 'Rorty Tom', and 'Coster Bill' were performed in venues
such as Melbourne's Apollo Hall and Brisbane's School of Arts.
Their characters also spoke in colloquial 'flashery' and hit heads
to 'smashery' for fun. Similar characters appeared in the theatre. In
1884, for example, the horse-racing melodrama *The Blue Ribbon of
the Turf* featured a Cockney punter described by a reporter as leary
in style.[36]

The reasons that leary stage acts appealed to young workers
are obvious enough. Their performers adopted the standard low-
comic practice of pandering to the rowdiest members of their
audiences – 'playing to the gallery', as the saying goes. If British music-hall performers are anything to go by, the Australian
performers of leary songs in pub singing-rooms may well have
peppered their songs with lewd insinuations delivered with a wink
or a raise of the eyebrows at their fans. Being more constrained
by censorship and propriety, leary performers in the theatre drew
on other low pursuits to forge a rapport with the gallery. In *The
Blue Ribbon of the Turf*, the Cockney comic relief hammed up his
agonies over losing a bet, attempting to draw guffaws from patrons
who had experienced the same.[37]

Given how often larrikinism has been linked to Irish-
Australianness, it is fascinating that Cockney figures should have
exerted such an appeal. It is true that many (but by no means all)
larrikins had Irish heritage of some kind. If one looks at the lists of
defendants described as larrikins in police-court reportage, there
are more Donnellans and Doolans than Richardsons or Martins,
although the latter are still to be found. With the great majority
being the children of gold-era immigrants if not the descendants
of convicts, most larrikins were colonial-born. For this reason,
their first allegiance appears to have been to the place in which

they were raised rather than to the place of birth of older members of their family. For larrikins, being white-skinned, speaking English and having local ties seem to have been more important than whether one's roots came from Manchester or county Donegal.

Even for those who had Irish heritage and were proud of it, it was not as if being drawn to Cockney acts required one to reject one's Hibernian roots. Both Irish and Cockney characters were associated with low mischief on the stage. In some cases, they were even played interchangeably by the same performers. The fact remains, however, that coster types exuded a rough glamour which colonial-era larrikins preferred to stage-Irish slapstick as a model for their own self-presentation. It was no doubt fun to laugh along with Irish buffoons as they performed their noisy knockabout routines, just as larrikins also laughed at blacked-up buffoon parts in minstrel shows. It was Cockney acts, however, which most modelled the style admired by youths keen to impress in the absence of a decent earning potential. This is partly because of their leary humour and dress, and partly too because they presented an idealised independence free from the humiliations of jobbing wage labour. Stage-Cockney figures were intended to bear some relation to actual East London 'penny capitalists', in other words. They played on the similarities between juvenile colonial workers and their East London equivalents and pandered to desires to be a cut above the mass.

As a street-vendor who owned his own pony cart or fruit barrow, the protagonist in 'Costermonger Joe' was presented as a fellow free from wage slavery. He did as he pleased all day long, he boasted to audiences, possessed of 'spirits as light as air'. The girls all smiled at him because of this, far more than at the men working steady jobs indoors:

> Your tradesmen in their shops, who live on mutton chops
> Are often more unhappy, I'll be bound

Than I with bread and cheese, and a drive out at my ease
And the wholesale twenty shillings in the pound, in the pound
And the wholesale twenty shillings in the pound.[38]

This kind of call-your-own-shots chic offered exactly the escapist vision that appealed to the workers in brickworks and abattoirs and boot factories dreaming of an independent life. It also served as a role-model for the aspiring street-hawkers, marine-store scavengers, self-employed carters, street musicians, would-be stage performers and bottle-gatherers keenly associated with the larrikin *milieu*.

The currency of acts such as 'The Chickaleary Bloke' helps us understand why a subculture revolving around the ideal of leariness reached a critical mass in Australia's east-coast capitals from about 1870. It was not as if this street-based subculture was wildly different from earlier forms of urban rowdyism in the colonies. Nor was it hugely different from urban rowdyism in other parts of the world. Still, the fact that these young people were called 'larrikins' and associated with the word 'leary' made a difference to their self-identity. Larrikins' interest in savvy Cockney characters also seems to have made a difference to the way others thought about them. On tour in Australia in the early 1890s, for example, the English burlesque performer EJ Lonnen performed a series of larrikin acts based on leary Cockney routines. Melbourne comedian Will Whitburn also performed cheeky larrikin acts in blackface minstrel shows in the same period. In one of these, he described himself as a 'leary lad'.[39]

In highlighting the dream of streetwise independence and popular theatricals, I have foregrounded the role of culture in accounting for the rise of larrikins here. This is in ways glaringly obvious. Larrikinism was itself a cultural phenomenon, manifested through flamboyant dress, a self-promotional demeanour, a love of cheap amusements and 'villainous songbooks'. Because of its links to the de-skilling of certain trades and a kinked age distribution following the gold rushes, however, it has often been talked about as if it were only a social phenomenon before now. This is all the more the case because the first larrikins had such a tendency towards delinquency.

Since policymakers and sociologists have long been concerned with pinpointing social 'risk factors' for juvenile delinquency, similar factors have not surprisingly dominated past attempts to explain why larrikins appeared. Some labour historians have also presented larrikinism as a form of working-class protest made through acts of delinquency.[40] Though these youths came from labouring backgrounds, however, they were not consciously working class. Though this would change in the twentieth century, late-colonial larrikins reserved some of their greatest antagonism for working-class activities and peers. They were also animated more by desire than protest. Chief among their motivations was the desire to scoff at tradesmen like Costermonger Joe and to big-note themselves like the Chickaleary Bloke.

Above all else, what we find in the late-colonial larrikins is a group of disadvantaged youth trying to adapt to rapid change. Coming of age during the last decades of the century, these youngsters experienced aggressive demographic growth, the increasing commercialisation of leisure, the early stages of industrialisation, and an economy reliant on flexible employment and frequent fluctuations in supply and demand. Those in the early twentieth century would face new challenges: the acceleration of industrialisation and the demise of showmanship and street-based work. Amid all of these developments, larrikin youth worked hard to create their own identities, their own styles and customs.

Though we may not like much of what became part of the

larrikin scene, many of their practices were the forerunners of those featured in the mass youth cultures of the twentieth century and beyond. Long before it became common for youth to aim for streetwise chic, in other words; long before heterogeneous crowds danced to bands in commercial venues – long, too, before Generation Y became notorious for hopping from job to job – such things could be found among lowborn roughlings on late-colonial streets. In this sense, one might well choose to see the first larrikins as a cultural vanguard rather than either the hidebound creatures of working-class traditions. Like it or not, the first larrikins' efforts have echoes in the leary confidence and hedonistic display still apparent in youth cultures today – a very different thing from acting solely as the ciphers of public anxieties.

Chapter Two

The brazen girl

This account of the female larrikin, or larrikiness, begins like my story of her male counterpart: in Gertrude Street, Fitzroy. In March 1890 two adolescent girls, Elizabeth Fry and Ettie Dickens, met in this street and fell to quarrelling. Though it was autumn by then, one of Melbourne's palely fine, apple-crisp autumn mornings, Dickens was soon so hot under the collar that she hit Fry and blacked her eye. Since the street was busy and Fry hoped for vengeance, the girls headed to nearby open ground known as Jerusalem Square. By the time they got there, word of the impending dust-up had spread and a crowd of gleeful onlookers had come running from the streets around. 'All the rules of the prize ring were duly observed', the *Collingwood Mercury* reported the next day, 'viz. seconds, bottle holders, referees, and timekeepers being appointed'.

Onlookers would later claim that Fry and Dickens fought for 20 rounds. That may have been an exaggeration wrought by their predatory excitement, gripped by the sight of two young women trading blows. So too, perhaps, were the estimates that 300 people were present at the fight. Before Fry finally claimed victory, however, both girls had evidently kept at it for some time. She made her way jubilantly home when she was done, though 'cut about the face and bleeding'. Unfortunately for her, these injuries attracted the attention of police who stopped and quizzed her about their origins. As the story of the fight came out, Fry was seized and marched to the watch-house. A warrant was put out for Dickens; witnesses were interviewed and charges were laid. A day or so later, both girls were brought before the local magistrate charged with affray. Standing in the Collingwood court before admiring supporters, the bruises spreading opal-green about their eyes, each was sentenced to a fine of 20 shillings or in default, imprisonment for 48 hours.[1]

Three years after Dickens and Fry had their fight, 13-year-old Brisbane girl Rebecca Lacey went with three of her girlfriends to a tented boxing show. They confidently threaded through the sweating concourse of bodies, undeterred by the reek of armpits and testosterone, thrilled by each successive fight. They were even confident enough to approach one of the several showmen present and talk with him as the crowd began to disperse. For some time before this, Lacey had been living and working as a domestic servant at the South Sea Boarding House in South Brisbane. Carting slopping bed-pans and soiled sheets by day, she was released into the street each night to join with other girls her age. Dressed in skirts hemmed well above the ankle, the members of this 'larrikiness push' lolled about the shops in Stanley Street, South Brisbane's main retail strip, and went to entertainments when they had the money. On weekends, Lacey could also be found with her older sisters and a bunch of male larrikins, sometimes in the city, other times by the eel-brown river at North Quay.[2]

Historical accounts of colonial larrikinism rarely mention its female participants. Reading them, one could be forgiven

for assuming that male larrikins only fraternised among themselves – either that, or for supposing that young women were only
included in larrikin activities as sex-objects or punching bags. Girls
such as Elizabeth Fry and Rebecca Lacey challenge this view. They
show that poor urban girls were not just 'donahs', a slang word for
moll or girlfriend; the term used to describe them in most historical commentaries. Instead, they were an active part of the larrikin
scene. These young women engaged in their own unruly activities: drinking, staying out late, hiking up their skirts, getting into
fights, forging friendships and generally daring each other to act
rebelliously. They also socialised with male larrikins in any number
of capacities: as fellow revellers, rioters, sisters and neighbours in
addition to sexual partners and girlfriends. It thus makes sense to
speak of these young women as larrikins in their own right; not as
donahs, but as larrikinesses or larrikin girls.

From the outset, larrikinism placed a premium on hyper-
masculine qualities such as cockiness and fighting prowess. A
concern with male solidarity also became increasingly important
from the 1880s, when male larrikins began to form 'pushes', or
loosely composed gangs. These pushes were only ever the most
visible aspect of the larrikin subculture, however; the part that
drew the most attention from observers at the time. They were
always connected to a broader social network that included adolescent girls or young women in their early twenties. Larrikinism
cannot be adequately understood without a consideration of this
broader network and its female participants – particularly when
girls such as Fry or Dickens were growing up and coming of age.

Colonial larrikin girls were every bit as showy and vulgarly confident as the boys. They courted reputations for boldness among their
friends and behaved indecorously before outsiders when it suited
them. As far as their funds permitted, they also enjoyed brash entertainments in the city and inner suburbs. Some larrikinesses even

took pleasure in exhibiting masculine qualities, exulting in their own abilities in the bare-knuckle ring. Others were more inspired by brazen burlesque performers than they were by leary boxers or acts such as 'The Chickaleary Bloke'. Observers often described these girls' style as brazen, as good a word as any to capture its mix of knowing sexuality, toughness and sass. In either case, young women's involvement in larrikinism was powerfully motivated by the friend-ships it allowed them to form with like-minded girls. The popular notion that female larrikins were subservient donahs, simply existing as 'roots' for the boys (if you will pardon the ockerism), should thus be recognised for what it is: a *Bulletin*-style men's fantasy.

Almost as soon as the word 'larrikin' was taken up by the press at the start of the 1870s, cartoons of larrikins were created by comic artists. The *Melbourne Punch* featured them in topical caricatures that contributed to public debates about how to deal with the 'rowdy class'. Some also featured larrikin couples in *faux*-romantic repartee, mining a vein of humour about lowborn courting couples that had long been popular on the stage. By the 1890s, similar cartoons appeared regularly in the *Bulletin,* many under the heading 'In Push Society'. Most of these were drawn by Tom Durkin and Ambrose Dyson, *habitués* of Melbourne's bohemian scene. Along with Norman Lindsay and Ambrose Dyson's broth-ers, Ted and Will, they formed a clique with the boozy members of Randolph Bedford's Ishmael Club. Laughing at the world through wine-stained teeth, they embraced a jovially superior, intellectually contemptuous version of masculine *bonhomie.* In the early nine-ties, Tom Durkin was criticised for the 'hysterical prejudice' of his caricatures of female suffragists, effectively deriding them as frigid wowsers. He and Dyson portrayed the female larrikin almost as derisively. In their hands, she appeared as an unattractive 'donah' willing to put up with anything for her man.[3]

The *Bulletin* images typically depicted the larrikiness as a raw-boned girlfriend, her face like a proverbial fishwife's. As often as not, she was shown swapping less-than-courtly quips with a brutish male *amour*. Sometimes a group of these young women were depicted boasting of the shiners their fellers had given them the previous Saturday night. Dressed in large hats extravagantly crowned with cheap feathers, they talked in a dialect bearing a sketchy resemblance to any spoken in Australia at the time:

> **Poll:** There goes May. One of 'er lamps is blackened!
> **Liz:** Must a-been an acciden', then. She ain't got no bloke! [4]

A LESSON IN OPTICS.

BILL *(of the "Boovernoo push," to his "Chooky")*: "*Mag, your 'mince pies' (eyes) is as bright as a new 'druar,' your 'bones' (teeth) is as white as a sheet, and your straight tips (lips) is as red as a crawfish.*"

MAG : "*Yes! And you're as green as a cabbage.*"

BILL *("stoushing" her)*: "*And there's a black peeper for yer.*"

Figure 8. *Cartoon by Tom Durkin for the* Bulletin, *2 February 1895, p. 11 State Library NSW*

The extent to which the 'In Push Society' series was based on observation of actual larrikin types is an open question. At the time, many of the *Bulletin* set were making names for themselves on the basis of their familiarity with 'lower Bohemian' society. Ambrose Dyson's cartoons drew on pursuits widely reported among real larrikins: trips to dance halls, picnics at Chowder Bay, scenes of street drunkenness, vivid sartorial display, and the like.[5] At the same time, his caricatures were saturated by low-comedy conventions. The fact that their female characters towered over their male partners was influenced by the range of burlesque-style acts in which rough women were depicted as monstrously unfeminine. The same logic that made it funny for male actors to perform as Irish servants or dames in drag (the precursors to Barry Humphries' Dame Edna) was at work in these cartoons. Their jokes and scripts were also lifted from Cockney routines doing the rounds of Australian burlesques and vaudeville shows in the 1890s.

One of the most obvious sources for the narratives framing the 'In Push Society' series was a hit song by London's celebrated Cockney performer, Gus Elen. Called 'Never Introduce Your Donah To a Pal', it pressed the figure of the Cockney fellow and his 'donah' to emphatically comedic ends. The Cockney donah in this song was highly fickle and promiscuous, continually running off with a new man in an ever more startlingly be-feathered hat. Another famous song of the 1890s was 'The Coster's Serenade', first performed in London by Albert Chevalier in the West End music halls. Chevalier's Cockney figures represented a shift away from the leary types featured in earlier Cockney acts. Unlike the Chickaleary Bloke, his Cockney fellows were sweet-hearted street-hawkers who sang the praises of their donahs in a spirit more earnest than rough. Numerous renditions of these songs were offered by Australian performers during the 1890s and beyond.[6] There were also local

acts performed in Australian vaudeville shows that substituted larrikin figures for the Cockney and his gal.

A larrikin act modelled on a Cockney's serenade was performed
by the English burlesque star, EJ Lonnen, during a tour of Australia
in 1892. Back in London, Lonnen was famous for his mischievous
Cockney or Irish routines. His most popular act in the early 1890s was
the Cockney boozing-song ''Ave a Glass, Won't Yer?' (alternatively
known as ''Ave A Glass Along of Me'). It was highly popular with
Australian crowds. Also endearing to colonial audiences was Lonnen's song, 'I've Chucked Up the Push for My Donah', in which he
played a larrikin whose heart melted for a 'donah wot I met at Chowder Bay'. That song was an Australianisation of Chevalier's Cockney
oeuvre and was immediately picked up by local artistes. It became
so popular that it led to spin-off jokes and parodies in the press.[7]

EVEN CHUCKED HIS DONAH
FOR THE PUSH—.

Figure 9. Bird O'Freedom *(Sydney), 6 May 1893, p. 5*
State Library NSW

Larrikin characters based on stage Cockneys were common in the Australian press and popular theatricals in the 1890s and early 1900s. A chapter in Banjo Paterson's *An Outback Marriage* (1906) teemed with larrikin figures, all raw giggling girls and unmannered youths. It was even given the same title, 'In Push Society', as the *Bulletin* series. Both the *Bulletin* caricatures and Paterson's chapter provided Gus Elen-esque riffs on the fickleness of larrikins' 'donahs'. First published as stand-alone poems in the *Bulletin* from 1908, CJ Dennis' *The Songs of the Sentimental Bloke* (1915) followed more in the mould of Chevalier's romantic Cockney or Lonnen's 'I've Chucked Up the Push'. The latter was played as the accompaniment to screenings of the silent film of *The Sentimental Bloke* shot by Raymond Longford in 1919.[8]

Anyone versed in turn-of-the-century vaudeville comedy would have recognised the works by *Bulletin* contributors as amusing parodies. This was especially the case for *The Songs of the Sentimental Bloke*, given that its very title foregrounded its connections to musical theatre. Mostly, however, later generations of readers have failed to get the joke. In particular, a number of historians have approached these representations as if they were reflections of actual characters from 'push society'. They speak now as if female larrikins really were called donahs, and as if the young women in the *Bulletin*'s caricatures or in Dennis' poetry were based transparently on real larrikin girls.

The word 'donah' did not appear with any regularity in the Australian press until after 1892, when Gus Elen's 'Never Introduce Your Donah' and Lonnen's 'I've Chucked Up the Push' were appearing on the stage. An 1878 cartoon from the *Melbourne Punch* admittedly shows a male larrikin promenading with his 'dona' [sic] with an air of grave pomposity. Since this is the only example I am aware of prior to the 1890s, however, it is likely that the word only gained broad currency as a result of Cockney routines in that latter decade. It is also likely that 'donah' was never widely used among larrikins themselves. To be sure, Louis Stone used the word in his novel *Jonah* (1911), a rattling read based on observations of larrikins at Paddy's Market and in Waterloo. As with the 'In Push Society' cartoons, however, there are limits to the extent to which *Jonah* was 'true to life'. The eponymous hero himself, an orphan larrikin turned earnest father and wealthy businessman, offers cause for reserve. Stone's knowledge of the vaudeville theatres attended by Waterloo larrikins also ran no further than the Tivoli.[9]

Plenty of early 1900s theatres were better placed than the Tivoli to draw custom from Waterloo. Among these were EI Cole's Haymarket Hippodrome, playing to peanut-scoffing masses in Belmore Park; Harry Clay's once-weekly vaudeville shows in Newtown; and the others he held in the Masonic Hall and Royal Standard Theatre in lower Castlereagh Street.[10] The Tivoli, on the other hand, was located in upper Castlereagh Street, up near St James Church and the high-flying doctor's surgeries in Macquarie Street. It pitched itself at well-heeled crowds coming from the North Shore by ferry or across the Domain from the eastern suburbs rather than crowds from the southern factory suburbs. Though its cheapest seats were only sixpence (the same as in less salubrious venues), only small numbers of these were available. Given that donah routines appear to have played predominantly on the Tivoli circuit, the chances that the word was adopted by larrikins as a result of these acts were thus relatively slim.[11]

Any account of larrikin girls which relies on turn-of-the-century cartoons and fiction which were themselves heavily dependent on Tivoli larrikin acts and stage-Cockney songs must now be taken with a pinch of salt. We certainly need to question James Murray's claim that the young women who associated with male rowdies were larrikins' 'drabs'. They were of a sort who enjoyed being clobbered by their men, he wrote, and were

'strangely jealous of other women given such masculine atten-
tions'.[12] But, of course, it is not as if one can dodge all problems
of knowledge about female larrikins simply by shifting to non-
fictional sources. We are always going to be dogged by problems of
representation when looking for evidence of these girls, forced to
contend with sneering or plain uncomprehending comments that
observers made about them. Short of giving up altogether, however – or otherwise confining oneself to exploring public attitudes
towards female larrikins – one has to be content with making the
best of the historical material to hand. At the very least, this means
hunting up a diversity of sources, going beyond the usual quotes
from the *Bulletin* and the works of its contributors.

One of the most recurrent problems with non-fictional sources on
female larrikins is the number of times they describe *any* girl in
the company of a larrikin-like youth as a 'prostitute'. Concerned
citizens or police officers were forever speaking of the 'larrikins
and prostitutes' who contaminated certain neighbourhoods after
dark, getting into fights and shocking public decency.[13] Certainly,
there *were* male larrikins who went to brothels or were caught
on the town with inveterate streetwalkers, but in such cases their
female companions tended to be older than larrikin girls' mid-
teen to early-twenties age-group.[14] There were also younger girls
who moved in larrikin circles and earned money from time to
time through sex.[15] Usually, however, the phrase 'larrikins and
prostitutes' was used thoughtlessly by contemporaries. Like someone now referring flippantly to a pack of westies or bogans, it was
generally delivered in a casually elitist spirit, with little interest in
the details at hand. Most often the person speaking did not care
whether the girls concerned really were prostitutes or not: so far as
they were concerned, it was one and the same.

At the very least, references to 'larrikins and prostitutes' tell us that rowdy young men and women were often in each other's company. Reading them in this way, avoiding the assumption that the 'prostitutes' were only present as sexual conveniences for the boys, it is startling how much mixed-sex socialising among these people has left a trace in the record. There are also other sources which convey this same impression without resorting to sexualised insults towards the girls. Happily, some of these proceed on the assumption that girls could be larrikins in their own right rather than just hired squeezes or donahs to the boys.

On 29 April 1882, the *Collingwood Mercury* reported that four young members 'of a gang, or "push" as they term themselves' had been arrested for insulting behaviour. Each of these push members was between 15 and 17 years of age. They were well known for loitering in Smith Street, stubbornly ignoring shopkeepers' efforts to drive them away. On this particular occasion, they were found half-drunk at 1:00am in nearby St David's Street. They had set up for the night on an unused lot, shrieking with laughter while swigging from a communal bottle of beer. The names of these 'push' members were then listed: William Engleton, George Cook, Maria Clements and Jane Madelin.[16]

Complaints about mixed-sex larrikin groups appear more often than one might expect in the colonial press. Scandalised accounts of 'young blackguards of both sexes' were legion, especially in the 1870s and 1880s. They hung about the roadside, horsing about, dancing, puffing on small clay pipes and when they felt sufficiently mutinous, shoving nastily at passers-by. Roughlings of both sexes also milled around prison gates to cheer when one of their friends was released. In 1887 a group of Melbourne larrikins was even accompanied by a street band that played 'See, The Conquering Hero Comes' as their mate sauntered free. But such cheer squads did not just turn out for the boys. In Sydney, male larrikins frequently congregated outside Darlinghurst Gaol 'to meet female prisoners coming out after a term'.[17]

In the early 1880s, the 'brazen-faced larrikiness', Elizabeth Pollock, was brought before the Collingwood court. With her air of studied insouciance and inexpertly-cut fringe, this 16-year-old belonged to a gang of 'thieves and prostitutes' (it was said) which met up next to Fox's Hotel. A similar group of so-called 'male scamps' and 'female brothel-keepers' was prosecuted before a crowd of Collingwood sympathisers in 1880. In a heady and perhaps hunger-fuelled escapade, they had broken into a local butchery by night and run off with strings of German sausages and bacon.[18]

Figure 10. *Elizabeth Pollock, 'brazen-faced larrikiness'. At 16 she was sentenced to two months' imprisonment after being found 'idle & disorderly' in Collingwood. This is her mugshot, taken on 26 November 1880.*
Public Records Office Victoria[19]

Just weeks before she was arrested as a participant in that self-described 'push' in St David's Street, 15-year-old Maria Clements fought another girl in a Collingwood roadway. Like Elizabeth Fry and Ettie Dickens, the girls were urged on by onlookers, in this case a baying band of male friends. These friends included John Batty, later to be arrested for his involvement in a gang rape of Emma Hamilton, a 26-year-old Collingwood woman, at Studley Park in 1889. Back in 1882, however, when police arrived to arrest Clements and her combatant, Batty and his male friends tried to stop their arrest. 'We won't let our ＿＿＿ go that way; if the bobbies take them they'll have to take us', they cried.[20]

Frustratingly, we will never know the word that John Batty and his fellow male larrikins used to describe Maria Clements and her female adversary. It was evidently something like 'bitches', imparting the sense of possessiveness which these youths felt towards female 'push-ites'. Though obviously attesting to the casual sexism of male larrikins, this possessiveness also conveys the clannish feeling shared among these disreputable teens. For both male and female larrikins alike, in other words, risking arrest with fellow rowdies from their neighbourhood meant developing a feeling of belonging to a loose tribe. It meant sticking up for one another if threatened, taking one another's part in local jealousies, and feeling a glorious though short-lived sense of collective empowerment when banding together to defy police. In spite of the patent differences between male and female experiences of the larrikin scene, some part of the girls' motivation was thus the same as the boys' – a desire for the heady togetherness that came with acting up with one's friends.

In 1876 two girls called Emma Gould and Alice Lacey took part in an assault on Collingwood police. They had been hanging out in a mixed-sex throng in Smith Street, running into pedestrians while pretending to be drunk and afterwards collapsing in *faux*-tipsy hilarity. When officers tried to arrest some of their male companions, these young women gathered the rest of their group together and incited them to pelt the 'peelers' with stones. These larrikinesses and their female friends were the 'chief instigators' of the fracas, the court was later told.[21] Young women throwing themselves into the fray to prevent male friends from arrest were also recorded in central Brisbane and Bouverie Street, Carlton, during the 1870–80s.[22] A yet more spectacular instance of this took place in Sydney in 1890 at the harbourside pleasure-ground of Chowder Bay.

On the afternoon of Eight Hours Day in 1890 (the then-equivalent of Labour Day), a fully fledged ruckus took place in and around the dance pavilion at Chowder Bay. The scene of the melee was a picnic held by an Irish-Catholic friendly society to raise money for the Maritime Strike. Two larrikin groups described in the *Sydney Morning Herald* as the 'Woolloomooloo push' and the 'Gipps Street push' descended on this picnic and turned it into a fiesta of blows. They first fell to fighting among themselves in the pavilion, but forgot their differences once police and artillery-men were sent to bring them into line. More than 40 arrests were made after the whole group began beating the officers, some with branches torn from trees, others with a storm of bottles and stones. The majority of those arrested were young men aged between 15 and 27 years of age, but four young women were also brought before the Water Police Court the next day. They had been caught either as members of a large group that chased police or, in one case, trading blows with another larrikin girl.[23]

Intriguingly, three of the young women arrested alongside each other in the Chowder Bay riot had married the previous year. Each was in her early twenties and had married a young man her age in the central Sydney district in 1889. It is tempting to con-clude from this that these young women were part of a push that included themselves and their husbands. Even if this was not the case, a group of young men and women who seemed to regard themselves as a push were arrested at the Sir Joseph Banks pleasure ground at Botany, Sydney, the same year. On 29 December 1890, the 19-year-old labourer William Kellow, and 19-year-old Carter Douglas were charged with drunkenness or indecent language at Botany on Boxing Day. Alongside them were 22-year-old Emily Shoppes and 23-year-old Elizabeth Cummings, both machinists. All four had taken part in a fight between pushes said to come from Newtown and Waterloo. Upon being fined five shillings, Shoppes allegedly said: 'Oh that is nothing. On New Year's Day I am taking my push to Lady Robinson's beach, and will give the Newtown Court a job of 5s.'[24]

Girls such as Elizabeth Pollock and Emily Shoppes are known to us today because they were arrested for larrikin behaviour. Many more girls or young women were not arrested, however, because the police were preoccupied with running male larrikins to ground. In 1882, for example, a 'mob of male and female roughs' congregated at the intersection of Stanley and Wellington Streets in Collingwood one night and held 'high carnival' there. Four of these young men were rounded up by police and charged with insulting behaviour. The girls were allowed to spirit themselves away. Undoubtedly, there were countless other cases in which girls involved in larrikin hijinks were simply left to disappear in this way.[25]

Male larrikins' violence towards women is another reason why the presence of female larrikins was understated in the press. After the Kelly-gang murders and the gang-rapes of the 1880s, in fact, larrikinism was effectively defined as a problem of male violence. Reporters of cases in which young male rowdies beat women their age assumed that those assaulted were meek victims rather than fellows or adversaries. One can hardly blame them for this, given that plenty of incidents warranted description in those terms.[26] Considering the assault of 18-year-old Norah Swan and her female companion, however, it becomes clear that some of the girls who bore the brunt of male larrikin violence were neither submissive girlfriends nor luckless passers-by.

In June 1885, James Hayes was charged with assaulting Norah Swan and her friend Annie Schultries in Brisbane. According to the magistrate, Hayes was a young man of the 'larrikin class'. When he was apprehended he had been at Brisbane's notorious Gympie Hotel and was accompanied by a male friend who lashed out at the arresting officer. He also had prior convictions for rorty offences such as public drunkenness. A reporter for the *Brisbane Courier* duly wrote up the incident as yet another instance of unsuspecting female pedestrians attacked by a male larrikin. In actual fact, Swan and Schultries were acquaintances of Hayes. They came upon him in Brisbane's Albert Street as they walked towards Chiriani's Circus one Saturday night. Hayes was with a female friend, Kate Bowden, whom Swan and Schultries also knew. The four of them had acknowledged each other as they approached, but soon began to argue. Hayes seems to have caused their disagreement, poking fun at the way Swan and Schultries were dressed. They had tucked up their skirts to about knee height, aiming for a racy exposed-calf look. Enraged, Swan began throwing stones at Hayes and Bowden, roaring 'you young buggers!' Hayes responded by calling her a 'bloody whore' and knocking her to the ground. He lingered long enough to kick Swan in the head and punch Schultries before taking off, Bowden at his side.[27]

Hayes' assault on Swan and Schultries is yet another reminder that male violence towards women was common within larrikin circles. Nonetheless, the fact that Swan threw the first stone indicates that violence was also a more general larrikin phenomenon. It was not just something expressed by young men towards women or young men among themselves, but also by young women towards each other and their male acquaintances. These young people won cachet through the capacity to inflict pain and bear it without complaint; the girls as well as the boys. This hardly means that we should now deem it acceptable that male larrikins were violent towards female ones, or that it was acceptable for the *Bulletin* to make jokes about this, implying it was all in good fun. It does mean, however, that we can quit seeing those girls as drabs waiting hopefully for a bashing as proof of their boyfriend's regard.

In the end, the question of how to view girls' role in larrikinism depends on whose perspective one views it from. Youths such as John Batty may well have viewed their female companions as their 'bitches' (or rather, the late-Victorian equivalent of that term) and used this to cultivate solidarity among themselves. But those female companions did not see themselves as passive items of property. Nor did they regard themselves as somehow peripheral to their own social scene. If they entered into a relationship or had casual sex with a larrikin youth, that did not make them 'just a girlfriend' or 'just a root' so far as they were concerned. And why should we assume that girls always regarded their relationships with boys as the main game? Young larrikin women worked up their own sense of same-sex solidarity; their own friendships and animosities and rivalries. For many, the allure of these girl-on-girl friendships was a key impetus for their involvement in larrikin circles. It helped to compensate for the easy brutality of the boys and the contempt of colonial society at large.[28]

Prostitutes living and socialising together were a regular sight in the brothel districts of the late Victorian era. A 'supportive female subculture' thrived in such places, allowing women rejected by the rest of society to find companionship, share chores, and manage the physical risks involved. In Melbourne, such young women lived together and called themselves 'mates'.[29] Similarly supportive relationships were found among girls sent to industrial schools or reformatories. From time to time, groups of these girls staged daring escapes together; some also then ventured out for celebratory sprees on the town.[30] In the early 1870s, whole groups of adolescent girls sometimes escaped from the Biloela Industrial School together, an institution for female children and adolescents deemed at risk of criminality or abuse. Situated on Cockatoo Island in Sydney Harbour, an outcrop of land close to the workshops and boatyards at Balmain, this 'school' was the scene of both violent repression and fierce friendships among its occupants.

The violence at Biloela shocked a parliamentary committee when it was sent to interview staff and girls there in 1873. It is still shocking today. Staff frequently put the teenage inmates into straitjackets, gave them beatings and canings, and locked them in darkened rooms. The extent of the girls' rebelliousness in the face of this treatment is also confronting. When urged to reform herself by one earnest visitor, the late-adolescent inmate Rose Oswald rounded on him ferociously. She had no desire to be respectable, she told him – the minute she got out of Biloela, she would return to what she was before. At various times over the preceding years, Oswald and her friends had smashed windows, bashed staff, sang songs with filthy lyrics and drew lewd caricatures on the wall. Invariably, they maintained a collective silence once they were done. 'I have nothing to say only the same as Sarah'; 'I say the same as Sarah Bourke'; 'I have only the same thing to say as the other girls', were indicative responses when interrogated by their superiors.[31] Some of the girls also partook of sexual play or relationships with each other. Two in their late teens slept in the same bed every night in spite of their superiors' complaints that it was 'unnatural'. Another pair was caught in the midst of 'something very bad indeed' up against a gate after prayers one Sunday.[32]

Intense female friendships were formed among unruly girls living at home as well as those in institutions. Contrary to our stereotypes about Victorian femininity, dripping with high-collared lace and lavender perfume, plenty of 'fast little girls' walked the pavements of districts such as South Brisbane, daring each other to engage in risky behaviours. In spite of police reluctance to prosecute them, all-girl duos or trios were still sometimes arrested for jostling pedestrians off the footpath or behaving riotously.[33] Mary Ann M. and Nell D. from Waterloo were one such duo. When they were both 12 years of age, they went AWOL from home for several nights in a row. If the number of parents obtaining warrants for the arrest of abscondee daughters is anything to go by, this was not an uncommon occurrence, at least in certain suburbs.[34] During their time away, M. and D. enacted a sense of racy sisterhood together, having sex with a couple of youths. A year later, in February 1887, a constable discovered Mary Ann M. in bed with a young fireman at the Redfern fire station. She told the officer that she had had sex 'of my own free will' with three of the young firemen there. She also told him she had planned to go straight to Nell D.'s house when she was done that night.[35]

Apart from fighting and going on sprees together, larrikin girls acted with a pert-faced impudence in court. According to John Stanley James, the journalist who called himself the Vagabond, both larrikin youths and girls of 'a certain class' manifested a lively interest in the fate of their friends on trial. The moment such a youth or girl was brought in, he wrote, 'you will see that their first movement is to peep round the corner of the dock and exchange a wink with their sympathetic "pals"'. A 'brazen-faced hussy less than 15' certainly did this in 1882. Charged with vagrancy on the basis that she had been consorting with larrikins, she waved away her parents' tearful protestations to the court. 'I'd rather live as I have been living than go home with them', she told the Melbourne magistrate. She then went out 'defiantly swinging her bonnet' after being sentenced to a year in a reformatory. In Brisbane, Norah Swan, the girl struck down by James Hayes, exhibited similar insolence. Two years after her assault *en route* to Chiriani's

Circus in 1885, she was charged with obscene language. Upon being found guilty, she 'bounced out of the court with what was intended to be a very crushing "thank you" to the bench'.[36]

Though girls acting devil-may-care in court had plenty in common with male larrikins, their gestures and expressions were not the same. Instead of the boy's half-smirking leary swagger, they went for saucy gestures: tossing their bonnet, walking with bouncy sass, delivering a 'crushing "thank-you"' to the magistrate. These behaviours were often called brazen by contemporaries. As caricatures of a sexually precocious 'low' femininity, they were indeed influenced by brazen female performers of burlesque. Late-Victorian burlesque meant something different to the striptease-cabaret we now associate with the term, I hasten to add. Delivered in rhyming couplets and littered with puns, a burlesque then was a play or skit that sent up something serious through overstatement and absurdity. It was still concerned with pushing the limits of bodily display, famous for its dancers in 'fleshings' which gave the impression of naked skin. But there was nothing *avant-garde* or necessarily glamorous about it. By the 1890s, in fact, many theatre critics decried burlesque as tacky and *passé*. 'Tasteless as a meal of stewed umbrella with hat sauce', is how the *Bulletin* described it in 1892.[37]

The burlesques perhaps most affordable for larrikin girls were short acts in blackface minstrel and variety shows. They featured burly men cross-dressed as women. Often they contained a barrage of jokes about bodily functions – the forerunner of later crudities such as the Benny Hill Show. Far more famous than these, however, were multi-scene burlesques starring women cross-dressed as 'boys'. As in pantomime, these performers presented themselves either as sexy hoydens or homely tomboys. The voluptuous American, Emmeline Zavistowski, was an example of the former. Touring Australia as one of the Zavistowski Sisters in 1871, she played a succession of burlesque princes and foppish military generals with fetching buxomness and 'go'. Two of Australia's so-called principal boys, Maggie Moore and Kate Howarde, belonged to the latter category. Each played the English thief and prison escapee, Jack Sheppard, in 1890s productions of the burlesque *Little Jack Sheppard* (incidentally the play that brought the song 'Botany Bay' to the world). Playing Jack Sheppard in Brisbane in 1898, Kate Howarde sang a ditty called 'As Bad as They Make 'Em', boasting of her toughness and misdeeds. In her version, the stout-legged Moore sang the rollicking tomboy number, 'Jack Keeps 'Em All Alive-O'.[38]

Figure 11. *Emmeline Zavistowski, voluptuous burlesque star of the late 1860s–early 1870s*
Houghton Library, Harvard College

Figure 12. Maggie Moore as Jack Sheppard c. 1895
National Library of Australia

Cross-dressed roles in which women played with masculine conventions were not the only burlesque style available to female
performers. Some specialised instead in rompingly vampish display.
After Lola Montez's so-called 'Spider Dance', the most well-
known Victorian-era act of this kind was 'Ta-ra-ra-boom-de-ay'.
First made famous by the London music-hall star Lottie Collins, it
featured a girl who pretended to be demure in her father's presence
but misbehaved the moment his back was turned. That song was
a hit in burlesques at London's fashionable Gaiety Theatre when
Collins performed it there in early 1892, frenetically flashing her
scarlet drawers. Packed audiences also attended performances of
'Ta-ra-ra-bum-de-ay' (as one wag christened it) when it appeared

in the colonies. Not only was it included in the London Gaiety Theatre Burlesque Company's Australasian tour in late 1892 – it was also copied and parodied in almost every other Australia performance venue of that year.[39]

Burlesque performances acted as case-studies in brazen femininity for female larrikins. This was important because young women from the social echelons occupied by Norah Swan had little to give them positive reinforcement. If their mothers worked long hours, skimping on themselves to make ends meet, they were unlikely to have had the time or allure to provide inspirational examples of feminine style. Representations of lowborn women as hefty-shouldered drabs or 'bloody whores' offered little by way of encouragement. On the other hand, charismatic performers displaying sassy vampishness or cocky 'badness' provided attractive alternatives for poor urban girls. They offered a girl tips on how to present herself as more self-assured than she actually felt; appearing in court, for example, or facing up to a shopkeeper trying to oust her from outside his door. For those of a tomboy bent, they also provided hints about how to play up one's masculine qualities, and perhaps even how to mock the pretensions of one's blokish friends.

Few female larrikins, of course, would have had loose cash for burlesques and variety shows. Domestic servants earned between five and eight shillings a week in this period. Younger girls in the clothing industry earned even less. In both cases, boys of equivalent age performing commensurate work were paid significantly more.[40] Even the sixpence for the gallery of cheaper venues would thus have been difficult for a larrikin girl to find. Still, a young woman only had to go to a play or show every now and then for it to leave a powerful impression. And there *are* examples of housemaids or factory girls going to the theatre, even in the paltry sources available.[41] Since uneducated women were the key recruits to burlesque choruses and cheap variety shows, some would also have performed burlesque on stage themselves. In early 1890s Sydney, a prostitute who sold sex to Chinese immigrants was working as a part-time dancer in fleshings at Chiriani's Circus. Though she was not a larrikin, her presence points to the lowborn status of female performers in entertainments of this kind.[42]

Another way that poor young women came into contact with burlesque conventions was through the circulation of theatrical songs. At Biloela Industrial School, for example, the girls sang constantly as they went about their work. Their long hours of labour in the school's laundries were made less monotonous if they sang together over the slap of hot cloth and the stoking of the boilers. Some of these girls had beautiful voices. According to staff, they could sing a hymn or love-song charmingly if they pleased. At night when they were locked in their dormitories, however, they preferred to perform acrobatic tricks and energetic song-and-dance routines. One of the songs they were singing in 1873 was a piece of frippery called 'Love Among the Roses', first performed in Australia by the Zavistowski Sisters in 1871. In a burlesque take on a romantic song, it required a girl-singer to adopt the guise of a lovestruck young man:

> A bewitching smile was on her face,
> As charming as the posies,
> I felt the smart of Cupid's dart,
> 'Twas love among the roses.

Whenever a newcomer arrived at Biloela, the older girls swarmed expectantly around her, begging her to teach them any new songs she knew. Their assumption that newcomers would be up on the latest acts perhaps indicates that these girls went to theatres more often than just suggested. Girls who could not afford a

ticket themselves might nonetheless get hold of one through
petty theft or occasional prostitution, or otherwise be treated by
male companions. Alternatively, it suggests that such acts circu-
lated by other means. An unruly young woman might encounter
theatrical songs in pub singing-rooms, brothel piano-rooms, by
friends' amateur renditions, or at circuses or sideshows.[43] Melbourne resident Catherine Frederickson was indeed managing a
sideshow which travelled around Richmond and like suburbs in
the early nineties which included a garter-flashing dance among
its other attractions. Playing in vacant lots or at fairs and sporting
grounds, it featured 'lady boxers' and 'girl high kickers' alongside
weight-lifters and sword-swallowers – or did, until a policeman
scandalised by the female boxers took Frederickson's licence
away.[44]

On a Saturday night, drunken streetwalkers and other older brazen women in places such as North Melbourne or Collingwood
were often reported making spectacles of themselves, kicking up
their skirts *a la* 'Ta-ra-ra-bum-de-ay'. During the London Gaiety Theatre Burlesque Company's tour, the *Bird O'Freedom* also
reported that a number of young Sydney women indulged in 'an
al fresco skirt dance to the huge delight of a mob of larrikins' in the
vicinity of Woolloomooloo. The same paper ran a comic cartoon
of a group of larrikins dancing to 'Ta-ra-ra-boom-de-ay' during
the Broken Hill miners' strike that year. Since so many Sydney
police had been sent to Broken Hill (the paper suggested), the
city's larrikins were literally kicking up their heels. A few years
later, three drunken young women and a man were arrested in the
inner-Melbourne suburb of Carlton for holding a high-kicking
competition in a park one Saturday night.[45] Such incidents provide a glimpse of the influence of brazen burlesque dance routines
on inner-suburban life.

Figure 13. Bird O'Freedom, *17 September 1892, p. 1*
State Library NSW

Cross-dressing was another burlesque convention carried out of entertainment venues into the streets. This practice played a role in the development of a homosexual subculture in late nineteenth-century Australian cities, but did not just appeal to men or women with same-sex desires.[46] Cross-dressing also functioned as a way to send up demure femininity or effeminate masculinity among young rowdies. A mob of Sydney larrikins who went for a naked swim in the harbour in 1881 indulged in this kind of mockery. Once they had finished swimming, the boys dressed themselves in the girls' underclothes and minced about on the sand to the guffaws of their friends. A few years earlier, two Sydney girls of about 17 years had paraded King and Erskine Streets in the city dressed as larrikin boys. Kitted out in trousers, high-heeled boots and 'indented billycock hat', they swaggered about boldly meeting the eyes of passers-by.[47]

It was once common for Left commentators to celebrate aggressive street subcultures as a form of resistance to the dominant social order. This was certainly how some regarded London's punks in the 1970s, not to mention the mods or 'sharpies' of the Vietnam years. On the whole, the male commentators championing these delinquent youths paid little attention to their female associates. In Australia, historians have similarly talked up the anti-'wowserism' of early male larrikins while overlooking their female colleagues.[48] If a rejection of authority or respectability is to be one's yard-stick for judging larrikin culture, however, then surely many of its female participants would score higher than the boys. Girls such as the inmate at Sydney's Shaftesbury Reformatory, who in 1891 boasted that she could 'fight with any man', departed far more flagrantly from social expectations than boys waging bare-knuckle bouts. And few young men could have delivered a more patent 'up you' to respectability than that delivered by the Biloela girls who threw off their dresses during a riot in the early 1870s. These young women ran bare-breasted onto a beach and threw stones at a hooting ship of sailors, damning their ogling and cheers.[49]

Though the behaviour of the Biloela girls was consciously sexualised, it was not just concerned with trying to be sexually attractive to men. Honed by their familiarity with burlesque, most female larrikins were aware that brazen precocity could be used to do other things. They knew that it came in handy if one needed to be courageous in court and as a way to reject demure femi-ninity. Some young women may also have drawn on burlesque in order to offer their own version of masculine rakishness and bravado. Thinking about these girls turning performance styles to their own ends helps us to imagine them as something more than a cartoon donah or prostitute. Thinking about their friend-ships with each other also gives us a richer sense of their lives. The brazen girl's audience was never just the male larrikin with his leary swagger and arrogant belief in male prerogative. Her audi-ence included other young women like herself: fellow combatants, rivals, neighbours and relatives, mates and partners in adversity.

Chapter Three

The pull of the push

In 1901 Ambrose Pratt, a Sydney lawyer turned writer, published an article in London's *Blackwood's Magazine*. Called '"Push" Larrikinism in Australia', the article was framed as a journalistic scoop in which Pratt laid bare the inner workings of a notorious larrikin push from the Rocks. Pratt claimed to have been initiated into the secret doings of this push after its 'king' adopted him as its solicitor. For some time, he said, he represented members of the push whenever they came before the courts. By this means, he became the only outsider to penetrate the mysteries of Sydney's vicious push culture. Not all larrikins belonged to 'pushes', a word which was early nineteenth-century cant for a crowd but used for youth gangs in the 1880s. If larrikins did join a push, however, then they came to exert an extraordinary influence over Sydney society. The city's most formidable pushes held sway in the back rooms of parliament, had a stranglehold on organised crime, owned large club-houses for their private enjoyment, and murdered police and recalcitrant members with impunity.[1]

As soon as Pratt's 'scoop' appeared, it was rubbished as a scam by

Henry Copeland, New South Wales' Agent-General in London. According to Copeland, Pratt's claims were worthy of the arch mountebank, Louis de Rougemont, a Swiss conman who claimed to have been appointed king of an Indigenous Australian tribe in a scurrilous memoir. Though they stopped short of calling him a rogue, a raft of Australian journalists also branded Pratt's article as preposterous. Perhaps Pratt was not a liar, they speculated – perhaps instead he had been led astray by mischievous informants who had played on his credulity. It did seem that these were the only possible explanations for his assertion that larrikin pushes were ruled by tyrants who enforced oaths of sobriety and monogamy on their members, and either had them whipped with sand-filled socks or kicked to death if they broke their vows. It also seemed that the only way to account for the fact that Pratt attributed serious political clout to some of the poorest members of Australian society. 'Not since the world was enlightened as to the flying habits of the wombat', the *Sydney Morning Herald* declared, 'has so much information of the fancy kind been unloaded on a startled world'.[2]

Henry Copeland and the Australian press were right to be cynical about Pratt's article, for he was indeed a lying rogue. At the time he wrote his piece for *Blackwood's*, he had published one novel about Sydney larrikins and was on the promotional trail for his next. The first of these was *King of the Rocks,* his literary debut, published in London in 1900. The second was *The Great 'Push' Experiment,* published in 1902. The latter work featured the 'Dogs Push', a wicked larrikin gang based at Miller's Point near The Rocks. Pratt imagined that this villainous larrikin 'order' was ruled by an affluent pawnbroker old enough to have a nephew in his teens. This larrikin 'king' was conducting an experiment through which he hoped to gain control of the New South Wales parliament. His plan was to rear his nephew to attain a high position in society, allowing him to influence the city's richest and most powerful citizens. To this end, the king had his nephew educated in a private school and afterwards sent him to the University to fraternise with the sons of the Sydney elite.

With this plotline one would think that *The Great 'Push' Experiment* would immediately have been recognised as a mess of narrative pottage when it first appeared. As Henry Copeland's scoffing response indicates, there were some who recognised it as such. In his preface, however, Pratt claimed that the Dogs Push really existed under a different name; that the details concerning it in the novel were a faithful representation of fact; and that anyone who was 'curious to learn more authoritatively of the secret murder clubs of Australia [should] . . . refer to my article, "Push Larrikinism in Australia"'.[3] The fact that Pratt published a non-fiction article in London's reputable *Blackwood's Magazine* meant that many were prepared to give him the benefit of the doubt. Surely such a respected publication would not have printed his piece if it had been a crock of untruths?

Not long after publishing *The Great 'Push' Experiment,* Pratt admitted it was a work of fantasy. In 1904 he brought a libel claim against a newspaper which had cast aspersions on his integrity as a solicitor. This case had nothing to do with his larrikin article or novels. Since his integrity was at issue, however, he ended up being questioned over the truth of those works at the trial. In cross-examination, Pratt confessed that he had never worked in Sydney's police courts as he had alleged in *Blackwood's Magazine.* He also admitted that he had made up many of his allegations about larrikinism in *The Great 'Push' Experiment* (and by implication, in his article as well), 'employing some far-fetched ideas'. 'Did you in that book say that in Australian cities there were gangs of larrikins who influenced Parliament, terrorised the police, and at times murdered their own members, just as Charles Lamb told the British public of the origin of roast pork?', his cross-examiner

continued amid laughter in court. 'That was fiction', Pratt conceded. 'So was my work'.[4]

Figure 14. *Ambrose Pratt c. 1930*
State Library of Victoria

A few years after Pratt's confession, stories of a Melbourne push
surfaced which appeared to give credence to his account. In February 1908, most of the Australian dailies reported on a group of
'youthful desperadoes' who called themselves the Heart and Arrow
push. Based in the predominantly working-class suburbs of Footscray, these youths had been tattooed with a heart pierced by an
arrow, the insignia of their push. This tattoo had been given to
them during a solemn initiation rite in which (it was said) they
had sworn loyalty to their leader and dedication to 'the promotion
of crime'. The identity of the leader of the Heart and Arrow clique
was shrouded in secrecy. He was referred to by his minions only as
'Mahdi' or 'His Nibs', his ceremonial names.

At first glance, the story of the Heart and Arrow push promised
to reveal a villainous conspiracy against law and order similar to

that in Pratt's *Blackwood's* article. Scanning the opening descriptions of this clique, some readers might have imagined that Pratt had been right after all – that his descriptions of clandestine pushes were more accurate than even he had realised. Perusal of the fine print, however, revealed a gap between the lurid suggestiveness of these reports and the paltry nature of the Heart and Arrow push's crimes. These desperadoes from darkest Footscray, who were 'a terror to the neighbourhood of Seddon', each with what the papers called a 'totem' inscribed on their limbs, were charged with the theft of fifteen pence from the Seddon railway station and four eggs from a neighbour's back yard.[5]

Much like our fascination with gangland *exposés* today, a market for stories portraying pushes as 'murder clubs' obviously existed at the turn of the century. Emphasising the pushes' 'totems' and mumbo-jumbo lingo such as 'Mahdi', these stories implied that push larrikins were on a par with savages, exotic and uncivilised. Invariably the sensationalism of these racialised stories outran the facts – in the case of the egg-stealers of Footscray, to an almost farcical degree. While they were overblown at the time, however, these accounts continue to influence views of the early pushes to this day. In his still widely read *History of Australia,* Manning Clark even repeated sections from Pratt's article almost word for word. He assured readers that the pushes were ruled by tyrannical kings who disciplined errant members through beatings with sand-filled socks – a form of torture which Pratt admitted to inventing during his libel case. Other commentators have similarly relied on Pratt for their accounts of pushes, Isadore Brodsky and James Murray among them. Others again continue to describe the pushes via a racialised vocabulary. They claim that the pushes were headed by 'chiefs' and that they ran whole neighbourhoods as 'suzerainties'.[6]

Suggestions that the first pushes were involved in organised crime, or that they reigned in terror over their local communities, are as hyperbolic as the plot of *The Great 'Push' Experiment*. In the first place, they overstate the organised criminality and internal discipline of any larrikin push. In the second place, they overlook the fact that the time period matters when discussing these early versions of youth gangs. Contrary to the popular view, a push from the 1880s was not the same as one from the early 1900s. Nor were any of these pushes the same as the unwieldy mobs of colonial roughs notable in Sydney in the mid-nineteenth century. Rather than jumbling examples from these different periods together, it is important to recognise that the push had its own history: a changing story that unfolded over time.

These days the larrikin pushes most likely to be remembered are the ones with fantastically picaresque names. Among these are Richmond's Dirty Dozen push, the Fitzroy Murderers, the Battle Ridge push, the Devil's Thirteen, the Montague Flying Squadron and the Gore Hill Tigers – their very names reinforcing a sense of their exotic savagery.[7] These pushes are often associated with the nineteenth century in historical commentary, but the majority were in fact from the early 1900s. Back in the late 1800s most pushes had workaday names referring to the places in which their participants lived: the Waterloo push, the 'Fitzroy forties', the Greenwich forty, and so on. It was not really until the early twentieth century that an inward-looking push culture emerged whose constituents were preoccupied with their prestige *vis-à-vis* other pushes and who gave themselves flamboyant titles.[8] It was only then that territorial battles were regularly fought among larrikin pushes whose names brandished capital nouns like bruised fists.

One reason for the shift toward a more coherent push culture in the Federation era was the fact that the popularity of team sport was on the rise. In the early twentieth century, the passion for group sport, especially football, influenced the way pushes presented and conducted themselves. In the late nineteenth century, however, the pushes were more chaotic than this. Their composition was dependent on the night of the week and who happened to be living in the neighbourhood at the time. Their energies were also directed less at promoting their collective identities than at disrupting communal activities and baiting officers of the law. The late-colonials pushes were thus characterised by a tendency to delinquency to a greater extent than those of later years. This was a form of criminality, yes – but one quite different from an involvement in organised crime.

In September 2000, the Australian Institute of Criminology issued a discussion paper entitled 'Young People and Gangs'. In his foreword to the paper, the institute's director Adam Graycar drew attention to the 'Cabbage-Tree Mob' from mid-nineteenth-century Sydney as one of Australia's earliest youth gangs. The so-called Cabbage-Tree Mob has often been treated in this way: not just as a forerunner of larrikin pushes, but of Australian teen gangs more generally. When one looks closely at reportage from the mid nineteenth-century, however, it becomes apparent that observers were not actually talking about a specific group when they spoke of the 'cabbage-tree mob'. When they used that term (almost always without capital letters) they did so generically, referring to any collection of callow youths wearing hats made from the leaves of the cabbage-palm tree. Being one of the cabbage-tree mob meant being one of the sundry rowdies who loitered outside the Royal Victorian Theatre in Sydney's Pitt Street, at the race course or George Street night market, or who otherwise harangued carriages of ladies *en route* to Parramatta for a fancy-dress ball.[9]

When they first appeared in the 1870s, descriptions of larrikins were couched in similarly generic terms to those used for the cabbage-tree mob. Throughout that decade, larrikins were mostly

presented in the press as a kind of lumpen mass, *sans* distinguish-
ing names or features. Anonymous larrikins were said to 'patrol the
paths in mobs', to gather in 'tribes' in vacant lots, and to amass in
clod-throwing 'crowds' on Saturday afternoons. The term 'gang'
was also used, but mostly also in a careless fashion, simply to denote
a loose gathering or group. In December 1871, for example, the
Argus reported that the streets of Carlton had for some time been
'infested by a gang of young rowdies of both sexes, whose amusement appears to be to promenade the streets at night'.[10] The same
kinds of description continued to be made in the early eighties.
Once the Salvation Army arrived in 1882, for example, bands of
larrikins gathered to disrupt their open-air meetings. Some hurled
a medley of elderly vegetables, soot, rocks, flour, even on one occasion a dead cat. Others issued volleys of jeers and burlesques of the
Salvos' hymns. In most cases the larrikin troublemakers seemed as
miscellaneous as their missiles: knots of 'rough blackguards' joined
by children and passers-by.[11]

Published in January 1881, the *Bulletin's* infamous article 'The
Larrikin Residuum' was of its day in portraying an amorphous
larrikin group. Written by the journalist William Henry Traill, the
article railed against a parcel of larrikins which had descended on a
privately-owned pleasure resort at Clontarf, a harbourside suburb
of Sydney, the previous Boxing Day. According to Traill, this party
of young men and women, girls, lads and children had engaged not
in an excursion but an 'orgy', taking part in activities that would
have made Horace blush. They had knocked back drinks and
romped promiscuously in the dance pavilion, their actions lewd as
a 'camp of black-gins'. This account is memorable not only for its
high dudgeon and racist metaphor, but also because it referred to
a gathering much too motley to be considered a larrikin push.[12]

Groups of larrikins were not always described as motley crowds
in the 1870s and early 1880s. Some descriptions of larrikin tribes

or bands gestured at something more specific than a casual collection of friends. In 1874, for instance, a journalist reported that
a group of larrikins frequenting Little Lonsdale Street kept a fund
for bailing each other out from gaol. Two brothers, William and
David Leary, were prominent among this group. In Sydney, too, a
Redfern man told police he had been struck by 'four or five "forties", or larrikins' on his way home from work in September 1876.
Possibly based on an antiquated form of measurement, *forty* was
slang for a patch of territory as well as for a group which had made
it their stamping-ground.[13] One gets an inkling from these cases
that at least small numbers of larrikins were forming proto-pushes
or self-conscious gangs. Such instances were still relative rarities
during the 1870s, however – indeed, the word 'push' itself only
began to be used in relation to larrikins in the 1880s.

According to James Hardy Vaux, a roguish convict who compiled
a dictionary of criminal slang in 1812, the term 'push' was once
thievish cant for 'crowd'. In his *Dictionary of the Flash Language*, a
push was described as 'any crowd or concourse of people'. By the
early 1880s, however, 'push' seems to have become a more specific
form of slang. In his memoir of sentences served in Irish gaols in
1882–3, the political dissident Michael Davitt indicated that his fellow inmates had used 'push' to refer to a prison labour gang. The
lexicographer Edward Morris later speculated that the word was
being used in the same way and in the same period in Australia, and
that it quickly migrated from the prisons into the streets as a term
for a larrikin gang. This was certainly suggested by an article on
Darlinghurst Gaol published in the *Sydney Morning Herald* in 1886.
The word 'push', the *Herald* explained for the benefit of readers
unfamiliar with it, referred to a gang or clique or clan formed in the
neighbourhoods around the gaol. A good number of Darlinghurst's
inmates spoke of belonging to pushes, the paper continued, including the 'Haymarket bummers' and the 'Woolloomooloo push'.[14]

To the best of my knowledge, the first printed use of 'push' in
connection to larrikins was in Melbourne on 29 April 1882. It
was on that date that the *Collingwood Mercury* referred to the 'gang,
or "push", as they term themselves' that included the 15-year-old
girls, Maria Clements and Jane Madelin. Interestingly, however, the
term only had a small circulation in Melbourne until the mid-
1890s, when it suddenly seemed to be everywhere. If groups such
as the Fitzroy forties and Bouverie forties are anything to go by,
the term 'forty' seems to have been preferred in the southern capital before then.[15] In Brisbane, 'push' took even longer to catch on.
It only began to make a showing in the 1890s, and even then was
not used much until the new century, when the city's population
finally exceeded 100,000. In Sydney, however, the term took off
in the last half of the 1880s. Readers from the harbour city were
treated to a rush of references to pushes almost as soon as the ink
was dry on that article about Darlinghurst Gaol. Including talk of
the Harris Street, Abercrombie Street, Waterloo, Woolloomooloo,
Paddington, The Rocks, Miller's Point and Gipps Street pushes
(the last associated with a street now called Reservoir Street in
Surry Hills), these read like a Baedeker's guide to the inner suburbs
and city fringe.[16]

The apparent explosion of pushes in the second half of the
1880s raises the same question as the uptake of the word 'larrikin' in 1870. Are we dealing with something new among young
people here or simply with new ways of talking about them? Are
we charting developments actually taking place on the ground,
or only in the way that police and journalists chose to represent
them? Since these questions go to the very heart of historical
knowledge, they can't be answered in any simple way. We will
never know how many gang-like entities were formed by lower-
class youth before 'push' became available to describe them. Nor
will we know the extent to which police or the press exaggerated

the push phenomenon once the word came into use. Journalists presumably felt the same pressure to find pushes at every turn then as *Today Tonight*-style reporters feel when discussing 'gangs out of control' today. The difficulties that even a conscientious observer might face when trying to distinguish between a youth gang and what sociologists call a 'non-gang youth group formation' also applied then as today.[17] Even so, it does seem on balance that the main reason 'push' came into use was because there was a genuine need for the word. Male larrikins really did begin forming more self-conscious allegiances during the 1880s, in other words. The push would also come to exert an increasing attraction for larrikins over the following years.

Seventeen-year-old Tom 'Wobbitty' Smith was not someone who needed convincing that the pull of the push was real. He had no doubt that they were something more than a device for reporters to drum up interest in their stories. In September 1886 he was hunting for snakes with friends in Sydney's Moore Park, hanging out on a scrubby knoll called Mount Rennie, when he saw a crowd of youths rape a 16-year-old girl. Hiding breathlessly in the bushes to watch, he later helped identify the perpetrators, doing a deal with police to avoid arrest. Smith told police that he knew most of the youths involved by sight, 'as they belong to the Waterloo "push"'. As an unemployed jockey with a prior conviction for disorderly behaviour, he was from the same social background as the young men charged for the crime. When he was not scavenging for snakes or rubbish in Moore Park, he socialised in the dance halls and roadways around 'Irish Town', the part of Waterloo adjoining the park. It was in Irish Town that he had come into contact with the larrikins he called the Waterloo push.[18]

Three years before the Mount Rennie Outrage, the Waterloo larrikin William Boyce was using the term 'the talent', a Sydney term used interchangeably with 'push', to refer to his set of friends.

Boyce was one of the youths executed for the rape at Mount Rennie. He ended his life on the gallows in January 1887. Back in December 1883, however, he was looking for his clique in the streets of Waterloo one Saturday night. To this end, he wandered behind the Duke of Wellington Hotel and approached two of his mates sitting on the grass. 'Where is the talent?', Boyce asked them. The reason this incident was recorded was that the pair on the grass were later arrested for the rape and murder of Margaret Owen, a 53-year-old prostitute, that night. Like Wobbitty Smith, one of this pair decided to 'turn dog' (as larrikin slang had it) in return for police dropping the charges against him. Though he admitted raping Owen along with his friends, this youth disclaimed knowledge of her murder. Owen must have been killed after he and his mates were done, he maintained. The youth then mentioned his conversation with Boyce after the rape by way of an alibi.[19]

Almost a decade after Margaret Owen's death in Waterloo, a Melbourne larrikin bragged to police that he belonged to a push. This young man was arrested at Fitzroy's Royal Sovereign Hotel in May 1892. As he was being led outside he shouted dramatically to his arresting officers: 'if you don't know who I am you soon will, I am one of the Stephen Street Push'. A few years before this, the Wollongong youth John Woods was also arrested, in his case for raping a barely pubescent girl. After being dragged off his 12-year-old victim behind a Salvation Army barracks, Woods stated: 'I knowed fine that I would sleep in a gaol tonight. I saw it in the cards this morning'. He then added: 'I am sorry I went for the girl. I thought it was her sister Annie. I did not get half an inch into her. The others in the push put me on to her and I went for her just the same as anyone else would do'.[20]

When larrikins used the term 'push', they were referring to a group of friends which met four basic criteria. They used 'push', that is, to refer to a group whose members were predominantly if not exclusively male, shared certain qualities, spent regular time together, and most importantly, looked out for each other's interests and backed each other up when aggrieved. Pugilistic talent and leary style were higher on the list of qualities valued by push-ites than they were among larrikins at large. The term 'the talent' is possibly indicative of this. One imagines that it referred to a group who prided themselves on their cockiness and fighting ability. In 1885, too, the press reported that a group of Ultimo larrikins who supported the Sydney prize-fighter Chris Dunn went by 'the euphonious title of the "Cow Lane push"'. So-called 'Cow-laners' were still hanging around Paddy's Market some fifteen years later. In 1900 their name appeared in connection to a melee with artillerymen near the market during celebrations for the end of the Boer War.[21]

Considering the lives of famed pugilists Larry Foley and Albert 'Griffo' Griffiths raises the possibility that some pushes formed in boxing gyms. Having started his career as a 'knuckle fighter' in the late 1860s, Foley was a hugely successful boxer with his own pub and gym in the 1880s. Once attracting the homage of Ned Kelly at an 1878 match, he had a huge larrikin following who cheered him whenever he took vanity parts in melodramas or set foot in the ring. As manager of his own boxing school, Foley also acted as mentor for young pugilists. One can imagine that some of the Sydney youth who trained in the gym attached to his White Horse Hotel might have come to refer to themselves as a push. The same probably applied to larrikins at other gyms: youths putting on the gloves after work, barracking for each other at matches, and gradually coming to think of themselves as a 'talent' or push.

Foley's one-time *protégé* 'Griffo' was one of the young men who trained at his White Horse Hotel gym. Griffo may not have been a push member himself. As an adolescent living at the Rocks in the 1880s, however, he would at least have been friendly with push-ites.

He first came to the attention of pugilists by waging knuckle fights in Sydney lanes and reserves, watched by hundreds of fellow bruisers. He then set himself on a path to boxing celebrity by attending successive Sydney gyms. Foley's gym in George Street was only one of these. Another was run by Ed Johnson above a wine saloon; another again, the Pelican Club, was next to Playfair's butchery in George Street.[22]

Griffo's background suggests that pugilism played an important role in the lives of rough youth across the 'larrikin belt'. Whether via outdoor knuckle fights or gloved matches in small boxing rooms, the sport was an important focus for rowdy youngsters of the inner suburbs in the late 1800s. It is thus more than plausible that sweaty gyms such as the Pelican Club acted as crucibles of push culture. Pushes may otherwise have formed from groups who met to test their fighting mettle on weekends. Crucially, boxing (unlike bare-knuckle fighting) was not against the law. Its legality allowed for a semi-organised round of matches and training rooms to develop during the 1880s, the very decade in which pushes or 'talents' emerged. Significantly, too, Sydney had a more thriving pugilistic scene than the other cities at that time. This may also help to explain why pushes developed more rapidly there than elsewhere in the late-colonial years.[23]

The growth of pushes marked the rise of a more self-conscious interest in masculine solidarity among male larrikins. The 'young blackguards of both sexes' visible on footpaths in the 1860s and 1870s would gradually become less common, with all-male groups taking their place. There would still be places where rowdies of both sexes would meet in the new century, football matches and cinemas among them, but the pull of the push had made male-on-male bonds more conspicuous by then. Even so, the fact that observers tended to overlook the existence of female larrikins

Figure 15. *Shops in the vicinity of the Haymarket/Paddy's Market area in 1901, not long after the 'Cow-laners' fought artillerymen celebrating the end of the Boer War.*
City of Sydney Archives

almost certainly meant that they exaggerated the male-only character of the push. This was the case in the 1880s when pushes were only just beginning to emerge. It was not just young men who could be skilled with their fists or enjoy watching a prize fight, after all. One of the few young women explicitly named as a push member was arrested for a bare-knuckle fight with another girl in 1882. This young woman was 15-year-old Maria Clements of Collingwood, who fought Annie Cronin in a public roadway surrounded by shouting male friends.[24]

Years after Clements was arrested for her disorderly match against Cronin, a young woman called Harriet Adderley was also arrested for participating in a street fight. She had been carousing with Valentine Keating and John Collins, both well-known members of the Crutchy Push, in North Melbourne's Baillie Place. After a constable arrived and tried to arrest Keating, a man on crutches widely considered a leading figure in the Crutchy Push, Adderley tried to stop him. 'You put a finger on him, and I'll split your skull!', she shouted. Keating and Collins then wrestled the constable to the ground, allowing Adderley to kick him viciously in the face several times.[25]

Figure 16. *Harriet Adderley, 1904*
Public Records Office Victoria [26]

Even if they were not expressly acknowledged as such, bellicose young women such as Harriet Adderley may have come to be treated as honorary males and thus as *de facto* push members over the years. Others may have acquired similar standing by virtue of their brazenness and demands on male push members' loyalties. In 1891 the *Age* reported that the Bouverie forties were accompanied by 'a number of girls, who are always on the look out for "game" for them'. Ten years later the *Collingwood Observer* reported that 18-year-old Rose Tucker and 19-year-old Mary Bourne were 'prominent members of the Swamp Push'. This was a group who hung out in the malodorous Collingwood swamp by night. Two years after this, in 1903, a Sydney woman was charged by a female neighbour with use of threatening words. The neighbour told the court that this young woman had punched her during an argument and then shouted that she would fetch 'a talent' to smash her home. Since her opponent was a kind of 'push queen', the neighbour explained, she now lived in fear of payback from the male 'talent' with which she kept company.[27]

The intimidation dealt out by the so-called 'push queen' of Sydney is only the tip of the iceberg so far as larrikin paybacks are concerned. Revenge was a key ethic in larrikin circles. This had been case since at least the early 1880s. On one memorable occasion, the friends of a Fitzroy larrikin up for assault sent a letter depicting 'a coffin, pistols, and bowie-knives, &c' to a magistrate before his trial. Luckily in that instance the larrikins' promise of retribution was an idle threat, but this was unfortunately not always the case. The gang rape and death of Woolloomooloo woman Elizabeth Phillips in 1883 was shrouded by rumours that one of her assailants had been motivated by revenge. He had wanted to 'get her back', it was said, after Phillips had helped put him away for indecent assault. The Collingwood gang rape of Emma Hamilton in 1889 was similarly fuelled by revenge. One of the arrested youths, Arthur Wren, had been keen to repay the 26-year-old victim after she had successfully prosecuted him for indecent language the previous Christmas. Coolly watching one of his friends rape her, this youth, Wren (brother of SP bookie, John Wren), told the victim: 'It serves you right you bugger. I have my revenge. You will remember Christmas time'.[28]

Phillips' assault in Woolloomooloo was committed by an opportunistic collection of friends rather than a known push. The Collingwood larrikins who raped Emma Hamilton may not have been a push either: certainly there is no mention of it in the court reports. Nonetheless, group retribution for individual grievances seems to have played an important part in push allegiances. An extreme example of this was when young men belonging to the 'Miller's Point talent' or 'Miller's Point push' kicked wharf labourer Thomas Pert to death in 1893.

In the weeks before he died, 35-year-old Pert had been the subject of a recriminatory campaign led by two members of this push. Nineteen-year-old Henry Doohan and 26-year-old James Maguire were both convinced that Pert had informed on them over an earlier crime. Doohan challenged Pert about this in the presence of other members of 'the talent' several times. On one occasion, he showed Pert a slingshot and told him: 'you'll have a taste of this before long'. On another, he went up to him outside the Palisade Hotel and announced: 'I want to have a fair dinkum fight with you'. Maguire was also heard boasting to a local publican's daughter, saying: 'we will lay him out as sure as his name is Pert'. This pair was ultimately joined by upwards of 20 others one Sunday morning in the beating that cost Pert his life.[29]

At the inquest for Pert's death, a young coal lumper, James Dever, was called as a witness. Asked whether he belonged to the Miller's Point push, he avoided a straight response. 'Yes, I do go with some of them', he said initially. He had often socialised with the accused and other members of the Miller's Point talent. But at the same time, Dever added, he had disagreed with the others' animosity towards Pert. He had even quarrelled with Henry Doohan because of it.[30] Dever may, of course, have been trying to exempt himself of complicity in Pert's death by answering in this roundabout way. Since no one was claiming that he had been involved, however, it is more likely that he was signalling the significance of his disagreement over the push's desire for revenge. If agreeing to avenge others' grievances was a prerequisite of membership, then Dever's refusal to attack Pert may have disqualified him from belonging to the Miller's Point push.

That some pushes actually carried out vendettas helps to explain why Pratt's allegations about their vicious internal discipline came to be so widely believed. His claim that push members intimidated court witnesses also resonated with an actual case where this had taken place. This concerned the death of the seaman, Knut Anderson, at The Rocks on 31 January 1892. A cabman had witnessed Anderson being fatally punched and kicked by several young men that night. Afterwards, one of their friends warned him that he would be 'topped off' if he identified them. Eventually, he was subpoenaed to give evidence at the committal hearing for three of Anderson's alleged murderers, the boxer Thomas Dinney and musician Henry Jansen among them. The cabman testified that he knew the three prisoners by sight and believed them to be members of the Rocks push. He also testified that he had seen them speaking angrily to Anderson just moments before the attack. One of the assailants appeared to be a skilled pugilist, he added ('sir, Dinney is a boxer, and from the way the men was fighting I should think that one of them was a boxer'). In spite of this, he refused either to confirm or deny the prisoners' involvement in Anderson's demise.[31]

The brouhaha following Anderson's death, for which no one was ultimately put on trial, was the inspiration for Henry Lawson's poem 'The Captain of the Push'. Published in the *Bulletin* in March 1892, this poem told the story of the 'captain' of an apocryphal Rocks-based push called the Gory Bleeders, who required prospective members to swear an elaborate series of oaths. Among other things, anyone wanting to join the Bleeders had to swear that they would punish a disobedient member, either by death or by 'kicking him to a jelly on the ground'.[32] Lawson's poem evidently influenced Pratt's *Blackwood's* article as well as the willingness of many Australians to believe its claims. Though it bore some relation to the Anderson incident, however, 'The Captain of the Push' presented a highly embroidered version of the reputed facts. For a start, none of the witnesses had suggested that the Rocks push had been formed through explicit vows. It was not even certain from the evidence that the accused actually belonged to that push. The figure of the tyrannical captain also appears to have been plucked from Lawson's fancy, much as white colonists had once errone-ously imagined Aboriginal tribes to be ruled by powerful kings.

It is always possible, of course, that isolated pushes such as the Heart and Arrows played with ceremonial rites and titles, perhaps even ironically inspired by the ideas popularised by Pratt or Law-son's 'Captain of the Push'. (Back in the 1870s, of course, youths had sometimes even played with the title 'King of the Larrikins'. In those cases, however, they were boasting about their street-credibility rather than claiming command of a gang). It is also possible that some pushes were dominated by a charismatic member who amounted to a leader in practice though not in name. The finest pugilist in the group may sometimes have effectively enjoyed this status, earn-ing the respect of his peers by besting other fighters outside the Eastern Markets or in an unused sporting ground. The vast major-ity of pushes evolved through casual rather than formal measures, however, and were not authoritarian in character. Though an act of revenge admittedly takes a degree of premeditation, there was always far more opportunism and flexibility about late colonial pushes than there was planning and ceremony. Like most youth gangs today, they operated according to evolving principles and rules of thumb rather than constitutions or fixed behavioural codes.[33]

That nineteenth-century pushes were essentially *ad hoc* entities can be seen in the Miller's Point push trial. Witnesses were hard-pressed to name how many members the push had. According to the victim's brother Robert Pert, a long-time resident of the area, the numbers which made up the Miller's Point talent differed from day to day. 'Sometimes there are 25 or 20 or 16 together', he said.

The coal-lumper James Dever agreed. 'I don't know how many are in the push. Sometimes there are 20 or 30', he declared. Like Dever, the wharf labourer John Kyneur testified that he had often fraternised with members of the Miller's Point push. Before getting married he had regularly socialised with the nine accused and others, having 'a yarn with them together at night'. He had since stopped associating with them quite so often, but still went with push members to the theatre occasionally.[34]

The picture one forms of the Miller's Point push from testimony such as Dever's or Kyneur's is of a core of a few close friends – in this case, James Maguire, Henry Doohan and Doohan's older step-brother, Edward Rich – who regularly mixed with between ten and 20 other young men. Brothers and other relatives often formed the core of a push. Training partners at a local boxing gym may have acted in the same way. These small groups were then surrounded by a looser collection of youths whose membership varied from time to time. Most larrikins associated with the nineteenth-century pushes would have fallen into this last category. They would have moved in and out of a push (or pushes) more or less as it suited – depending on whether they wanted to participate in the group's activities, whether they had to shift neighbourhoods or had decided to fraternise with different friends. This was certainly William Boyce's experience of push society before he was executed in 1887. The group of youths he called 'the talent' in 1883 was not the same as the 'Waterloo push' with whom he was associating three years later. Rather than tight-knit clans, nineteenth-century pushes were makeshift alliances which were continually being reconfigured, often dissolving and recomposing, in response to their participants' needs.

Not long before the first reference to a larrikin push appeared in the press, Ned Kelly drew attention to larrikins' growing tendency to act aggressively towards police. For Kelly, the larrikin was essentially a younger, less physically impressive version of him-self: a stripling city cousin who shared his determination to resist oppression from the law. 'It takes eight or eleven of the biggest mud-crushers in Melbourne to take one poor little half starved larrakin to a watchhouse', he declared in his Jerilderie letter in February 1879. 'I have seen as many as eleven, big and ugly enough to lift Mount Macedon out of a crab hole, more like the species of a baboon or gorilla than a man, actually come into a court house and swear they could not arrest one eight stone larrakin . . . without some civilians assistance'. Though armed with 'battens and niddies', Kelly continued, police were often 'going to hospital from the effects of hits from the fists of the larrakin'.

It was not of course as if all larrikins fought police. Plenty kept well clear of the officer's baton, running away if one drew near. Others contented themselves with leary wisecracks as soon as a constable's back was turned. But Kelly was right that resisting arrest had become a larrikin practice by the end of the 1870s. There are any number of cases in which aggressive lairies fought an arresting officer, first knocking him over and then 'jumping him' as he lay prostrate on the ground. Even more larrikins gathered outside the courts the next day, cheering their police-resisting friends as they were led smirking inside.[35]

One of the fiercest push fights with police took place at Bondi. On the morning of Boxing Day 1884, more than 20 young men hired a horse-drawn van from the Haymarket and asked the driver to take them to the beach. Upon arrival, some of the revellers went to the dance pavilion, climbing through the ladies' dressing-room window instead of paying at the door. As soon as police threw them out, 'a regular Donnybrook' broke loose. Hearing their shouts, the rest of their friends came bolting from every direction, arm-ing themselves with rocks and sticks as they ran. The afternoon was overtaken with the crash of stones on the pavilion roof, the thwack of fists and batons, the thud of boot-tips on bone. Showers of rocks hit police and other revellers; people were screaming as they rushed to escape the barrage. The riot ended as abruptly as it began when a constable was knocked in the head and fell, apparently dead, to the ground. 'The bugger is dead, let us pack!', his attacker cried, prompting the rioters to take off up the road.

Police lost no time in rounding up suspects in the Bondi riot case, as it became known. Some 20 youths were put on trial the following January, sweating in the dock of the Water Police Court at Circular Quay. Among the line-up was James 'Rorty' Grey, Walter 'Shoppy' Burns, Jeremiah Sullivan, two brothers, William and George Kellow, and James 'Jago' Jones, a youth who fought the riot in trousers and hat but no shirt. In a courtroom jammed with 'feminine relations and friends of the prisoners', a police witness testified that most of these young men lived in Surry Hills and styled themselves as 'the talent' or 'Bummer Gang'. What they meant by this, he said, was that if one was arrested he called out 'bummer!', and those within earshot would attempt a rescue.[36]

Figure 17. *Jeremiah 'Jerry' Sullivan, one of the 'bummers' who took part in the Bondi riot. In 1889 he was arrested for 'jumping' a Redfern police officer, this time, with a different larrikin group.* [37]
State Records NSW

Larrikins' animosity towards police bloomed amid a rapid expansion of officers' powers. In the heady years of the boom, colonial parliaments made police responsible for a quite astonishing range of activities. The force still had to keep up its traditional role of maintaining public order: arresting drunks, disorderly persons, and so forth. Amid the influx of immigrants in the 1880s, however, its brief grew with the speed and luxuriance of a tropical vine. Police were now required to exert functions we would consider the domain of social welfare agencies, including the management of the destitute and the protection of children considered neglected or at risk. They were made responsible for preventing truancy at a time when primary school had only just become compulsory. They were also charged with controlling horse-racing, gaming, betting, cock-fighting, bare-knuckle fighting, prostitution and even leisure on Sundays.[38] These responsibilities set them at odds with a sizeable number of city residents – and none more so than underprivileged youth.

Police friction with larrikins was exacerbated by the fact that they appeared to view criminal proceedings as ends in themselves. They handed out arrests and summons with dogged zealousness, as if the rising numbers on police court lists were the key measurement of their efficiency. The colonies' arrest rate in that decade (or, in the case of Queensland, the early 1890s) was the highest in Australian history. In New South Wales, 75 arrests were made for every 1000 people in 1881 – a much higher rate than the average of 45 per 1000 that prevailed in the twentieth century.[39] Most arrests or summons were for petty offences such as drunkenness or insulting behaviour, for which fines were the most likely sentence. Such was the zero tolerance approach of the day, however, that anyone unable to pay a fine served a default stint in gaol. The prisons groaned under the weight of poor petty offenders thus sent to their cells. At its high water-mark in August 1884, Darlinghurst Gaol had 947 inmates, far more than it was ever intended to house. This number had fallen to 773 by early 1886, but was still well above the prison's supposed capacity of 650 inmates.[40]

When the Irish dissident Michael Davitt visited Darlinghurst Gaol in the early 1890s, he found that there was a special category known as 'Class Seven' assigned to young prisoners. This was referred to informally as the 'larrikin class'. Class Seven inmates were supposed to be secluded from visitors and other prisoners. This policy had been put in place for their own protection and presumably also to prevent pushes forming in gaol. Its unintended effect was to heighten larrikins' sense of being unfairly targeted by the law. They expressed this aggrieved sense of injustice by lashing out at police. An especially bitter example of this took place in Regent Street, Redfern, in April 1886. Less than two years after the Bondi riot, a group of adolescents calling themselves the 'Chippendale clan' came across an officer shopping off-duty with his wife and baby in Redfern. 'Don't wait for the others, let this bugger have it', one of the clan shouted to his friends. The group immediately surrounded the officer and his family, scooping handfuls of rocks from the road. After a frightened pedestrian cried 'do not hurt the child!', they allowed the officer's wife and baby to step aside. These two then watched as the clan stoned the officer and other police who ran to help him, jeering 'we will give you Bondi!'[41]

Australians have often assured themselves that a fair number of their forerunners nurtured a loathing for police. Knowing of the country's convict origins and Ned Kelly's hatred of 'mud-crushers' – knowing too of confronting attacks like the Chippendale clan's – one could be convinced of this view. There were certainly many citizens with good reason to resent police in the late colonial years. In actual fact, however, the majority of residents in inner-suburban communities actively supported police. Their support was sometimes almost as raw as the resistance offered by pushes such as the Bummer gang.

Outside certain pubs and dance halls, it was not unusual to find civilians willing to risk injury to help police arrest larrikins. During a ruckus in Little Latrobe Street in 1895, for instance, Melbourne officers were assisted in arresting a number of larrikins by 'a woman who more than once has aided the police in street fights'. In November 1888, a long-time resident of Chippendale was hurt helping police arrest larrikins outside a dancing saloon in Abercrombie Street. Two of the men wounded alongside police in the Chowder Bay riot of 1890 were members of a friendly society raising money for the Maritime Strike. They had literally thrown their weight behind the law after rowdy youth began trashing their picnic that day.[42]

Civilians helping police fight larrikins came from a range of social backgrounds. Tempting as it might be to assume that they were always middle-class respectables, this was simply not the case. Wildly disparate attitudes towards policing could be found among working people. For every larrikin prepared to 'jump' or stone a constable, there were scores of ordinary workers who welcomed officers' presence in their streets. Conflicting attitudes to police could even be found within larrikin homes. In Newtown, Sydney, a surprising number of cases have been found in which struggling parents initiated summons under industrial schools laws in the hope that police might help them find runaway children or remove them to reformatories. A fair number of these were step-parents hoping that police would support them to create order within their newly 'blended' families. Parents pleading for help dealing with errant children could also be found in the courts. In the waterside Sydney suburb of Balmain in 1888, the mother of 17-year-old Elizabeth Loudon implored a local magistrate to do something about her daughter. Loudon had been charged with vagrancy after staying out at nights with 'a gang of larrikins'. Her mother told the court that she 'could do nothing with her for the last two years, and wished her sent to an institution'.[43]

Fights within families such as Loudon's allow us to imagine a painfully intimate dimension to larrikins' resentment of police. They show that these youths' hostility to the 'peelers' was enmeshed in other struggles with their neighbours and sometimes also within their homes. A pair of larrikin siblings would certainly have had extra reason to resent an officer if he was acting on the complaint of a hated stepfather when breaking up their late-night street party. A larrikin girl such as Loudon would also have despised her arresting officer all the more if he had colluded with her mother in taking her away. These youth would also have had reason for enmity towards community organisers if they knew they were liaising with police about keeping them in check at public events. Organisers of picnics and marches often arranged for friends to be sworn in as special constables in case of larrikin disturbances.[44] This may well have been a reason that pushes so often made trouble at such events.

That larrikins blurred the distinction between police and other members of colonial society can be seen in the most infamous push riots. The Haymarket bummers did not just fight officers at Bondi on Boxing Day 1884 – they also did their best to disrupt other revellers. After climbing through the dressing-room window of the Bondi pavilion that morning, Jago Jones and his friends had headed into a far corner of the dance hall, singing at the tops of their voices. Jones then pretended to have a fit, throwing himself onto the ground, rolling about and aiming spiteful kicks at the couples nearby. Revellers at Chowder Bay were similarly menaced by larrikins so often that the owners of the dance pavilion built a ten-foot fence around it in 1895. Those at the Sir Joseph Banks ground at Botany were the subject of further disruptions from pushes from Redfern, Waterloo and Newtown. In each case, the youths involved seemed to have sought the discomfort of other civilians as well as cathartic fights with police.[45]

Both intimate conflicts such as Loudon's or public stand-offs like the Chowder Bay riot give us a sense of just how unsettled inner-suburban localities were in this period. A restless passage of people moved in and out and through larrikin districts in the late-colonial years. Some had just arrived at the ports, others were *émigrés* from country towns, others again were casual workers tramping the streets in search of a wage. The buildings in their thoroughfares were as much a motley as their inhabitants. Factories, shops and houses were strewn higgledy-piggledy, brothels jostled against churches, tumble-down 'Irish Towns' abutted meticulously kept homes. With Middle Eastern immigrants moving into Redfern in the 1890s and enclaves of Chinese in places such as Waterloo and Alexandria, the inner districts were also more ethnically diverse then than they would become in White Australia days.[46] Amid this diversity we should hardly wonder that struggles about who belonged, about whose interests really counted, took place in larrikin localities. Nor should we wonder that police were caught up in this strife. Police were obviously involved when they prosecuted youth for racist attacks on Chinese street-sellers, when they acted on complaints by parents or local women and when they were called to protect community groups from marauding youth at a dance.

Criminal justice activists have long argued that law-and-order crackdowns are counterproductive: that they act as incitements rather than deterrents to crime. They also suggest that these crack-downs can contribute to the formation of disorderly juvenile gangs. If we needed another example of this, the early larrikins provide it. They responded to overpolicing and prisons engorged with inmates with a sometimes breathtaking ferocity towards officers of the law. Their tendency to form pushes from the 1880s may also have been encouraged by a consciousness of being unjustly targeted by the force. But the pull of the push was not solely caused by lawmakers or police. It was influenced by the boxing scene that gained momentum in the same decade and the aggressive masculinity celebrated within the ring. These pushes' disorderliness was also influenced by other conflicts within larrikins' neighbourhoods: by fights over policing, over what behaviours were acceptable, and who had a right to belong.

There is no one-size-fits-all explanation for why youth gangs form in particular places and moments in time. Nor can one theory ever hope to explain the emergence of as complex a thing as juvenile delinquency. In late colonial larrikins' case, however, the chaotic nature of their neighbourhoods goes some way towards this. At the very least it gives us insight into why late colonial pushes targeted such a mixed-bag of victims: not just police but do-good civilians, assertive women, foreign immigrants, parents and peers who 'turned dog'.[47] The chaotic nature of these districts also sheds light on the makeshift nature of the pushes themselves. Far from swearing allegiance to all-powerful 'kings', most male larrikins had only the loosest connection to a push. Spilling out of pubs and dank boxing gyms, lolling on greens and around Paddy's Market, their messy alliances were a far cry from the exotic 'murder clubs' imagined by Ambrose Pratt. Plenty of push-ites would scarcely have known where they would be living the following month, let alone have been in a position to forge 'til-death-do-us-part bonds. With this in mind it is time to finally put Pratt's hoax to rest, setting it aside along with other accounts reliant on his false *exposé*.

Chapter Four

The Mount Rennie outrage

When the bohemian writer Marcus Clarke published a piece called 'Melbourne Larrikins' in 1870, he presented a brutal picture of the breed. Larrikins were youthful scoundrels who moved in company, he said. They came from the gutter and they sent people into it, knocking them down wherever they chose. Because of this, Melbourne's larrikins reminded him of Sam Hall, a fictitious murderer in a music-hall song. In the song, Sam Hall sat defiantly on death row. 'I'm going to hell, hell, hell', he sang, 'Damn your eyes!' The larrikin felt much the same way. Only the other day it was discovered, thankfully before a train came by, that someone had laid bricks on the railway line. Soon enough, a young rough had confessed to the deed. The spectacle of 'a steaming confusion of blood and brain and brickdust' would have been just the thing to gratify the larrikin mind, Clarke mused. These ruffians didn't give a fig about others' feelings or morality. The rest of the world could hang for all they cared.[1]

Clarke's caricature of the larrikin as *enfant terrible* of the colonies was chiefly meant to amuse. Reading his piece was supposed to be like watching a performance of 'Sam Hall': fast-paced, funny and a little thrilling at the same time. Had it been published in the 1880s or 1890s, it would have been received with less levity. The Kelly gang had really tried to burst up a train at Glenrowan, after all, aiming (to borrow a phrase from Kelly himself) to scatter 'blood and brains like rain'.[2] For this, the gang was the object of hero-worship among city larrikins. In the years that followed, larrikins were also responsible for a trail of attacks on police, vengeful assaults and gang rapes; crimes considerably more frightening than the misdemeanours Clarke described.

Some of the violence in which larrikins were involved appears more chilling now than it did at the time. In May 1888, for example, some 50 larrikin-like youths aged between 14 and 18 years were at the forefront of an anti-Chinese riot in Brisbane. They led a crowd through the city, smashing Chinese-Australian shops and beating their keepers, shouting slogans such as 'Go for the Chinkies!' Though thwarted by police, a mass of Sydney larrikins and others similarly attempted to damage the shops of Chinese-Australian cabinet-makers and attack their occupants in the Rocks in December 1878. Racially motivated attacks on non-Anglo Celtic street-sellers and pedestrians were another feature of larrikin life. In 1879, for example, a pair of larrikin youths from South Melbourne chased 'two negro boys' up the street into the Montague Hotel before assaulting the publican. The following year, four adolescent rowdies from East Melbourne caused a Chinese-Australian man to lose his eye in November 1880, hitting him with rocks from a slingshot as he walked unsuspecting down the road.[3]

Larrikin attacks on non-white Australians remind us that the racism of youth driving cars with 'Fuck off, we're full' bumper stickers is far from a recent phenomenon. My focus here, however, is on the sex crimes committed by male larrikins in the 1880s, most notably the 'Mount Rennie Outrage'. This gang rape of a

16-year-old girl took place in Sydney in 1886 by larrikins known as the Waterloo push. Unfortunately it was not the only such crime. Three years earlier, in 1883, two Sydney prostitutes had died after being 'ravished like dogs' (as one of the perpetrators put it) by larrikins in separate incidents. In the first of these, 35-year-old Elizabeth Phillips was gang raped, burned on her buttocks and thighs with a hot iron, then left naked to die in a vacant lot in Woolloomooloo. In the second, 53-year-old Margaret Owen was found bludgeoned to death in a Waterloo paddock adjoining Our Lady of Mount Carmel church.[4]

Though the Mount Rennie Outrage did not involve the death of the victim, it was by far the most infamous larrikin sex crime of the late colonial decades. It overshadowed other incidents from Melbourne and Brisbane: the gang rape of a 16-year-old girl in North Melbourne in 1887; of 26-year-old Emma Hamilton in Collingwood in 1889; and of 17-year-old Violet Moorcroft in Brisbane's Mowbray Park in 1907. One of the reasons for the notoriety of the Mount Rennie rape was that its victim, Mary Jane Hicks, was a teenage orphan from a convent in rural Bathurst; a more attractive victim than the drunken prostitutes victimised in 1883. There were also unsubstantiated rumours that the rape had involved more than penile penetration, that rocks and hoop-iron had also been used. No doubt the shocked prurience which attended these rumours contributed to the crowds which packed into the court and eagerly thumbed reports of the trial. More sensational yet were the death penalties the defendants received.

Back in 1883, the trials for the Waterloo and Woolloomooloo Outrages had each foundered due to lack of evidence. The youths accused of murdering Margaret Owen at Waterloo were acquitted in March 1884. Only one, the drayman Edward Williams, was convicted over Elizabeth Phillips' shocking demise. In the

Mount Rennie case, on the other hand, 16 teenagers were gathered together after an irregular investigation by the police, 11 of whom were subjected to a scandalously short trial. Nine were then convicted and sentenced to hang. The four youths who eventually died in a partly botched public hanging were almost the last to be executed for rape in Australia. (The very last was Charles Hines at Maitland Gaol, New South Wales, hung for raping his stepdaughter in 1897). Their executions took place after a hard-fought campaign against the death penalty which raised passionate feelings in the broader Sydney community.[5]

The so-called Mount Rennie Outrage has remained a *cause célèbre* over the years. It is not hard to see why. Any case raising the spectre of an unfair trial of socially disadvantaged offenders is bound to spark controversy. Add to that the little matters of capital punishment, gang rape and the vilification of the female victim (Hicks was painted as a conniving trollop by some of the campaigners against the sentences), and its volatility is assured. The fact that the incident has contemporary resonances is another reason it continues to attract comment today. Hearing about it now, the gang rapes in Sydney led by Bilal Skaf during 2000, the gang rape and murder of Anita Cobby in 1986, the rape and murder of schoolgirl Leigh Leigh in 1989, and the Bali Nine spring to mind.[6] Along with this ability to speak to current issues, the case also helped shape two warring images of male larrikins in late nineteenth-century public life.

The prevailing image of the larrikin throughout the Mount Rennie scandal was of a colonial Sam Hall. Each of the young men who participated in Hicks' rape was a 'villain of the vilest type', as the *Evening News* put it during the trial. These villains were so given over to their base masculine urges that they were more 'depraved fiends' than men, the press claimed. The neighbourhoods in which the prisoners lived, Waterloo and Redfern, were similarly maligned. Like Woolloomooloo after Phillips' death, they were reviled as jungles of iniquity. Understandably the residents of these places were distressed by this calumny and tried to defend their suburb against the bad press. A number of the campaigners against the sentences went further than this. Not only was Waterloo a decent place, they claimed, but the prisoners were nothing but 'poor dear boys'.[7]

According to Reverend TJ Curtis, a Presbyterian minister based in Redfern, the character of at least of two of the youths convicted of raping Hicks was 'exceptionally good'. He knew William Hill and George Read personally and was certain they were innocent of the crime. He had always been impressed by their 'quiet, moral behaviour' and aptitude for 'honest industry'. The worthy Waterloo gentleman, TM Williamson, defended the prisoners on similar grounds. As a Catholic MP who ran a free legal service in Waterloo, he represented some of the Mount Rennie defendants at their initial police court appearances. Far from being fiends, he claimed, six of the accused had been to a mass at Our Lady of Mount Carmel Church not long before the crime.[8]

In these defences of the Waterloo push, the image of larrikins gang raping a girl or shouting 'damn your eyes!' to society simply melted away. It was as if such images were simply the stuff of diseased fantasy. The term 'moral panic' had not been coined in 1886, but if it had, youth advocates such as Curtis and Williamson might well have found it appropriate. So far as they were concerned, an irrational fear of a larrikin menace unleashing itself on the city had been worked up by the judge and journalists and blown out of all proportion to the threat actually posed. As anyone who worked with them would know, larrikins were really just the sons of decent labouring families struggling to do the best with their lot. Give them a chance, and they would end up making something good of their lives.

One reason that views of the Waterloo larrikins were so polarised was that for the general public these youths functioned not as people but as types. The *Evening News'* depiction of them as 'villains of the vilest type' was an obvious example. A tendency to view the so-called lower orders as either villainous or virtuous indeed dominated Western public life in this period. More often than not, the labouring classes and non-white peoples were divided into sweeping categories: the hard-working and the idle, the respectable and the rough, those who wore collars and those who did not – as if those labels could describe their whole selves.[9] With such a categorical view of the 'lower classes', it is little wonder that visions of the Mount Rennie Nine were so starkly juxtaposed. The prisoners could either be respectable workers or rough beasts: not both at once, and not something in between.

We may well smile indulgently now at the two-dimensional approach to the toiling masses that predominated in the Victorian era. Those were the days before democracy was predominant, when eugenic ideas were what passed as serious psychology – how naïve those Victorians were, we might tell ourselves! Before feeling too smugly progressive, however, it is worth bearing in mind that plenty of biographical commentary today is still posed as it was back then. Stark juxtapositions are still rife in our discussions of individuals accused of violent crime: 'Serial Killer or Family Man?'; 'Devoted Husband or Ruthless Player?' 'Villain or Victim?' Much news reportage today also replicates the mode of social description once applied to the Victorian 'nether world'. During the riot at Sydney's Macquarie Fields in 2005, for example, journalists depicted that suburb in a disturbingly similar way to representations of Waterloo in 1886. In particular, the Glenquarie housing estate where the riot had erupted was portrayed as a benighted badlands, the haunt of idlers and thugs. Other responses to this reportage tended to the opposite extreme. They suggested that the rioters were the innocent victims of police harassment – none of them villains, all of them poor dear boys.[10]

The problem here is not just the oversimplification of the issues whenever we encounter underprivileged groups given to violence. Nor is it just that we still resort to the language of Victorian melodrama or slum-*exposé* reportage when writing about poverty-fuelled crime. It is also the failure of imagination that kicks in as soon as one tries to hold notions of humanity and horrible violence together at the same time. Confronting a crime such as the Mount Rennie Outrage, it is exceedingly hard to conceive of the perpetrators of gang rape as people rather than stereotypes. It is easy to think of them either as melodramatic villains or victims of injustice. It is much harder to picture them as individuals with real lives and relationships who nonetheless committed 'one of the grossest crimes on record'.

In late November 1886, 19-year-old labourer George Keegan was sweating it out in Sydney's Darlinghurst Gaol. With eight of his friends, he had been sentenced to death for the rape of Mary Jane Hicks. The rape had taken place on the afternoon of Thursday, 9 September after a number of young men dragged Hicks through the scrub from Bourke Street, Waterloo. They took her to a rump of bush in the sprawling expanse of Moore Park; the small knoll known ludicrously as Mount Rennie where the Moore Park Golf Club now stands. Some time later, Hicks was discovered by Darlinghurst police wandering the area in a bloodied, semi-coherent state. She told the officers who found her that she had been raped by eight men, George Keegan among them – although since there were others present, and she had fallen unconscious for a period, the number may have been more than this. Some of her attackers had held her legs open, she said. Others had covered her mouth while their friends raped her; others again had gathered to watch nearby.

The police had been alerted to Hicks' presence in Moore Park by a young shipwright called William Stanley. He had burst into Redfern police station shouting that a girl was being raped at Mount Rennie. Stanley told the police that he had seen Hicks being pulled screaming into the scrub by three assailants. At first he had managed to rescue her from these youths, but was then beaten away by a hooting pack of their friends wielding sticks and knives. Over the next couple of days, Stanley identified numerous boys in their late teens brought before him by police. So did another witness, Tom 'Wobbity' Smith. Almost all of those identified were known locally as larrikins and members of the 'Waterloo push'. They hung out together in the streets around Paddy's Market, at dances in Waterloo's 'Irishtown', at Redfern skittle alleys, and in vacant lots and parks – including Moore Park – near their homes. Some had been before the courts before: Keegan, for one, had been charged with riotous behaviour with a friend in Waterloo earlier that year. Most too were in uncertain employment at the time. Two of the group, Leslie Douglas and Michael Mangan, worked for themselves carting building materials. Others helped family members or local greengrocers sell produce; another again had recently worked handling bloody sheepskins at Geddes wool wash.[11]

Given the public anger that erupted upon reports of Hicks' rape, George Keegan must have held little hope of escaping the noose as he sat in his cell on death row. He started to change his mind over the following days, however, as a campaign against the death penalties led by religious leaders and journalists got underway. Prompted by this support, he and the others pleaded for a reprieve from the New South Wales Governor, Lord Carrington, and the rest of the New South Wales Executive Council. Seventeen-year-old Joseph Martin had already confessed to having sex with Hicks, predictably arguing that she had been a willing party. Seventeen-year-old

George Duffy had also confessed to this, naming others as having done the same. Keegan, on the other hand, prepared a statement that attempted to provide an alibi for himself and Hugh Miller, his particular friend. It set out a welter of detail about their whereabouts on the afternoon of the rape. Eighteen-year-old Michael Donnellan made a similar statement, adding an extra flourish of bravado at the end. He did not ask for clemency, he told the Governor. Rather, he asked for justice, 'which I have not received up to the present. I will say no more. My last struggle for my rights'.

Figures 18 and 19. *George Keegan (left) and Michael Donnellan (right) State Records NSW*[12]

It is no understatement to say that Keegan and Donnellan produced a welter of detail about their whereabouts on 9 September 1886. Their statements may have been compiled in dramatic and tendentious circumstances, but it is hard to read either of them without tiring of their laboriously rendered sequence of events. The opening sentences of Keegan's statement set the tone: 'On the day of the alleged outrage I met Hugh Miller and William Foster at the corner of Elizabeth and Phillip Streets, Waterloo. We then remained there until about half-past 10, and we proceeded to the Strawberry Hills bus stand towards Sydney'. From the bus stand, Keegan added, he and his friends headed to Cleveland Street Public School and loitered outside for a time. At about 12:30pm or 1:00pm, they returned home for dinner – or rather, Miller went home for dinner while Keegan and Foster waited for him on a nearby green. Once Miller returned, the three went to another corner and hung about while one of them took a scarf pin to be gilded at a local jeweller's. After this, they went to a house in Alderson Street for a drink of water, chatted to Thomas Knowles and Lizzie Fizzell on yet another street corner, and then stood about talking to the drivers of wood-carts and drays in the roadway. Sometimes a boy or man that they knew came by and were asked for a drink or a nub of tobacco: one even threw them a handful of oranges. Other times, it seems, they simply chatted desultorily and watched traffic go by.

Michael Donnellan's statement is just as full of quotidian comings-and-goings as Keegan's. It relates a visit to his aunt's with a pair of trousers to be mended; helping his Irish-born mother Honora to tap beer for the hotel she ran in Buckland Street; and supervising a 'Chinaman' collecting manure from the rear of his mother's house in Botany Road. Donnellan also describes doing various small jobs: first at Mr Adams' yard, then at Mr Stokes' 'bus stables, then at Coates' produce store. He further recounts conversations in the street with a young man, Alfred Anderson, and with two peers called John Farrell and Ellen O'Donnell on their way back to work after lunch, each 19 or 20 years old. Finally, Donnellan speaks of a failed attempt to *rendezvous* with a group of workers from a nearby bakery. They had intended to walk to a picnic being held for bakers' employees at Botany that day.[13]

Donnellan, Keegan and Miller received a reprieve of their death penalties on 16 December 1886. Two more of the Mount Rennie

Nine were reprieved on 6 January 1887. The remaining four were hung the next day. It is not clear whether or not Lord Carrington and the Executive Council had been convinced that Donnellan and Keegan had been telling the truth when they offered them their reprieve. They may have been motivated by political considerations instead. Over the many years since, however, numerous commentators on the case have expressed a belief in their *bona fides*. In his widely read *Scandals of Sydney Town* (1957), for example, popular writer Frank Clune suggested that at least some of the Mount Rennie Nine had been innocent – Donnellan in particular. Clune also argued that the accused were denied procedural fairness during the police investigation and trial. His account has influenced views of the case ever since. Most recently it formed the basis for Deborah Beck's sympathetic portrait of the convicted youths in a history of Darlinghurst Gaol. Providing a detailed report of their families' grief and the distressing spectacle of their executions, Beck referred to them affectionately (and erroneously) as the 'Rennie boys'.[14]

Frank Clune was right when he suggested that the Mount Rennie Nine only received death penalties because they were poor. The sons of affluent families would neither have been arrested so hastily nor sentenced so aggressively. It is thus obvious that they received shameful treatment by the judicial system and that those four young men should not have been hung. One can disagree with the sentence and the way proceedings were conducted, however, without disputing the guilty verdict. It would certainly be unwise to place much store by Clune's effort to exonerate the Mount Rennie prisoners, based as it is on a number of mistaken claims. For a start, he incorrectly suggested that the accused were identified solely by a trauma-addled Hicks and the garrulous jockey, Wobbity Smith, whom he considered untrustworthy. In fact, the shipwright Stanley also identified Keegan and his friend

Miller. Stanley told police that they were among the three men trying to rape Hicks when first he arrived on the scene. A cabman and a bread-carter also identified Donnellan as one of the youths at Mount Rennie that afternoon.[15] Significantly, too, Donnellan later changed his version of events. He told a Catholic priest that he had been innocently picking flowers with Hicks in Moore Park before marauding strangers took her away.[16]

While a detailed reading of the evidence suggests that Donnellan and Keegan were guilty, one might be tempted to form the opposite view from a simple reading of their statements. It is easy to imagine that these documents swayed the Executive Council in the youths' favour. This is because for the most part they recount things that really happened: errands their authors ran, conversations they had and places they went to, some of which was backed up by witnesses at the trial. The question of exactly *when* those things took place was crucial, however, and it was at this point that mistruths were almost certainly involved. Nonetheless, the quiet recounting of mundane happenings in these documents creates an aura of verisimilitude which clings to them stubbornly, like newsprint blacked on the fingers.

The sheer ordinariness of the material in Donnellan's and Keegan's statements and some of their witnesses' evidence is another reason why it is hard to imagine their creators as criminals. During the trial, 18-year-old Lizzy Frizell gave evidence that she referred to Keegan as 'Tommy' and Miller as 'Hughy', and that she had chatted to them on 9 September as she did on many days.[17] The pair thus appear to have had more connections to their local peer group than their reputation as depraved fiends suggests. Donnellan's reference to his aunt and mother also infuses his account with an element of domesticity immediately difficult to reconcile with an image of him as a pack rapist. It is precisely for this reason that victims' advocates are so often critical of attempts to humanise the perpetrators of brutal acts. The depiction of a person in the midst of banal activities tends to have an exculpatory effect in and of itself, in other words. It makes it nigh-on impossible to continue to think of the perpetrator in the same condemnatory way.

The power of ordinariness to banish lurid visions of larrikin districts has been put to good use by social historians over the past decades. Melbourne historian Janet McCalman used this technique when she produced her account of early twentieth-century Richmond in the 1980s. Back in the early 1900s, she tells us, Richmond was a predominantly lower working-class suburb with a reputation for banditry. When you actually spoke to people who had then lived there, however, this reputation became hard to sustain. Most Richmondites worked hard to stay clean and 'nice' in the face of material privations, and supported each other to do the same. Ordinary life in this suburb was about careful economy and hard work and staying away from the drink, McCalman insisted – a far cry from the popular notion that Richmond was the place where the 'bandits' lived.

Grace Karskens has said similar things in her work on The Rocks in turn-of-the-twentieth-century Sydney. Contemporary bohemians and later social historians alike have long cast the Rocks as the 'wicked waterfront', she notes. The prevailing image of the area during the Federation era is of a slum teeming with vice and plague-ridden rats. The sky did not, however, lie in a Dickensian fug over this sunny harbourside locality. Nor was life at The Rocks conducted in the bleak tones of a slum *exposé*. Archaeological digs have instead recovered pretty dolls, painted china and delicate combs from its humble dwellings, showing that many of its residents had aspirations to domestic comfort and respectability.[18]

The 1893 trial of the Miller's Point larrikins for the murder of Thomas Pert at The Rocks in many ways supports Karskens' account. Each of the witnesses at this trial had known each other, the dead man, and the defendants for years – in some cases, the whole of their lives. In spite of the numbers of new immigrants and transients in the district, these long-time inhabitants managed to cultivate an almost village-like familiarity among themselves. Like Keegan and Donnellan, the accused were friendly with plenty of the people around them: waitresses, publican's daughters, lift boys, coal lumpers, and other wharf labourers. Some, like 20-year-old drayman George Reid, were considered 'hard-working' and 'industrious' young men. Eighteen-year-old Thomas and 19-year-old Dave Howell were also regarded as decent brothers from a good Catholic family who only hung out with the Miller's Point talent on Sundays and Saturday nights. According to one witness, Dave Howell in particular was a regular bloke – 'just the same as any other young fellow'.[19]

The 'inside' view of larrikin suburbs conveyed by archaeological digs and local accounts is vital when evaluating the character of larrikin groups. It shows us that we need to adjust the conventional image of these young people as a pack of outcasts incapable of longings for respectability or any sort of finer feeling. Even so, it is important not to become so keen to talk up the ordinariness of these youths and their neighbourhoods that we underplay the violence at hand. Even though the Howell brothers only mixed with the Miller's Point push on weekends, they were still among the pack that knocked down a wharf labourer and kicked him to death. Though Donnellan and Keegan had plenty of friends in Waterloo, this did not stop them joining in a spree of sexual violence at Mount Rennie with the Waterloo push. Whichever way we look at it, these communities gave rise to a youth subculture characterised by an ethic of revenge, violence towards women and non-white Australians – an observation scarcely invalidated by their possession of china teacups and collared shirts. It is important that we do not put so much emphasis on the 'humdrum immediacy' of an offender's life and locale that we gloss over hard questions raised by his violent acts.[20]

Larrikins' admiration for being street-smart raises another point: they had their own interest in sensationalised caricatures. Though they were people rather than types, they still took pleasure from the stylised villains and vamps in the popular culture of the day. They went to some lengths to ape the style of stage crooks and brazen hussies in each others' company, acting devil-may-care after the manner of theatrical pickpockets or 'rorty gals'. That sort of play-acting up was part of what they did to earn each other's respect and enjoy themselves. Because of this, one can well imagine a group of them exultantly shouting the words to 'Sam Hall', enjoying the thrill of defiant togetherness it gave:

> And now I'm going to hell, going to hell!
> And now I'm going to hell, going to hell!
> And now I'm going to hell,
> But what a bloody sell
> If you all go there as well!
> Damn your eyes!

The final sentences of Michael Donnellan's statement to the Governor in 1886 gives us a fleeting impression of the bravura that male larrikins performed in each other's presence. 'I defy any man on the face of the earth, to speak conscientiously, to say I was there, or within two miles of the place on that dark day', he wrote. That was the sort of thing tough showmen said when they were bluffing, standing out the front of an obviously bogus spectacle and daring the audience to prove them wrong. Larrikins in court provide us with other examples. In 1887, 11 youths in their late teens went on trial for a non-fatal stabbing at Balmain's Temperance Hall in Sydney. The stabbing took place during a fight between pushes at a dance the previous Christmas Eve. Like most cases in which larrikins were tried over a well-publicised crime, the court-room thronged with their neighbours and peers. In addition to the defendants in the dock, a number of their male friends were put on the witness stand. Several of these caused 'much amusement to the lookers on' by giving an elaborate display of innocence about what had gone on that night. They acted as if their testimony was an in-joke to be shared with their friends in the gallery. Another youth spat a great chaw of tobacco onto the floor of the witness box, making a show of what the Chickaleary Bloke would have called 'not giving a flatch'. He was verbally raked-over by the magistrate because of this, but was no doubt later congratulated by his friends for his audacity.[21]

With its redolence of leary stage acts, the performance of the witnesses in the Balmain stabbing case highlights the importance of disorderly theatricality to the larrikin identity. This point is significant, because as soon as we start thinking about the larrikin persona as a form of role-play it becomes possible to move away from simplistic debates about these youths' characters. Not everyone in the Victorian era considered respectability or disreputability to be permanent codes of values governing every aspect of their lives. Many instead saw them as roles which could be put on and off at will.[22] For this reason it was possible for certain members of the Waterloo push to impress a Presbyterian minister with their 'quiet, moral behaviour' one morning and afterwards run amok with their friends. We don't have to choose between an image of dear boys and vile villains when thinking about these young men, in other words, because they were capable of appearing as both in different social contexts. Accepting this obviously requires us to move beyond caricaturised views of larrikins as slumdog brutes. Yet at the same time it insists on the value they placed on acting disreputably in company, sometimes to seriously vicious effect.

The stories that long-time Brisbane residents told Ronald Lawson about the 1890s affirm the significance of role-play in young rowdies' lives. One old-timer interviewed by Lawson was a man who I will call Richard Grigson (Lawson's records conceal his first name). Grigson told Lawson that he was born in 1874 in Petrie Terrace, a district close to the city centre with a mix of small business-owning and working families. He lived in humble but by no means abject circumstances. His father was a stationer – a white collar worker, no less – and the family owned its own home. Even after Grigson's father's died in the late 1880s, his mother managed to stay respectable by cutting costs and taking in boarders.

When he was at home with his mother, Grigson did his best to be the dutiful son. Every Sunday he took the money she and a pious boarder gave him for the Home Missions Society and headed off in the direction of a Wesleyan Sunday school. As soon as he was out of sight, he took off to a two-up school in a seedy laneway near the Roma Street markets and gambled the money away. Every Saturday night he also went to minstrel or vaudeville shows in the city, saving for the ticket during the week from his job as a city messenger boy. No doubt he learned tips there about how to style himself when hanging out with his disreputable two-up mates. Most of these were spruikers and pickpockets with loutish monikers: Bush Burgess, Molly Moran, Slab Brennan, Nigger Telford and Gringer Hutch.

In some ways Grigson is poor example of how the dynamics of roughness and respectability might work in male larrikins' lives. Given that he was not from an unskilled labouring family, he had more social capital than most members of larrikin groups. Nonetheless, recognising that he was able to play both the role of good son and raffish gambler helps to explain how divergent views might be formed of a single individual, each of which speak a certain truth. The same can be said for one of the self-confessed larrikins who also spoke to Ronald Lawson towards the end of his life.

The Brisbane larrikin George Richardson (again, I have made up his first name) was born in 1883 in Red Hill, a suburb not far from Petrie Terrace. His father was a self-employed carpenter/joiner, a skilled workman, but the family rented rather than owned their own home. When his father died in 1893, Richardson, his mother, two brothers and a maiden aunt moved into cheaper housing in Kelvin Grove. His mother worked full-time as a midwife to support the family until she died five years later. Richardson's granny then emigrated from England, bringing enough money to buy a house in Red Hill. Things might have improved for the Richardson boys at that point, but their granny was also soon to die.

After his grandmother's death, Richardson moved alone into a boarding house in Owen Street, Woolloongabba, aged only 17. He had been working for a couple of years by then: first in a city boot factory and then as a piece-worker in a furniture-making workshop. In his spare time he borrowed popular books from the library, went to occasional melodramas and to vaudeville twice a week. He also trained at a boxing school, attended prize fights and fought in the streets as a member of a larrikin 'mob'.

As a homeless orphan struggling to keep a permanent job, one can imagine that Richardson enjoyed the sense of community he found among fellow larrikins. With his boxer's arms and labourer's hands, he no doubt also looked the part during his mob's street fights. He was good at playing parts. Not only did he avidly attend vaudeville; he would later become a performer of illustrated songs at a cinema in Normanby. With such a capacity for role-play, it is quite possible that Richardson presented himself as something other than a larrikin in certain contexts. He may have come across as an earnest young man when he borrowed books from the library, and possibly also when he sang on stage. Illustrated songs were usually sentimental in character because they worked well with pretty images projected behind the performer as he or she sang.

Whatever Richardson performed at the cinema, he certainly cherished sentimental feelings for his mother throughout his life. 'Mother a great woman', he told Lawson wistfully, decades after she died. Capable both of familial feeling and street violence, this young man was not a two-dimensional street rough, cherishing nothing but the chance to knock people into the gutter when he chose. He was simultaneously the 'good' grieving son and the 'bad' street-fighting larrikin – and no doubt other things besides.[23]

After their death sentences were commuted to prison terms in December 1886, George Keegan and Michael Donnellan lived very different lives. Keegan was sent to Parramatta Gaol and spent two years in the mental hospital there. Donnellan, on the other hand, became an earnest and studious young man. He was not at all a fellow to luxuriate in going to hell Sam Hall-style. Instead, he attached himself to the Catholic chaplain at Bathurst Gaol and learned to play the organ at services. He also learned to write in shorthand and keenly interested himself in the 'rights' of prisoners and 'youth issues' at large. (The rights of female victims of rape appear to have been rather lower on his priorities).

Serving the last portion of his sentence back at Darlinghurst, Donnellan became sacristan in the chapel and worked in the prison library. When he was released ten years later on 26 November 1896, he immediately returned to Waterloo and busied himself with good works. Taking on the role of organist and sacristan for Our Lady of Mount Carmel Church, he wrote occasional articles for the Catholic *Freeman's Journal* and later married and fathered two sons. Incredibly, he was also elected as an alderman to the local council in the early years of the new century. In this capacity,

Donnellan helped establish a Workmen's Club on Botany Road, the very street in which he had been living before he went to gaol.[24]

For Donnellan's supporters it was vital to believe in his innocence. This was a man with an apparent desire to help the people of Waterloo, a man who came from what they insisted was a 'refined' local family, whose sisters kept a store down the road. How could he have been the depraved fiend the press had made him out to be? Waterloo's prestige was caught up in this, for if Donnellan had been unjustly convicted then the suburb had also been unfairly maligned when it was called a den of iniquity. Unfortunately, however, human character does not work in this unambiguous way. Neither the fact that Donnellan's early life was mostly spent in humdrum activities nor his later role as a pillar of the community proves his innocence of raping Mary Jane Hicks. As a young man he was attracted to the masculine fellowship he found in the Waterloo push, and he almost certainly acted this out at Hicks' expense on that long ago 'dark day'.

Chapter Five

Larrikin style

Featured in websites such as *Things Bogans Like, Bogan Bingo* and *bogan.com.au*, the term 'bogan' has a broad currency in Australia today. Once it functioned as a non Sydney-specific version of the term 'westie', designating youth from the outer-suburban fringes who exulted in ugg-boots and flannelette shirts. Now it has a more flexible meaning, denoting anyone or indeed anything sufficiently crass. Among its enumeration of bogan enthusiasms, *Things Bogans Like* includes reality TV, Palazzo Versace Australia, Buddhist statues as home furnishings and Louis Vuitton bags bought in Thailand. The official website for the *Kath and Kim* TV series adds to this list Gucci Envy Me clutch sprays and tan-in-a-can. These days, it seems, the point of reference for 'bogan' is more Sutherland Shire than Mount Druitt, more Gold Coast than Logan, more McMansion than public housing estate. In its current form, bogan name-calling reflects a disquiet about the expansion of credit-fuelled consumption and the push for easy-come celebrity in Australian society. It also springs from a desire to prove the superiority of their own consumption by those who describe others via the word.

Since the bogan phenomenon is concerned with recent developments, one might think it inappropriate to compare it to larrikinism
in the late 1800s. For a start, 'bogan' is not age-specific: it can be used
for the old as well as the young. It also refers to people with decent
disposable incomes (or more to the point, credit cards), something
nineteenth-century rowdies could not have hoped to possess. Still,
the fact that *Things Bogans Like* and *Kath and Kim* include malaprop-
isms on their bogan hit-lists makes it clear that the concept draws on
a comic tradition stemming back at least as far as the 1890s. Caricatures and written pieces poked fun of larrikin style in that decade in
a way not dissimilar from bogan jokes today.

Mockery of larrikins was a frequent aim of poems published
in the lowbrow Sydney paper, *Bird O'Freedom,* in the early 1890s.
With names such as 'How Mee Fadir Beet the Push', 'A Push
Picnic', 'Bill Brisket' and 'Why Sally Fell Out With Her Bloke',
they related riotous larrikin outings at the Balmain skating rink or
'out St Peter's way'. English travel writers, the *Bulletin* and popular
stage comedians contributed to this *oeuvre*. The blackface minstrel comedian-turned-vaudevillian Will Whitburn began playing
larrikins to comic effect in the late 1880s. Wearing a short coat,
emerald-green bootlace tie, flared trousers and blacked face, one of
his favourite numbers concerned a larrikins' 'hop':

Did you ever see a larrikins' hop,
When the lads and girls on the floor all flop,
And a 'rorty' MC out the figures does bawl,
And the 'push' go skipping around the hall,
With their well-oiled heads and their high-heeled boots,
Bell-bottomed pants and very loud suits!
The girls with bustles that bob up and down,
They think themselves the swells of the town!
Round and round they hop, they never stop

Till quite out of breath, their faces do mop,
Sit round by the wall, and do a little mash,
Their talk's of the kind that's known as flash![1]

The caricatures created by Tom Durkin and Ambrose Dyson for the *Bulletin*'s 'In Push Society' series made similar jibes at larrikin style. Published in 1895, Durkin's 'At the Larrikins' Ball' played up the contrast between a pair of larrikin youths' oafish looks and the exquisite gaudiness of their dancing attire. It portrayed the duo in bootlace ties and pants simultaneously tight and voluminous, a flower adorning one of the youths' lapels. Another image by Dyson sent up female larrikins' headgear. In it, a pair of larrikin women snigger at an aesthete in an out-sized hat while wearing hats sprouting shrub-sized plumage of their own. 'Struth Liz', one of the women exclaims, 'jist fancy a bloke wearin' a 'at like that in the street!' Designed to draw attention to these young people's sartorial tackiness, there are obvious parallels between these cartoons and present-day ridicule of bogan tastelessness.

Figure 20. *'At the larrikins' ball'*, Bulletin, *13 July 1895, p. 15*

Figure 21. *Cartoon by Ambrose Dyson,* Bulletin, *18 August 1900, p. 14*

After seeing caricatures of larrikin regalia, it can be something of a shock to come across prison mugshots of youthful rowdies in the late nineteenth century. One only has to think of dour Harriet Adderley or George Keegan and Michael Donnellan to recognise that a gap existed between *outré* descriptions of larrikin dress and how most actually appeared. Police descriptions of youths explicitly dubbed 'larrikins' reinforce this notion of a gap between what many larrikins wore and the rococo coats and hats in the *Bulletin*'s images. In 1872, for example, a young man described by police as a larrikin was accused of stealing clothes from a house in Emerald Hill (South Melbourne). He was said to be of 'shabby appearance', dressed in 'dark tweed sac-coat, light-coloured trousers, [and] old slouched felt hat'. Other accounts mentioned larrikins looking 'careless in attire', sporting dirty suits or a slovenly look.[2]

Since larrikins were among the least affluent in colonial-Australian society, we should not be surprised that they should fail to live up to the stylised vision conjured in the popular press. Given that their bodies were still growing and their parents may have struggled to feed them, many younger larrikins would scarcely have had a full set of clothes. Descriptions of barefoot larrikins make it clear that some had no shoes, let alone boots with narrow toes and high heels.[3] Obviously, too, caricatures such as the 'In Push Society' series relied on exaggeration for comic effect. The tightness of male larrikins' pants and the size of female larrikins' head-plumage in those caricatures were not meant to be taken literally.

They may have been exaggerated, but caricatures of Saturday night larrikin style were not entirely off the mark. They would not have been funny if they had borne no relation to actual larrikin dress. Mugshots showing larrikins in prison garb or everyday clothes do not necessarily give us a sense of what their subjects wore when they really went to town, after all. And in any event, there are examples of larrikins described by police or photographed by prison authorities looking distinctly florid in style. In April 1874, for example, the *Victorian Police Gazette* described the Collingwood larrikin, Garney Cooper, dressed in a 'black cloth sac-coat, soft black felt hat with white horseshoe in band, light tweed trousers, and a showy striped scarf'.[4] In 1872, bootmaker's assistant George Jenkins, a late-adolescent youth arrested for theft, was photographed wearing a patterned scarf of this kind. Twenty-one-year-old John Kenworthy sported an alternative look upon his arrest in 1871: a striped shirt and *Bulletin*-esque bootlace tie.

In 1891, a Port Melbourne youth wanted for robbing an ice-cream man was noted by police to have been wearing a 'grey tweed sac suit, larrikin make, buttons at back'. This suggests that there were many youths wearing coats like it at the time. Given the buttons on the back, this style of coat may have had what Norman Lindsay called a duck-tail. Lindsay later recalled that a flash groom who had worked for his family in the Victorian goldfields town of Creswick had worn such a coat, with buttons and a distinct flare at the rear. Possibly, too, the tweedy cloth of the ice-cream thief's suit may

Figures 22 and 23. George Jenkins (1872) (left) and John Kenworthy (1871) (right)
Public Records Office Victoria[5]

have been of the large-checked sort sketched by New Zealand artist JS Allan during an Australian visit in 1895:

Figure 24. *JS Allan, 'The larrikin', 1895*[6]

The sheer range of artists and observers who portrayed male larrikins in high-heeled boots, striped/checked or flared trousers and tight short jackets suggest that these were really worn by a range of larrikins. Others suggest that an alternative style of jacket was a loose sac coat decorated with shiny buttons or braiding, in some cases even with 'mysterious pieces of scalloped velvet on the tail'. Police reports and other accounts of adolescent girls similarly suggest that brash young women really did favour big hats with coloured ribbons or feathers. 'Wanted' descriptions of young women who had run away from home with girlfriends suggest that they were wearing dresses trimmed with fur or flounces, some black with flashes of scarlet and others all over deep pink at these times.[7] Rather than treating these as a representation of what all larrikins actually wore, however, we should approach them as indicative only of the most overt larrikin street-look. They represent the style adopted by the most 'fullblown' or resourceful larrikins rather than what all young people who moved in larrikin circles wore. For those without sufficient funds or chutzpah, this style would simply have been something to covet, or to try and achieve in less successful ways.

When trying to picture larrikin dress in a less-than-caricaturised fashion, trying to imagine what young people actually wore on the streets, it helps to think about the ways that they strove to achieve a streetwise look. Making clothes at home was an obvious way to begin. Those female larrikins who worked for clothing factories would have had the skills to make their own clothes. It is not hard to imagine male larrikins urging these girls or other female relatives to run them up a shirt at low cost. Altering hand-me-downs was another common trick. An example of this may be found among the most daring inmates at Biloela Industrial School for Girls in the 1870s. Aged in their late teens, these young women tore off the bottom of their regulation-issue dresses so that the hemline rose as high as the knee. Young men who worked for bootmakers may have had access to tools with which to embellish their boots. Others made accessories with a knife and piece of bone. In 1882, a journalist noted larrikins on the streets of Hotham (North Melbourne) wearing bone scarf pins covered with elaborate designs they had carved while serving terms in Pentridge.[8]

Secondhand clothes at the pawnbrokers' or stalls at markets were another source for larrikins who could not afford new clothes. In his Sydney-based novel *The Workingman's Paradise* (1892), William Lane described Paddy's Market as a place where clothes both old and new could be found. Boots and cheap jewellery could also be bought there: 'anything by which a penny could be turned by those of small capital and little credit in barter with those who had less'. It is possible that Paddy's was where the Waterloo larrikin Hugh Miller bought the cheap scarf-pin that he took to be repaired by a local watchmaker during the week of the Mount Rennie Outrage.[9]

For those larrikins who really wanted to make a statement, expensive items such as jackets or new shoes could be purchased from these market stalls or shops on instalment: what we would now call lay-by. This practice was widely available to city residents in Australia in the late nineteenth century. In the early 1890s, for example, a blackface comedian talked of buying clothes by instalment in an act for the Coggill Brothers, two Australian performer-managers who catered to the lower end of the theatrical market. Called 'I Owe Ten Shillings to O'Grady', the act featured a hapless fellow who cheerfully enumerated his many debts to the crowd. Presumably he was aiming for a knowing laugh from those patrons who knew what he was talking about firsthand:

A brand new suit I've ordered from a tailor on our block,
I bought it on the new time-payment plan;
I paid him just five shillings, that left me owing ten,
Pat O'Grady was the little tailor man.[10]

Stealing was a time-honoured but risky way in which a young man or woman could achieve a streetwise look. In March 1885, the youth Harry 'Tatter' Walsh, described by Sydney police as a 'smart and active . . . larrikin', was wanted for stealing a pocket book and paget coat from a cart in the street. A similar incident took place in 1871 when a number of waistcoats went missing from a tailor's in Melbourne's CBD. Police found the larrikin culprits not long afterwards, 'foolishly wearing the stolen items as they paraded around the streets for their peers'. Young women who stole goods were also known to celebrate by going on shopping sprees, buying hats and brilliantly hued raiments together with their ill-gotten gains.[11]

The fact that some larrikins boarded with other families or took rooms in lodging houses increased their opportunities for stealing from peers whose clothes they admired. One night in late 1890, for example, a Fitzroy carpenter found his best suit, scarf-pin and silver watch missing from the house in which he had been boarding with a younger man. Though his fellow boarder had disappeared, the tradesman later saw him outside the Opera House (a venue used for variety shows in Bourke Street), coolly dressed in the stolen suit. Similarly, an 18-year-old seamstress from Newtown in Sydney was charged with stealing a pink dress and cape from an acquaintance in early 1899. She told the court that she had taken the clothes with the intention of wearing them to a dance and had planned to return them the next day.[12]

As anthropologist Danny Miller notes, sartorial style involves the construction of an aesthetic based 'not just on what you wear, but how you wear it'. Even sloppily handmade clothes could acquire panache if worn with the right attitude. A racy tilt to a hat, a swagger to the walk, a toss of the head and the 'jaunty air affected by larrikin in the presence of justice' could provide an outfit with a streetwise twist. For most larrikins, putting on style would indeed have been more about gestures than clothes. A larrikin style could also be complemented by a catchy nickname that drew attention to a young person's cock-a-hoop qualities. 'Lippy Sam', 'Plucky Jim', James 'Rorty' Grey and Frances 'Cocky' Danby are all larrikin monikers emphasising these, the last adopted by a 16-year-old factory-girl from Woolloomooloo.[13]

Dancing was another arena in which larrikins exhibited a brash look through bodily means. According to a Melbourne journalist in early 1892, 'the larrikin has a [dance] style peculiarly his own . . . It is an education . . . to see him walking through a quadrille with his hands shut and elbows turned well out, his shoulders rounded, and his whole body thrown forward by his regulation heels'. In the 1870–80s, at least, it was common for male larrikins to dance together at some venues. That too was a sign of being plucky or rorty – especially after dance-hall managers tried to stamp out the practice in an effort to attract more female patrons. The practice of partnering together probably stemmed from the popularity of step-dancing among boisterous, mostly humbly born men. Youths having dance-offs in public places, trying to prove who was best at the quickstep and double shuffle, were occasionally reported in the colonial press. The high-heeled boots prized by larrikins were also associated with step dancing. They enabled a young man to tap out a rapid ostinato with his heels on a cellar flap or dance floor.[14]

Many underprivileged youth who could not afford top-to-toe flamboyance could still focus on small sartorial details as a way of signalling leary or brazen desires. It is for this reason that creative use of scarves or handkerchiefs appear in so many descriptions of male larrikins. Along with Garney Cooper in his 'showy striped scarf', 15-year-old Collingwood youth James Hansen, alias Plucky Jim, was wearing 'light trousers with brown stripe down side, black wideawake hat, and red silk necktie' in December 1874. After the

Figure 25. *Photograph of prisoners at Darlinghurst Gaol in the late nineteenth century. Given that they are in prison garb, the way that stance or attitude could create a distinct sense of style is vividly illustrated here. The prisoners fourth and second from the right perhaps provide the best embodiments of flash attitude.*
Mitchell Library, State Library of New South Wales[15]

Mount Rennie Outrage, the jockey Tom 'Wobbitty' Smith said that one of the perpetrators had been wearing a red silk handkerchief around his waist and a white handkerchief at his neck along with 'laced-up water-tight boots' on the day of the crime. (Evidently a keen observer of sartorial detail, he also noted that another was dressed in 'light shirt, greyish brown trousers, [and] brown vest with pearl buttons').[16]

Experiments with hair oil and scissors or razors were yet another component of larrikin style. Those male larrikins old enough to grow facial hair would sometimes fashion thin moustaches which they would wear above their pipes or practiced leers. Throughout the late-colonial period, a 'greasy forelock brushed flat and low' was regarded as a sign of larrikin desires. This was the style affected by John Kenworthy (see his mugshot earlier) and the Waterloo larrikin, William Boyce. Jeremiah Sullivan, one of the 'Haymarket bummers' who took part in the Bondi riot in December 1884, also dressed his hair this way. An altogether more adventurous hair experiment than these could be found in the case of James Dever, the Miller's Point larrikin who gave evidence during the trial over Thomas Pert's death in 1893.

Figure 26. The coal lumper and larrikin, James Dever, 1888
State Records NSW

Before appearing as a witness in the trial of the Miller's Point push over the Pert's death, Dever had been imprisoned for assault or riot-ous behaviour several times. On one of these occasions in 1888, he was photographed with greased hair and a shaved section on one side of his head, achieving what we might call a semi-Mohawk. Dever's hairstyle complemented his exhibitionist demeanour, on display when he boasted of his criminal history to the packed court during the trial. 'I have a faculty for causing rows', he announced dramatically. 'I am particular about what I hit a man with . . . I was in Darlinghurst [Gaol] for assaulting a publican. I've been up a few times for breaking up hotels and assault. When I'm on the job it doesn't take me long to clear a bar'. A Melbourne inmate called Alfred Moran similarly appears with hair shaved from the sides of his head in his mugshot. A contemporary description also exists of a youth sporting a similar style in a London police court, suggesting that Dever's 'do was not as idiosyncratic as it first appears.[17]

Tattoos were another way that larrikins ornamented themselves in the absence of decent financial means. Many of the young people mentioned in this book had tattoos. These could act as a form of love-token, lucky charm or private memorialisation of a significant event. They spoke an iconographic language that would have been understood by the wearer and their intimates. The anchor, for example, meant 'hope', while an anchor beside a cross meant 'I have hope in salvation'. Since most larrikins would have been given their tattoos by or in the presence of friends, however, tattoos were also badges of leary fellowship among brash juveniles. In Brisbane, George Howard was sporting a heart and anchor tattooed on his right arm and a heart with a date of birth on the left in the late 1880s. Back in Brisbane, the adolescent larrikiness Norah Swan had an eagle and rosebush, the initials 'BCBJS', a flash star and the words 'I love RJ Columba' adorning her right arm.[18]

The term 'flash' was often used when describing colonial larrikins. Even more than most slang, this word was extraordinarily versatile. Back in 1812, the convict lexicographer James Hardy Vaux indicated that it was used in at least four different ways. In the first place, he wrote, 'flash' referred to the dense slang or cant used by thieves and 'the Fancy', the disreputable types who followed bare-knuckle prize-fights. In the second place, it was a verb meaning to show or expose something. 'Don't flash your sticks' thus meant 'don't show your gun'. Thirdly, 'flash' meant being wise or 'awake' to any matter: to a trick, criminal racket or *double entendre*. To be flash in this sense meant to be street-smart: the opposite of being gullible and naive. More significant yet was the use of 'flash' to refer to any attention-seeking enterprise. 'A person who affects any peculiar habit . . . merely to be taken notice of', Vaux wrote, 'is said to do so *out of flash*'.

The various colloquial meanings of *flash,* some of which were synonymous with 'leary' or 'fly', point to a powerful link between being streetwise and being showily dressed in colonial society. The very concept of being street-smart combines these qualities. Back in the early 1800s, groups of convicts calling themselves 'flash' also brought together the same qualities. A group of convict women calling themselves the 'flash mob' wore rings and coloured handkerchieves while engaging in standover tactics with their fellow convicts at the Female Factory in Hobart in the 1830s. Certain convict men in Sydney also called themselves flash mobs. One such group took part in Major Thomas Mitchell's expedition into the interior in 1846. Its members 'spoke the secret language of thieves' and were fond of cant songs and prize fights. In the same period, the eccentric police superintendent William Augustus Miles produced what he called a *Registry of Flash Men* in the 1840s. It recorded his surveillance of roguish thieves and 'flash girls' (well-dressed prostitutes) in Sydney's shadier zones. Some of the men that Miles shadowed at The Rocks also called themselves a flash mob.[19]

The intimate assocation of criminality and flash style was continually in evidence in the early nineteenth century. Convicts with fast proclivities wore 'frilled shirts, tailored nankeen trousers, expensive shoes and hats' in old Sydney's streets in those days. The roughs who wore be-ribboned cabbage-palm hats and lingered in mobs outside the Royal Victoria Theatre also longed to look flash. So did Charles Dickens' fictional thief, 'flash Toby Crackit'. He strutted the pages of *Oliver Twist* (1838) in a coat shiny with brass buttons and hands heavily laden with rings. Along with dramatisations of the career of real-life outlaws such as Jack Sheppard, *Oliver Twist* was banned from the stage in England in 1845 out of

concern that the lower classes would attempt to emulate its thievish characters' deeds and style.[20]

Growing up in the 1860s and 1870s, the Kelly gang and their
friends had direct links to the criminal tradition represented by
convict flash mobs. Even before he became a bushranger, Kelly
was often called flash by police. He displayed this quality by affect-
ing 'a jaunty air in the presence of justice' and a roaring talent
on horseback. Kelly's flashness was also achieved by a showman-
like rhetorical style (he once memorably described himself as a
'rambling gambler') and by his skill in bare-knuckle fights. As
members of a group of youths who called themselves the 'Greta
mob', Kelly's brother Dan and friend Steve Hart tied sashes at
their waists, donned high-heeled boots and wore their hat-straps
beneath their noses in an effort to look fly.

Figure 27. *Portrait of Steve Hart with handkerchief at waist and neck
and high-heeled boots*
State Library of Victoria

Once they became bushrangers, the members of the Kelly gang consciously fashioned themselves as flash outlaws. They sang bold songs together, offered largesse to worthy victims, sent taunting letters to authorities and attended Larry Foley's illegal knuckle fight in Echuca in 1878. Significantly, too, they also made 'regular bush dandies of themselves' with stolen clothes and perfume. Kate Kelly, Ned's sister, was a fine embodiment of flash femininity. Admired for her brazen demeanour and prowess on horseback, she exhibited herself for money after Ned's death astride her pony, Oliver Twist.[21]

Like the Kellys, larrikins were beloved of pugilism and boldly-worded songs. Melbourne larrikins were noted singing re-tooled versions of outlaw ballads on street corners in praise of the Kellys' deeds while the bushrangers were still at large. Ned Kelly first heard of one of these, 'The Kellys Have Made Another Escape', after a barmaid sang it to him in a bush pub. Known as Mary the Larrikin, the barmaid had come across the song during a recent trip to Melbourne, where it had possibly been sung to her by city-larrikin friends. Melbourne larrikins later treated the Kelly family as royalty during the campaign against Ned's death sentence in 1880. Whenever they left their hotel in Hoddle Street, Jim Kelly and Wild Wright were followed by a 'rough-looking retinue' from the area. It is tempting to speculate that this retinue included larrikins who called themselves the 'Hoddle Street lairies' and boasted of becoming a 'second Kelly gang' in the weeks after Ned's death.[22]

Perhaps mindful of early colonial associations between criminality and flash style, historians have sometimes described larrikin dress as a form of social rebellion over the years. Echoing similar ways of describing punks in the 1970s, for example, cultural historian John Rickard once spoke of male-larrikin style as designed to mock 'the image of the respectable male bourgeois'.[23] There is some truth in this. The most extravagantly dressed larrikins would have discomfited a good number of respectable citizens as they swaggered past in the street. They must have appeared shocking to sober professionals in heavy frock coats, to church-going women in subdued finery and shabby-genteel clerks in painstakingly laundered clothes. Though they had connections to convict flash mobs and the classical rebelliousness of the Kelly gang, however, these youths' style emerged in a more modern urban context – one in which flashness was becoming more mainstream. Because of this, not all late colonial citizens would have been scandalised by larrikins' dress. Quite apart from the Durkin types who found it amusing, there were others who admired their flair.

That larrikins were far from the only showy dressers in colonial society is clear from the many descriptions of flamboyant dress on the goldfields back in the 1850s and 1860s. The streets of Bendigo and Castlemaine were said to throng with miners dripping with jewellery and women in colours so garish they hurt the eyes. Mostly written in the 1860s and 1870s, Marcus Clarke's essays for the Victorian press make it clear that Melbourne had its own instances of exhibitionist dress. Hilarious but deeply snobbish, Clarke's non-fiction pieces were in many ways the direct antecedent of the *Things Bogans Like* phenomenon today. Their favourite target was the city's newly cashed-up mercantile class. Clarke lambasted the typical Melbourne merchant's wife as a plump woman a-quiver with baubles, and the merchant himself in gleaming hat and red neck-tie, his 'big coarse hands twinkling with rings'.[24]

Gaudy exhibitionism was not confined to Melbourne and Australian goldfield towns. In England, the twin arrival of the sewing-machine and aniline dyes led to the production of brilliantly hued ready-to-wear clothing at cheaper prices in the 1860s than had been the case in earlier decades. By the 1870s, such clothing was increasingly to be found on the backs of clerks, shop assistants, apprentices and factory workers of both sexes:

people who were neither well-off respectables nor lowlife thieves. In America, the end of the Civil War in 1865 brought a similar hankering for eye-catching clothes. Well before the war, 'free blacks' fleeing to northern cities had made a name for themselves as pavement strutters in colourful attire. Now celebrating their emancipation after the war, gorgeously attired African Americans once more took a place beside other brassy dressers on city streets. So widespread did conspicuous masculine dress become in the 1880s that new slang was even coined to describe it. 'Dude' and 'masher' entered the American lexicon in this decade, effectively translating as loudly dressed cad or *roué*.[25]

Popular culture was fascinated with urban spectacles of self-display by the time larrikins appeared on the colonial scene. In London, for example, performers such as Alfred Vance had impersonated exuberantly dressed lordlings in the music halls during the 1860s. With names such as Champagne Charlie and the 'Comet of the West [End]', these characters were debauched aristocrats who wore *haute couture* to gambling dens. They were followed onto music-hall stages by a cavalcade of more overtly low figures from the end of the sixties. These characters dressed in outfits which borrowed from Champagne Charlie-style fashions but gave them a determinedly streetwise appeal.

The Chickaleary Bloke, also played by Alfred Vance, was a classic example of a low swell in late nineteenth-century popular culture. Vance is said to have introduced him to London audiences by telling them that the Bloke was the son of bovver-boy Bill Sykes from *Oliver Twist*. In this way, he flagged the character's relationship to a long line of flash crooks. At the same time, he included an advertisement for the Shoreditch tailoring firm Edward Grove when performing him in East End music halls. 'At Groves you're safe to make a sure pitch', Vance's Chickaleary Bloke sang. '. . . There ain't a shop in town / Can lick Groves in the Cut as well as

Shoreditch!' The Chickaleary Bloke was thus a hybrid character: a bridge between the old argot-ridden criminal flash tradition and the emerging mass consumerism of his own day.[26]

Blackface minstrel shows provided other examples of low 'masher' or 'swell' types. Black toff characters had first appeared in American blackface minstrel shows before the Civil War as a mocking commentary on the pretensions of free blacks flocking to northern cities at the time. With monikers such as Zip Coon, Blue-Tailed Fly and 'Dandy Jim ob Caroline', they were made to look ridiculous in their frenetically-hued attempts to imitate New York high society. In the post-Civil War decades, however, the satire offered by blackface swell routines took a wider aim. While the characters were still obviously racialised, routines such as 'The Dandy Coloured Coon' and 'The Man With the Seal-Skinned Pants' played to the broad multi-racial interest in dandified dress then apparent in urban life. They sent up the interest in buying luxury items such as seal-skin jackets by instalment and amused those who enjoyed wearing gaudy clothes themselves and could handle a bit of self-mockery. Some blackface characters also embodied the alluringly fly street-credibility still associated with African-American masculinity. An example of these was 'De Coon Dat Had De Razor', a character played in early 1890s Australia by the athletic African-American performer, Irving Sayles.[27]

The late nineteenth-century fascination with 'swells', 'dudes', 'mashers' and 'fly coons' allows us to picture a whole range of people who did not dress with scrupulous conservatism, or certainly not all of the time. Some of these were like the merchant family mercilessly skewered by Marcus Clarke: the women a-bob with ringlets and the men in rings and 'masher'-like hats. Others, like male larrikins, went for the edgier look of the Chickaleary Bloke or De Coon Dat Had De Razor. Portrayed in theatrical acts, discussed in newspapers, displayed in the streets and possibly shop windows, there are thus plenty of indications that flash style had become more mainstream in the late-colonial years.

That larrikins rubbed shoulders with other fast types in billiard halls and performance venues was another factor that made a difference to their style. According to the Vagabond, sharp young cads with decent incomes could be found in the stalls of Melbourne's Theatre Royal, "'dressed to kill'", with slouched hats *à la* larrikin, and paget coats'. Photographs of end-of-the-century boxing matches also show a range of men in tilted hats and neckties. These images evoke a *milieu* in which male larrikins and men from different social circles tried to impress each other with their streetwise clothes. Occasionally, larrikins were also said to wear 'masher hats' – the sort worn by the performers of swell songs that appealed to up-and-coming merchants and clerks. Though these young rowdies enjoyed creating a recognisably larrikin look, their clothes had things in common with other colonials' efforts to put on style.[28]

Thinking about nineteenth-century larrikin style brings larrikins' restless combination of social alienation and aspiration into view. These young people must have enjoyed turning up to a dance pavilion with their tight coats or short skirts and watching respectable dancers clear a space on the floor. They were very obviously disaffected youth, who sought ways to spoil these good citizens' pleasure on public holidays. Yet they also had longings to be admired. In singing rooms and boxing halls, larrikins hoped to draw approving looks from cads and cafe belles 'dressed to kill'. It was these efforts to impress that amused cosmopolitan types like Ambrose Dyson. He and his fellow *Bulletin* contributors treated these young hopefuls' style with the superior flippancy of a Marcus Clarke, poking fun at their tasteless finery.

To get a sense of how colonial larrikin style appeared at the time, it helps to think of it as the forerunner of today's most

outrageously bogan looks. One might well bring to mind Corey
Delaney Worthington, the Melbourne teenager derided as a bogan
after making headlines for bad-boy antics in 2008. Photographed
for the Fairfax press in fur-lined hoodie and cap, this lairy poser's
rude swagger gives us an inkling of why colonial-larrikin style was
the subject of jokes and displeasure from those outside the scene.

Figure 28. *Seventeen-year-old Corey Delaney Worthington and friends,*
January 2008
Fairfax Syndication

Chapter Six

All the world's a football field

In October 1899, an anonymous author published an article in the Melbourne *Argus* declaring that larrikinism was among the 'lost arts'. Certain youths still formed pushes and tried to act the part, the writer conceded. Carlton's Freeman Streeters were an example of these. So were North Melbourne's Crutchies, 'an extraordinary combination of one-legged youths'. Yet none of these pushes were a patch on those of the previous decade, the very names of which – South Richmond's Irishtown push, the Fitzroy forties, and South Carlton's Bouveroos – had struck awe into those who heard them. Unlike the weedy offerings now at hand 'there were giants in those days and many of them', the author wrote wistfully.

In March 1910, a decade after this requiem for the push was published, a similar article appeared by another anonymous writer in the *Argus*. Called '"Pushes": Larrikinism a Lost Art', it too was characterised by a full-throttled nostalgia for larrikinism's bad old days. 'Larrikinism as we used to understand it is dead', its author proclaimed. Back in the nineteenth century, larrikins had included

toughs such as 'Gunny' Hughes, 'a great leader and a hard hit-
ter' who had led the Little Bourke-street push into battles with
rival gangs. At the turn of the century, they had included South
Melbourne's Flying Angels, a band of 'hard-fisted, foul-mouthed,
desperate scoundrels'. Compared to these raw'uns, Melbourne's
current pushes were a bunch of 'dirty little boys', the author
sneered, 'not a man amongst them'.

Fourteen years after that *Argus* writer lamented the loss of Melbourne's tough pushes, another journalist reported a fight involving
bike chains and fence pickets between the North Melbourne Coffins and the North Fitzroy Checkers push. Police had assured him
that this and other present-day skirmishes were nothing like the
larrikin battles of the 1880s, he wrote in 1924. There was a quali-
tative difference between current pushes and those of yesteryear.
This was because 'the pushes nowadays are youths bubbling over
with unchecked energy, where[as] in the good old days they were
grown men who never worked'.[1]

The misguided romanticism apparent in articles such as
'"Pushes" – Larrikinism a Lost Art' makes them a dubious basis
for drawing conclusions about larrikinism after the turn of the
century. That 1910 piece was infused with the then widely held
anxiety that modern life was causing men to become soft. Before
the First World War generated its own legends about Australian
masculinity, claims that the city was turning all its young men into
weedy hoodlums appeared repeatedly in public life.[2] Allegations
that current-day larrikins were pale shadows of their colonial forebears thus tell us more about these broader currents of thought
than they do about larrikins themselves. Nonetheless, push larrikins did become less antagonistic towards police and public
order in the early 1900s. They became more interested in struggles among themselves than in attacking police and others in their
neighbourhoods. This did not mean, of course, that all larrikins

were now dirty little boys. Nor did it mean that pushes (or 'mobs', as they were increasingly called) simply vanished from view. The very fact that a piece was being written about Melbourne pushes in 1924 shows that earlier rumours of their death had been greatly exaggerated, to paraphrase Mark Twain. Rather than the demise of the push, what took place was a decline in fears about pushes and the emergence of a more insular push scene.[3]

Push larrikins became less antagonistic towards police and the broader society because the public began adopting more tolerant attitudes towards larrikinism. These two developments were profoundly interlinked. Also relevant were the appearance of more cohesively working-class communities within the 'larrikin belt' and the rise of football. Outstripping pugilism as the favourite larrikin sport, football encouraged a territorial consciousness among push members at the same time as it helped integrate them into a sense of place and working-class identity. The intimate relationship between pushes and football was most spectacularly the case in Melbourne, where 'Australian rules' enjoyed a popularity that exceeded rugby union and continued to exceed rugby league once it was played north of the border from 1908. In part because of the rowdyism associated with Australian rules, Melbourne was restored as Australia's larrikin centre in the Federation era, having ceded that title to Sydney over the previous two decades.

When the anonymous author of '"Pushes": Larrikinism a Lost Art' published his piece in March 1910, he had in mind two contemporary pushes: the Emu push (named after the Emu Hotel in Carlton) and another from North Melbourne. In the month before the article appeared, these pushes had waged a series of Friday night fights in the streets around Victoria Market. These melees did not herald a return to the disorderliness of the colonial period, he informed his readers. He had spoken to a policeman who had subdued both pushes singlehandedly and had barely found it a stretch. Given that another report described multiple officers preparing to bring the skirmishers to heel, it is doubtful that this was correct. Even more doubtful is the writer's claim that larrikinism had all but disappeared by 1910. Less than a month after '"Pushes": Larrikinism a Lost Art' was published, in fact, a classically larrikin incident took place. Early that April, some 40 youths associated with the Emu push gathered to watch a knuckle fight in Carlton's Lincoln Square. They were cheering for 19-year-old John Kirkby when a police officer arrived. They then helped Kirkby resist the officer until a passing fireman joined the fray and enabled his arrest to be made.

A few weeks before he was caught knuckling up in Lincoln Square, John Kirkby had been arrested over a scuffle in a Carlton pub. The scuffle itself was once again classically larrikin: drunken and with police readily on hand. This time, however, two less typical elements were involved. The first was that Kirkby was caught with a concealed firearm, something that larrikins had shown little interest in before then. The second was that the police prosecutor introduced him at his later court hearing as 'the captain of the football club of the local Emu push'. Both these things were harbingers of developments that would play a bigger role among larrikins in the following years: the use of guns in push skirmishes and a close relationship between pushes and football.

Carlton police court was to hear another mention of the 'football club' belonging to the Emu push towards the end of 1910. In October that year, it was told that 'the football clubs of the Emu push, Carlton, and the Collingwood push' had fought each other one Thursday night, prompted by a dispute over a game. Apparently, the Collingwood push had formed a line along the edge of the tram track in Nicholson Street, opposite the Carlton Gardens. A contingent of the Emu push had then emerged from the gardens and similarly formed into line. For a moment the two faced each other belligerently, each trying to stare the other down. Then someone shouted 'charge!', and a wild scrap full of rock-hurling and picket-splintering ensued.[4]

It is hard to know exactly what was meant when it was said that the Emu and Collingwood pushes had their own football clubs. Perhaps the fact that a steady stream of complaints had been made about football-playing youths over the preceding decade gives us a clue. Youths playing ball in the street had become a public nuisance during the Edwardian years (1901–1910) and continued during the 1910s and 1920s. According to a man later interviewed by Janet McCalman, a larrikin push with its own football team had been at large in Richmond in the early twenties. Its members called themselves 'the Coppins' after Coppin Street in Richmond, and played matches around the district in vacant lots. One afternoon they challenged this man and his friends, then in their teens, to a game. The Coppins duly lost and turned vicious, chasing their victors down the street in a swirl of curses and bike chains. It is quite possible that this was what was meant by the Emu and Collingwood pushes possessing their own 'football clubs'– that they went about challenging locals to impromptu games.

The Collingwood push known as the Don mob went in for similar antics to the Coppins' in the 1920s. In the 1980s, Victorian Football League (VFL) historian Richard Stremski interviewed Harold Rumney, a former Collingwood Football Club player born in 1907. Rumney told him that two members of the Collingwood seconds had belonged to the Don mob in his youth. When this mob were not hanging around the Don Billiard Hall near the corner of Johnston and Hoddle Streets, not rowdily barracking at matches or fighting rivals with bike chains, one of its members' favourite activities was to field a team for informal games on weekends.[5]

Close relationships existed between some larrikin pushes and teams in Melbourne's minor leagues. This is suggested, at any rate, by an incident in South Melbourne in 1918. Strolling down City Road with a female friend one afternoon, 18-year-old coal-lumper William Cook was punched by another youth, David Bourke, outside the notorious Wayside Inn. Bourke allegedly struck him as payback for testifying against one of his friends in a Children's Court trial. Given the pulpy severity of Cook's wound, a knuckleduster was almost certainly used. A police witness said that the vindictive Bourke was a member of the Adelphi push, a group of rowdies who socialised outside the Wayside Inn. During cross-examination, both Bourke and one of his friends denied belonging to an Adelphi push, but admitted to being members of the Adelphi football club. Bourke made no such attempt to deny the assault itself. 'I hit him, and I'm proud of it', he said of Cook with a jaunty larrikin air.[6]

The Bourke–Cook assault case suggests that a link existed between the Adelphi football club and a South Melbourne push known as the Adelphis, although there is no proof of this. As far back as the start of the century, a similar link seems to have existed between the infamous White Roses push and a junior Australian rules team known as the White Rose football club, both also from South Melbourne. In 1901, players from the White Roses club assaulted an opposing team-member with a fence paling on their way home from a game. These players likely included the brothers, John and David 'Denny' Tobin, if not other members of the White Roses push. Like their rivals in the Flying Angels push, the Tobin brothers styled themselves as hard-fisted scoundrels during the Edwardian years. Before one of their many appearances in court, on this occasion over a pub affray involving sling-shots in 1905, the brothers' friends alternated between threatening witnesses and entreating them not to 'go against the boys'.[7]

Before he became a star with the Richmond Tigers in the 1930s, VFL legend Jack Dyer (a.k.a. 'Captain Blood'), played in the Metropolitan Junior League. His team went by the push-like name of the Richmond Hill mob. Given that a group of larrikins called the 'Hill Mob' assaulted a youth in Swan Street in 1926, members of Dyer's team may even have been regarded as a push around Richmond. Late in life, Dyer looked back on his youth with a nostalgia similar to that of Edwardian commentators on the colonial push. The junior league was 'the breeding ground for the roughest, toughest assortment of players football has ever seen', he said in a memoir published in the 1960s. 'Every match was followed by a fight. You had to win both to stay in business'. It was foolhardy not to carry a knuckleduster for those after-match fights – especially when dealing with teams such as the Yarraville Stars or the Moray Stars from out South Melbourne way.[8]

Along with playing in junior football competitions, Melbourne larrikins flocked to watch premier league matches on Saturday afternoons. Going to the football on Saturday had become a larrikin institution in that city by the early 1900s. This practice had begun to develop in the late nineteenth century, back before the VFL was formed in 1896 and the only high-profile competition was run by the VFA (Victorian Football Association).[9] As early as 1885, the 'Fitzroy forties' had lent noisy support to Fitzroy's then VFA team when it played at its Brunswick Street oval. On 17 September 1885, reporters were disgusted that these 'forties' fought South Melbourne supporters after one of Fitzroy's home games. Violence at North Melbourne's Arden Street oval was the subject of even more opprobrium in the following decade. The most egregious example of this was after a match against Collingwood in July 1896, when an umpire was badly beaten for a decision against the North Melbourne team.[10]

In mid-1899, members of the indomitable Crutchy Push ('several of whom are cripples') were reported trying to scale a fence and rush the Arden Street oval during a North Melbourne VFA match. The Crutchies were wearing hats festooned with blue and white streamers and threw punches when police ejected them from the ground. In the next decade it became routine for larrikins to arrive at matches in club colours, flamboyant with umbrellas and flags. All of the clubs within the 'larrikin belt' became renowned for their rowdy supporters, with assaults on players and umpires disturbingly commonplace. As a consequence, many clubs constructed a wire-mesh 'race' between the field and the change rooms so that their players could pass unmolested by the crowd.[11]

While wire races gave players and umpires some physical protection, it did nothing to stop fights between fans. Chasing away-from-home spectators and throwing rocks at their departing transport became a more or less expected event after games in the early 1900s. This unruliness diminished during the war when the game was drained by the departure of players to the battlefield and controversy dogged those who continued to compete at home. But things picked up again as soon as the hostilities were an end. Bruising scuffles involving larrikin pushes continued to be a feature at matches after the armistice. In August 1919, for example, a disturbance at a North Melbourne match was attributed to the Coffins push. After another attack by North Melbourne rowdies on Hawthorn supporters in 1923, a local magistrate fulminated over the weekly assemblage of pushes at football games with rumbling expressly in mind.[12] As Jack Dyer's memoirs suggest, junior games were even more disorderly. With less money to spend on crowd control, the blood flowed almost as freely at some of these matches as the run-off from a Richmond tannery.

A close relationship between larrikin pushes and football took longer to develop in Queensland and New South Wales. This is because their premier football code was rugby union, or was at least until the 1910s. It was not that disadvantaged youth had no interest in playing or watching rugby union games before then. On the contrary: a steady stream of young working men donned rugby union jerseys or gathered to cheer from the sidelines. In the mid-1890s, a reporter for the Sydney *Referee* decried the numbers of larrikins who barracked at rugby union games. 'Wrecks of humanity' could often be found at matches, he said, sporting 'high collars, tan shoes and wide pants'. Yet in spite of this enthusiasm, rugby union's association with elite schools and the university restricted working people's identification with the code. It was not until the New South Wales Rugby League held its first premiership in 1908 that working-class communities outside Victoria found a game they could call their own.[13]

Sydney's first rugby league premiership was an impetus for the Queensland Rugby League. It was formed in 1908 and held its inaugural competition in 1909. After a brief period playing under rugby union rules, both leagues adopted the code played by England's Northern Union, an organisation that had broken away from England's Rugby Football Union in 1895. In Sydney it did not take long for rugby league crowds to overtake rugby union ones. Some accounts have this taking place as early as 1910. Things took longer in Brisbane, but had shifted in rugby league's favour by the end of the war. The new administration's offer to pay players and compensate them for injury (something refused by rugby union officials) was the key impetus for this. It meant that even casual workers could now afford to invest serious time in the game.

The areas in which the earliest rugby league clubs were formed suggest the level of enthusiasm with which working men took to the new code. In Sydney, the founding clubs included Balmain, Eastern Suburbs, Glebe, Northern Suburbs, Western Suburbs, Newtown and Southern Suburbs. The latter drew supporters from Surry Hills, Redfern, Alexandria and Waterloo, a key larrikin zone.

While Easts is now considered a silvertail club, it had a considerable following at the time from residents around the wharves at Woolloomooloo. The North Sydney Bears appealed not just to middle-class residents from Sydney's north shore but also labourers at the gritty tanneries and coal depots across the harbour from The Rocks and Balmain. Some of Brisbane's early clubs were also based in districts with large numbers of labouring residents: namely Milton, Valley, South Brisbane and West End.[14]

It was not, of course, as if all rugby league players were larrikins. Two of the new code's star players came from families who employed labour: Norths' Albert Broomham, whose parents owned a Willoughby tannery, and Easts' Herbert 'Dally' Messenger, whose father ran a boatbuilding workshop in Double Bay. Other players from different teams belonged to the aristocracy of labour, with close links to trade unions and the Labor Party. But youths of poor but roisterous stock undoubtedly flocked to the game. Many of Newtown's early players worked at St Peter's Brick Pits, a similar workplace to the one at which members of the push calling itself the 'red blacks' had once been employed. One of Balmain's early players also came from a larrikin-like background. Born in 1893, 'Junka' Robinson spent a hard-scrabble childhood with his seven siblings and single mother who took in laundry. He was twice sent to the Brush Farm reformatory for stealing before he worked his way up through junior teams to play for Balmain.[15]

With football offering ways even for rascals such as Junka Robinson to become heroes, we should not be surprised that the public came to view larrikinism less disapprovingly over time. Elderly residents from larrikin-belt communities give us a rich sense of this in memories of the 1910s and 1920s. Of these, it is also striking how many dismissed their local pushes as non-serious. As an old woman in the 1980s, for example, Melbourne resident Elizabeth

Haynes was interviewed about growing up in Collingwood in her youth. Born in 1908, she had been sent to learn the sewing trade at Foy and Gibson's in Smith Street as soon as she finished primary school. A number of larrikin 'mobs' frequented the district at that time, she recalled. Everyone knew about groups such as the Yarra and Don mobs and the violent contests that took place between them. What everybody also knew, however, was that these mobs were no trouble to anyone but themselves. As Haynes recalled it: 'you could go anywhere – the train, the tram – and you'd be quite safe . . . They never bashed somebody unless somebody did something to them . . . They [only] knocked each other about'.

Elizabeth Haynes' indulgent perspective on larrikin 'mobs', as she called them, was shared by one-time Sydney grocery-boy Bert Hickey who was born in 1905. 'Larrikinism as I know it . . . was confined to these mobs that used to be in the districts', Hickey told an interviewer in 1987. At night time, 'there weren't too many of those fellows around. A few did sneak out and play up a little bit but generally speaking they were much better behaved mobs than they are these days'. John Drummond, a Sydney man born in 1903, was of the same view. During his impoverished boyhood at The Rocks, he was aware that push fights took place in the laneways around the house in Cumberland Street in which he and his brother and widowed mother sub-rented a single room. The Cumberland Street mob, the Gloucester Street mob, and the 'Erkos' (after Erskine Street) were all known for fighting each other, he said. Drummond used to see pickets ripped from fences during these fights discarded in the road the next day. The push-ites did not really bother anyone else, however: 'if you stayed in your own place and minded your own business you were quite alright'.[16]

A belief that larrikin mobs were essentially harmless underscores the views even of those who recalled taking fright on seeing push fights in their youth. In early 1920s Collingwood, Thomas

Maybery, then 14 years old, saw a push battle in a vacant lot in Langridge Street. An apprentice shopfitter on his way to work at the time, Maybery would later remember it as a terrible spectacle. 'I can never forget it, really, you know, being young', he told an interviewer in the 1970s. 'It was one of the worst gang fights I ever saw'. The fight in question was between the Campbells push, named after Campbell Street in Collingwood, and the Coppins, the football-playing push from Richmond. All who took part in the fight were in their late teens. They met in vacant land near William's Boot Factory at about 7:30am one weekday morning and fell upon each other in a tumult of pickets and bike chains. Terrible as it was, however, Maybery appears not to have felt threatened by those involved. He was several years younger than the combatants and his circles centred on church and cricket, both of which left larrikins cold. The warring push-ites seem to have regarded Maybery as irrelevant because of this, and so left him alone.[17]

Claims that twentieth-century larrikins were better behaved than youths in gangs today should of course be treated sceptically. Aged subjects may be influenced by a different sort of nostalgia than the one expressed by Edwardian writers on larrikinism: a nostalgia for an age when they felt blithely invincible and nobody locked their doors. If they were not assaulted by larrikins themselves, they might easily form the mistaken view that everyone had a similarly benign experience. The idea that twentieth-century larrikins were harmless certainly seems mistaken when one considers the lot of Violet Moorcroft in 1907, a 17-year-old domestic servant raped in Brisbane's Mowbray Park by five youths whom police called larrikins. South Melbourne prostitute Lily Mitchell almost suffered the same fate when she was seized by members of the Flying Angels push in 1906. So did Kate Forfar at the hands of larrikins in Newtown, Sydney, in 1904.[18] Even allowing for this, however, memories such as Haynes' or Hickey's point to the fact that larrikin pushes came to be regarded with less fear and loathing over time.

The upheavals of war hastened the growth of tolerant approaches to push larrikins. If nothing else, teenage clashes paled into insignificance when compared to the carnage of Gallipoli or the Western front. The celebration of the Australian Imperial Forces' so-called larrikinism also helped to reduce harsh judgments of lower-class rowdies in civilian life. The development of criminal networks devoted to sly grog and cocaine further conspired to make the pushes seem small beer. According to John Frederick 'Chow' Hayes, a one-time larrikin who became a notorious criminal, Sydney police were uninterested in the push fights in which he was involved in the second half of the 1920s. With bigger fish to fry, they went the other way if they knew a fight was on: 'their attitude was to let the gangs crack each other's skulls'.[19]

Though the war and post-war developments had a profound impact on the push phenomenon, articles such as '"Pushes" – Larrikinism a Lost Art' show that attitudes towards it had started shifting well before 1914. Ambrose Pratt's scandalous article on push larrikinism admittedly prompted some to speak of an ongoing larrikin menace in 1901. Even then, however, anxiety on the subject was on the wane. That very same year, in fact, the murder of 21-year-old George Reginald Hill met a muted response. Dispatched by a blow from an iron bar to the head, Hill was rumoured to have been killed by a fellow member of the North Melbourne Crutchy push in September 1901. Three years later, in 1904, the death of 'Flying Angel' Walter Cranshaw caused barely more than a murmur of concern. He died after a fight with the White Roses push at a Greensborough picnic on Easter Monday, stabbed in the neck with a knife or jagged glass. The matter-of-factness with which news of these deaths was received contrasted sharply with the clamour for a larrikin crackdown after Thomas Pert's demise in 1893.[20]

Changing attitudes to youth itself contributed to the greater complacency towards larrikins. The idea of adolescence as a distinct phase of life between childhood and adulthood was gaining currency at the time. Admittedly, a rudimentary concept of adolescence had begun to develop before then. The larrikin phenomenon itself had concentrated attention on youngsters in 'the hobbledehoy or transition state' between childhood and adult maturity in the 1870s.[21] The term 'adolescence' only became widely used after 1904, however, when the American psychologist G Stanley Hall published a two-volume work with that name. His work popularised not just the word but the idea that adolescence was a period of 'storm and stress' in a young person's life.

Hall was convinced that a child was thrown into hormonal tumult once he or she hit puberty. Prey to antic desires and impulses, the adolescent needed careful guidance in order to emerge unscathed. This idea appealed to the so-called 'child savers' of the day. Reformers focused on rescuing underprivileged children from poverty and vice had been active for some decades by 1904. They had set themselves a cracking schedule, variously campaigning for compulsory schooling, the regulation of child labour, the provision of parks and kindergartens, and raising the age of sexual consent. In the wake of Hall's work, however, many of these reformers began to adopt a more specific focus on adolescent youth.[22]

If they were interested, poor adolescents could attend a world of bracing ball games followed by pep-talks in the Edwardian era. In Brisbane, boys in their early teens could join the Naval Cadet Corps at the Institute of Social Sciences, established in Fortitude Valley in 1907. Girls over 14 were eligible for the Working Girls' Club at the same Institute; males over 17 for the Young Men's Club. A realm of bright-lit billiard halls lined with Bible tracts and mentors was also offered to youngsters at the Central Methodist

Mission (now Wesley Mission) in Sydney, while in Melbourne, young newspaper-sellers could join Edith Onians' City Newsboys' Society to enjoy classes and hot meals by night.[23]

Some of the reformers responsible for the youth initiatives of the early 1900s would later make ambitious claims about their success in ridding Australia of the larrikin scourge.[24] Their efforts may well have had an effect on individual lives. Since pushes such as the Coppins were still active in the 1920s, however, one cannot credit any wholesale claims. Perhaps the most we can say is that these activists helped garner support for the view that wayward adolescents should be treated differently to adult criminals. Their advocacy brought about greater public acceptance of the idea that allowances should be made for these youths' 'storm and stress', with efforts directed at helping them live honest lives.

Australia's justice and prison systems were dramatically over-hauled at the turn of the century on the basis of the new wisdom about how to treat juveniles. As early as 1894, a *First Offenders Act* was passed in New South Wales, aimed at diverting young and petty offenders from gaol. It allowed prison terms to be suspended for first-time criminals convicted of a summary offence. Along with like measures in other colonies, it was followed by the *Justice (Fines) Act (1899)*. This reduced the numbers of people who had been imprisoned in default of a fine simply because they could not afford to pay. Further reforms were directed at the treatment of young offenders imprisoned on serious charges in adult gaols. They no longer received harsh corporal punishments such as the lash, putting paid to a measure once been seriously presented as a cure for larrikin delinquency. Children's Courts were also established in the eastern Australian states between 1905 and 1907. They dealt variously with offenders to the age of 16 or 17 years.[25]

The penal and judicial reforms were hardly an unalloyed good for rowdy juveniles. Attempts to ensure that they were diverted from prison led to the expansion of what criminologists call 'penal welfare' institutions: Magdalene Asylums, Salvation Army Homes, industrial schools, and the like. Young women considered at risk of sexual exploitation could be sent to these so-called schools or homes. So could Aboriginal youth considered at risk simply on racial and cultural grounds.[26] Penal welfarism had some positive consequences for rough white teens, however, particularly if they were male. Chief among these was that they were now more likely to be regarded as 'youths bubbling over with unchecked energy' than as hardened criminals.

The idea that larrikins were more 'poor dear boys' than vicious blackguards affected how they were policed as well as how they were treated in prisons and courts. Put simply, police became more prepared to deal with these larrikins via discretionary measures rather than arrest or summons. There was still greater surveillance of rough-looking youth than those considered respectable, but officers were now more willing to issue cautions or 'kicks up the back-side' in place of initiating criminal proceedings.[27] For these reasons, larrikinism experienced what might be called a *de facto* decriminalisation in the early 1900s – the very reverse of what had happened in the 1870s and 1880s. At the same time, policing stopped being the flash-point for social conflict that it had once been. Ned Kelly could not have boasted that eight-stone 'larrakins' regularly bested police of a Saturday night in the 1910s and 1920s. Nor could it have been said that jeering crowds routinely gathered to cheer police-resisters in court of a Monday morning. Because police and magistrates were no longer targeting larrikin types so pointedly, the same degree of resentment was not directed their way.

In May 1910, Dr Agnew, a magistrate at the Richmond police court, demonstrated compellingly how attitudes to larrikins had changed. Walking down Lennox Street, he was heckled by a smart-mouthed rough lounging on a corner with his friends. Instead of insisting that this larrikin be summoned to court for insulting his dignity, Agnew simply turned and punched him in the nose. Back in the colonial era it would have been unthinkable for a magistrate to publicly assault a young man like this. Now, however, Agnew not only resorted to blows but was glowingly commended for it in the press. The following day, the *Richmond Guardian* lauded the doctor, a keen Melbourne VFL fan, for dealing it out to 'a gang of North Richmond roughs'.[28]

Dr Agnew would have felt secure in his status within the Richmond community before indulging in this show of new century manliness. By that time, Richmond had only a sprinkling of professionals, most of them Catholic and probably the magistrate's close friends. Back in the nineteenth century, a larger and more diverse elite had presided over the area: big hotel-owners, industrialists, fashionable lawyers and medical men, all enjoying the easy proximity to the city and gracious boom-era homes. By 1910, however, the larrikin belt had undergone the opposite of the gentrification process it has been experiencing in previous years. During the 1890s depression, many of Richmond's larger residences were subdivided into a not-so-gracious warren of rooms-to-let. The same applied in other areas close to the central business districts, their owners either bankrupt or fleeing from the sight of hungry masses outside their door.[29]

The outbreak of bubonic plague in 1900 hastened the exodus from the inner suburbs. First appearing around Sydney's port in 1900, the Black Death Scare led to the demolition of lanes in areas such as The Rocks, Surry Hills, Pyrmont and South Brisbane over the next two decades. The fear of unsanitary housing even spread to inner Melbourne, where no deaths from plague transpired. Cleared to make way for modern factories, whole blocks were swallowed in brickdust and the grief of their former residents. As those who could afford it continued to move to less industrialised localities, those left behind were mostly labouring families, hunkered down amid plumes of soot and the pungency of factory scents on the air.

As districts close to the city became more uniformly populated with manual labourers, their communities embraced a working-class identity with greater gusto. The thriving political and industrial labour movement helped this rise in class-consciousness take place. Most suburbs ringing the cities became Labor strongholds in the Edwardian years. There must have been plenty of street parties thrown in South Melbourne or Pyrmont the night Australia elected the world's first Labor Prime Minister, John Christian ('Chris') Watson, in 1904. Trade unions grew just as robustly as the ALP. Between 1900 and 1914, their membership multiplied more than fivefold to over a half a million Australia-wide. This muscular growth had a lot to do with their success in negotiating for white male workers' interests once the federal Conciliation and Arbitration Court was established in 1904. The gains made by collective bargaining under the arbitration system brought droves of unskilled workingmen previously alienated from the labour movement into the union fold.[30]

Male larrikins were among those unskilled workers more likely to support the labour movement. They were also much more consciously working class. The tighter regulation of street commerce contributed to this. It was less feasible for them now to even dream of making a living from penny capitalist enterprise. The 'disappearance of a lusty and frenetic nineteenth-century street life' also meant they had less flash showmen, costermongers, 'cheap jack' hawkers and roving prize-fighters to offer models of learily independent style. Working in plain shirt-sleeves at the Colonial Sugar Refinery in Pyrmont or Yarraville, for Carlton United Brewery,

Whybrows Shoes, or any number of new factories, they were more inclined to resign themselves to being ordinary working men.[31]

As the larrikin belt became more socially homogenous, standards of decorum changed. The gap between the rough and the respectable lessened – or rather, a more elastic sense of what constituted respectability emerged. The greater acceptance of betting games was one outcome of this. Back in the 1870s and 1880s, the game of pitch and toss had been dogged by complaints from residents taking umbrage at its presence in their streets. By the 1920s, two-up, its successor, was regarded more leniently. Two-up was played on virtually every corner around East Sydney when he was young, the son of a horse-drawn bus driver, William Sarnich recalled. You had to watch out for police if you got involved – they gave you a 'smack across the earhole' if they caught you out. Few neighbours were bothered by it, however, because more often than not someone in their family liked to play.[32]

An admiration for Agnew-like shows of gumption was another marker of changed standards of propriety. As a Richmond man would recall, the basic rule in his suburb when he was growing up was that you 'daren't walk away from a fight'. It didn't matter whether you came from one of Richmond's tumbledown cottages in Irish Town near the Church Street bridge or the double-front houses in Twickenham Crescent. Wherever you lived, you had to be prepared to use your fists if you wanted to win respect as a man.[33] Beating others to the punch was even more imperative in Montague on the South Melbourne waterfront. Fights between men at a pub known colloquially as the Bloodhouse were a regular event in post-war Montague. So were 'blues' held to settle disputes by a bend in the Yarra of a Sunday morning. 'You could easy buy a fight' in Montague when he was young, former push member Tom Hills remembered. 'You moved in a strong working-class area, and it was really a question of competition for work, for living. Some shady things were done, one word would lead to another and . . . "Come outside with me!" It was the survival of the fittest. You couldn't afford to be a weakling'.[34]

Though public violence became more acceptable, the distinction between who was a push larrikin and who wasn't did not disappear. A line was still drawn between those who were willing to cause real damage in a fight and those who were not that game. Though Woolloomooloo resident Billy Pascoe used to fight youths from other suburbs, for example, he and his friends were what was sometimes known as a 'soft mob': they never fought too earnestly. There was no kicking or weapons in their street-spats, he said – not like those fought by the 'really, really, really, really tough boys of what they call "The Push" at Millers Point'.[35] Now that hard masculinity was more universally admired, however, larrikin push-ites could earn a certain respect for being tough even among those who thought they went too far. This admiration was most marked when old-timers reflected on past pushes such as the Bouveroos, endowing them with a lustre they had not possessed at the time.

Respect for toughness was felt by inner-suburban women as well as men. This was because it was prized as a way of responding to hardship, not just as a masculine quality. The residents of larrikin-belt communities certainly endured plenty of hardship. Even after the depression eased and the economy started to improve at the start of the century, the pre-war era was still one of tightened belts and toil. Much of the housing built in the 1880s became increasingly dilapidated over these years.[36] Women bore the brunt of this as they struggled to run a household falling down around their ears. And the war itself, of course, brought a whole new kind of privation. With loved ones dying or returning maimed and disturbed, it reaped a harvest far more bitter than anyone could have imagined in earlier years.

Since women as well as men had to shoulder the burdens of the day, they too placed a value on toughing out life's blows. Some developed a laconic femininity, a just-get-on-with-it feminine style, that many of us would have observed in elderly relatives or friends. This feminine toughness was perhaps one of the reasons that football attracted such a passionate female following in Melbourne's inner suburbs. No doubt women in inner-Sydney and Brisbane also admired tough rugby league players. But Melbourne's football code had a more conspicuous female fan-base. When that melee erupted at the end of the discreditable match between North Melbourne and Collingwood in 1896, for example, women were among those throwing punches at the beleaguered referee. Over the following years, others distinguished themselves through mad barracking, spitting and sometimes even jabbing hat-pins at players from rival teams. This unruliness was still evident in the 1930s when a Fitzroy policeman observed misbehaving girls at the Brunswick Street Oval on Saturdays. There would always be 'what you'd call the buck larrikins' who congregated behind the goals at VFL matches, he later recalled. Alongside them 'you'd get these certain type of girls that were like the buck larrikins, you know what I mean, only they'd be girls'.[37]

Saturday football games were one place where male and female larrikins socialised in the new century. Suburban cinemas were another. In 1911, a large crowd 'principally of the rough class' assembled at the Lyceum Theatre in Coventry Street, South Melbourne. Including members of a Montague push, this crowd shouted and cat-called throughout the evening's 'performance', which most likely included live acts as well as films. When the attractions ended, an altercation took place 'between some young girls and youths' that quickly devolved into a free-for-all. Mingling between the sexes also took place at a cinema at Paddington, Brisbane, in the 1920s. One Paddington old-timer remembered crowds from West End pouring

into the Paddington Picture Theatre in Given Terrace on Saturdays
during the football season. Nine times out of ten there was a fight,
he said – sometimes caused, perhaps, by flirtations between West
End youths and brazen Paddington girls.[38]

Parks and public toilets were another place for *rendezvous*
between male and female rowdies, in this case of a sexual kind.
Sixteen year-old Mary Higgins and 18-year-old Dorothy Langton
were caught 'fooling around' with some male larrikins outside a
toilet off Swan Street, Richmond, in 1911. The next year, police
found 18-year-old Ivy Maine and a female friend acting in an
'offensive manner' with two larrikin youths in nearby Yarra Park.
Maine was one of a group of '"buck" larrikins' that frequented
South Richmond, the court was told. Knowing that venereal disease was rife in Australia even before its soldiers returned from
war-time brothels, one wonders what became of these young
women and their sexual partners. According to Sydney doctor,
Herbert Moran, VD was rampant among male larrikins in the
pre-war years. Male larrikins wearing black felt hats were so often
among the outpatients he treated for VD that he and his doctor
friends used to snobbishly refer to them as 'venereal hats'.[39]

Though twentieth-century girls continued to socialise and have
sex with male larrikins, they did so in smaller numbers than in
the colonial years. Inner-suburban men recalling their youth in
the early 1900s suggest this. They spoke of an overwhelming seg-
regation between the sexes. As William Sarnich, an East Sydney
resident born in 1904, put it: 'they kept to themselves the girls,
not like today . . . They never interfered with what the boys were
doing'. Born in 1914, Ultimo man George Cairns said much the
same thing. The girls 'were different to what they are today', he
recalled. '. . . You know, how they mix together today. But them
days it was just the opposite. They never interfered with it, whatever, you know, like all the boys were doing'.

The luxuriant growth of male pushes was one reason for greater sex-segregation among inner-suburban young ones. Influenced by the rapid spread of masculine team sports, a heavier emphasis on all-male company could be found throughout the Western world, not just among Australian larrikins.[40] At the same time, rowdy young women were also choosing to spend more time in exclusively female company. The appearance of factories employing large cohorts of female workers was one reason for this. So too was the development of local dance schools, city dance halls, working girls' clubs and even all-girl sporting teams. These things meant that rorty gals of the 1900s had more opportunities than their colonial sisters to form networks independent of the push.

When George Cairns looked back on his early adolescence in Ultimo, traversing the wharves and parks around Sydney Harbour in the late 1920s, he recalled a maniacally precise subdivision of territory among pushes and 'soft mobs' of youths. You had to watch your back going anywhere, he said, because if another mob saw you stepping across an invisible line into their territory, 'they'd be onto ya' with bricks and fists. The grocer's boy Bert Hickey remembered watching tough pushes such as the Hegarty Street mob in Forest Lodge enforcing their stamping ground with the same exactitude. 'If that's the edge of the street and that was the edge of the street and you were in the centre there', he said in an interview in the 1980s – 'as long as you stayed there and didn't come over, you were right. [But] if you step over there . . . they get you, a dozen of them get you and rub you into the dirt'.

Territoriality of this degree of detail and militancy had not been a part of the late colonial larrikin scene. When pushes of that era staged violent ruckuses, they had rarely been motivated by a desire to win or protect a stamping ground. From all accounts, fights between nineteenth-century pushes had often been caused by

jealousies engineered by larrikin girls. Others were held in neu-
tral zones such as Melbourne's Friendly Society grounds or 'down
the Harbour' at Chowder Bay, whether as a test of mettle or to
settle some other dispute. It was only in Hickey's and Cairns' boy-
hoods that pushes regularly strove to stake out a home territory
and defend it against opposing mobs.[41]

The push to which Sydney's Chow Hayes belonged in his teens
had its own patch which it patrolled with hard-boiled vigour in
the late 1920s. Called the 'railway mob', its territory was the streets
around Central Station and Broadway. The railway mob actually
consisted of two groups known internally as the little and big
mobs. These young men's mental map of Sydney was a maze of
gang territories, as finely lined by push boundaries as the palm
of an old sailor's hand. 'The Surry Hills Mob was really the Ann
Street Mob, and its territory ran up from the Railway up to Darlinghurst and back through Riley Street and Surry Hills', Hayes
recalled. 'They were a really tough bunch'. Groups from Redfern,
Woolloomooloo and the Rocks had similar territories which they
protected from incursions by other larrikins. If you were caught
over one of these mobs' boundaries by night, its members 'kicked
the living daylights out of you'. In 1925, Hayes' older cousin Ezzie
Bollard was sent to the Emu Plains Farm for Boys for dealing it
out to a member of the Surry Hills mob in this way. At 17 years
of age, Bollard and a friend fractured the young man's skull with a
fence paling during a tit-for-tat fight.[42]

Guns became a part of territorial skirmishes between pushes in
inner-Melbourne in the years immediately following the war. The
best publicised of these took place in December 1919. It involved
two hands at a Collingwood boot factory, 16-year-old Harold
'Dodger' Smith and 14-year-old William 'Porky' Flynn, who killed
a rival larrikin with a pistol shot. The victim, Arthur Worseldine,
belonged to the Roses push from Rose Street, Fitzroy, Smith and

Flynn to the Little Campbells from Collingwood. Given their age, the Little Campbells were probably a younger satellite group associated with the older Campbells push. On Melbourne Cup Day, members of the Little Campbells had headed to Rose Street intending to 'give the Roses "a fly"'. Seeing Worseldine emerge from a lolly shop in Brunswick Street, they called out and gave chase. In the heat of the pursuit, ducking down laneways and through holes in fences, Flynn seized Smith's gun and fired. The shot hit Worseldine in the temple, felling him as he ran. He died shortly afterwards, pockets spilling gum-drops and all-day suckers, never having had the chance to eat the lollies he had bought as a Cup Day treat.

Figures 29 and 30. *William 'Porky' Flynn (left) and Harold 'Dodger' Smith (right), December 1919*
Public Records Office Victoria[43]

'Porky' Flynn and 'Dodger' Smith were convicted of manslaughter on 8 December 1919 and spent the next few years in the Castle-maine Reformatory. Their baby-faced looks were one reason so many people were now convinced that larrikins were younger than they had been in colonial days. It *was* the case that younger larrikins were getting involved in the push scene, possibly because older rowdies had enlisted and died on the Somme. But it was hardly as if all larrikins were now as young as Porky Flynn. Most were still in their late teens or twenties. In early December 1920, for example, a member of the push called the Wanderers shot another larrikin at the North Carlton Jubilee Picture Theatre. At 19 years of age, Alexander Abikhair, a motor mechanic, was no dirty little boy. Nor was his victim, Martin Millson, apparently a member of the Checkers push, whose age was reported as 26 years.

The Checkers were active in numerous push fights around the time that Millson was shot in the leg and hip in that Carlton cinema. Though at least one of these was waged with bike chains and fence pickets, others were fought with guns. Until tighter gun laws brought the situation under control in the second half of the twenties, pushes such as the Checkers, Woolpacks and Northcote Imps continued to hold pistol-fights. In 1925, the Wanderers even staged what we would now call a 'drive-by', a very modern form of gang combat. Seizing a milk truck left temporarily empty by its driver, they blazed a trail of pocked doors and smashed glass as they drove it down a street in Fitzroy.[44]

For a few years in the 1920s, it seemed as if almost every young blood in Melbourne, if not also Sydney, was parading the streets with a pistol in tow. There was far more posing than firing going on, however – and even when guns were fired, most of the shots were wide. As crime historian Peter Doyle points out, the homicide rate did not spike amidst the post-war gun craze. Since military training had been made compulsory for schoolboys and male Australians aged 18 to 26 years in 1911, we can assume this was not because gun owners did not know how to aim. Among push larrikins, at least, the rarity of deaths was more likely because of an unwritten rule against killing in gun fights. The same applied to fights without guns. Though waged with bike chains, pickets, knuckledusters and shang-hais (a word then used for 'slingshot'), they seldom involved glass or knives. Even among 'really, really, really, really tough boys' there was an effort to contain the fatalities that might come from push hostilities.[45]

Apart from the appearance of guns, another feature of the twentieth-century push scene was that it was more preoccupied with rivalries among its own members than attacks on non-larrikins. Fewer reports of pushes involved in diffuse forms of street violence can be found in this period. Assaults on non-white street-sellers, on neighbours who 'turned dog', on police and the civilians who assisted them were less to the fore. This was not because push members had become less aggressive or racist. Instead, larrikins had become more concentrated on skirmishes among themselves. There are interesting parallels to be drawn here between these pushes and present-day football hooligans. In the early years of this millennium, the sociologist Ramón Spaaij interviewed many self-described football (in this case, soccer) hooligans. Visiting Spain, England and the Netherlands, almost all the young men he spoke to considered it shameful to fight people outside the hooligan scene. So far as they were concerned, the only way to win masculine prestige was to pick on another hooligan, someone more or less their own size. A sportsmanlike code operated among these hooligans in many ways similar to the one among new century larrikins.[46]

Football enthusiasts have often told wistful stories about the early days of Australian rules and rugby league, back when skirmishes were common on and off the field. Full of reminiscences about how tough football players once were, Jack Dyer's memoir *Captain Blood* is a classic example of these. Like 'Pushes – Larrikinism A Lost Art', this narrative belongs to a tradition of romanticising the past as more full-blooded than the present, wilder and freer from the constraints of modern life. Reflecting on the extent that terri-torial boundaries once restricted the movements of larrikin youth, there is reason to challenge this view. Surely we should not lament the near-absence of guns among Australian youth, nor the fact that football losses are no longer avenged with rocks and bike chains. Given that the early 1900s was a time when inner-suburbanites struggled for dignity, when it was 'really a question of competition for work, for living' – there is little cause to look back with such wistfulness.

Chapter Seven

The demise of the flash larrikin

When Sidney Baker published his now classic work *The Australian Language* in 1945, a collection of ruminations on Australian culture and slang, he included a whole section on the first larrikins. This was considerably expanded in the second edition published in 1966. 'There was a hard, sleek finish to the [male] larrikin's Sunday-off dress', Baker wrote. It could be found in the larrikin's bell-bottomed trousers, his wasp waist, his shining black felt hat and high-heeled, highly-decorated boots, 'all of which brought those words *flash* and *lairy* to your thoughts'. For Baker there was an uncomfortable sexual ambiguity about this mode of dress. The larrikin might have expressed contempt for things effeminate in his speech and pastimes, he said, but he came 'perilously close to effeminacy' himself in his sartorial style.

If Baker felt a certain discomfort about colonial larrikins' clothes, he was downright squeamish when it came to Ned Kelly and his gang. So far as he was concerned, the Kelly gang were not so much sexually ambiguous as patently homosexual. 'After examining all the relevant evidence, I have little doubt that they were homosexuals', he maintained. The principal 'evidence' Baker relied on seems to have been that the gang once wore perfume, sprinkling themselves with it at Faithfull's Creek after robbing a hawker's cart in early 1879. He may also have had in mind the fact that they sometimes partnered with each other at dances, and that Steve Hart was rumoured to have cross-dressed.[1]

Baker's view of the Kelly gang and their larrikin contemporaries is problematic on several counts. Wearing perfume was a common practice among men during the Kelly era. If the Kellys were to be considered homosexual on this basis, a good proportion of the colonial population would need to be so described. Dancing together was also a common enough custom among uproarious youths in their day.[2] Further qualifications must be made to Baker's comments about larrikin dress. The key source he was relying upon when describing the 'hard, sleek finish' of male larrikin attire was Louis Stone's *Jonah*. Published in 1911 and set in the late Edwardian years, this novel dealt with a period in which male larrikin dress was more pared-back than it had been in previous decades. Colourful accessories such as red neckties or jewellery were rare by then; bell-bottomed pants and wasp-waisted coats had fallen out of vogue. Baker was thus mistaken when he combined Stone's description of a streamlined Edwardian larrikin look with talk of those flashy colonial items.

Over the years between the early 1890s and the publication of *Jonah* in 1911, male larrikin style became distinctly leaner and less ornamented – although attention was still paid to embellished boots. In the years after 1911, male larrikin dress changed again, becoming more literally down-at-heel. A number of factors brought about these alterations in style. The first was an anxiety about effeminate homosexuality. Like Baker, male larrikins became concerned about coming 'perilously close to effeminacy' from around the turn of the century. Also relevant was a general shift in men's fashions towards informality, and the fact that the larrikin identity became more working class. By the end of the decade, the larrikin's practice of proving himself a cut above the general labourer was all but replaced by his acceptance of being an ordinary worker. The emergence of the Australian digger during the First World War played a role in this. Celebrated for his cheeky scruffiness, the digger was to exert an influence over larrikin style and Australian identity that persists to this day.

When police descended on a brothel in Cleveland Street, London, in the English summer of 1889, they could hardly have known how far the resulting shockwaves would spread. The raid revealed that a number of adolescent messenger-boys for the General Post Office had been selling sex to elite men at this brothel by night. One of these men was Lord Alfred Somerset, equerry to the Prince of Wales. Though it was never proved, the Prince's son, Albert Victor, was rumoured to have been another of the brothel's clients. These rumours were amplified by the fact that Albert Victor had a reputation as an effeminate dandy. Called 'Collars and Cuffs' by his own family, he spent most of his time watching the world behind a languid pall of cigar smoke while dressed in impeccable suits. Before he died of influenza in 1892, just three years after the scandal, he kept himself as thin as the recently disgraced designer John Galliano, with an equally pencil-thin moustache. He was even thought to have once worn a corset beneath his military uniform to better cut an elegant figure on parade.

Before the 1890s it was not widely believed that effeminacy was linked to same-sex preferences in men. The very idea of homosexuality was not widely held at that time. It was of course known that some men engaged in 'unnatural acts', as indeed did certain women. Sodomy was considered a mark of depravity by anyone who knew their Old Testament, and had been a hanging offence in former days. But the knowledge of such acts did not translate into an understanding of a specific and stable same-sexual orientation. Nor were a particular set of characteristics ascribed to those who committed 'unnatural acts'. Over-the-top dandyism like Prince Albert Victor's was mocked as unmanly before the 1890s, but the general public did not consider it a sign of attraction to other men. All that was to change, however, in the wake of the Cleveland Street scandal. Following hot on its heels in 1895, Oscar Wilde's trial for gross indecency also played a role here. It received sensational publicity throughout Western society, in Australia as much as elsewhere, with high-profile reports of Wilde's sexual dalliances with young men splashed across the daily papers.[3]

The London-based scandals of the 1890s caused people to make connections between other stories and earlier rumours they had heard about same-sex acts. This led them to become convinced of the existence of a homosexual identity, and to start atttributing to it certain qualities. Wilde's penchant for velvet suits, scented carnations and flowing locks became particularly inseparable from the public imagination of homosexuality. In Australia, scattered incidents before and after the scandals contributed to this notion that homosexuality was associated with dandy dress and mannered effeminacy. After reading of Wilde's trial, for example, those who had been in Melbourne in October 1888 may have recalled reports of a young actor, Gordon Lawrence, who appeared in the central court on a charge of vagrancy. He had been arrested after being discovered parading in women's dress at the Centennial Exhibition. After a raid on his rented room, police had discovered more female clothes along with a glistening jar of oil. In court, an officer stated that Lawrence was from Sydney, where he formed part of a set of men 'who commit disgusting and horrible offences'. Another said that he had seen him wearing a 'masher' suit and powdered face in the city the previous Saturday night.[4]

Instances of men being prosecuted for same-sex practices began to appear in Brisbane with greater frequency in the years following the London scandals. The city's police were becoming more conscious of 'unnatural acts' among men, it seemed, or were at any rate more inclined to regard them as criminal matters worth pursuing in the courts. Legislators were also busy proscribing homosexual offences in Queensland's newly codified criminal law. Ironically, by raising the profile of homosexual acts these authorities contributed to the development of an embryonic same-sex subculture on the streets. Once it was publicised that certain places had been used for male-on-male sex – among them, a toilet behind a hardware store in Queen Street, Brisbane's main thoroughfare – other people would have been encouraged to use similar sites for the same purposes. Greater awareness of the styles of pick-up, slang and dress used by men seeking homosexual liaisons would similarly have allowed others to more knowingly participate in the same.[5]

The idea that dandified dress could be a sign of male homosexuality appeared in sundry articles in the Australian press after Wilde's trial. Late in 1895, a Sydney scandal-sheet known as the *Scorpion* ran an article called 'The Oscar Wilde's [sic] of Sydney'. It claimed that many of Sydney's pubs and billiard halls were frequented by flamboyantly attired homosexuals 'whose presence is advertised by effeminate speech'. Some years later, in 1907, a Toowong man accused of sodomy was questioned in the courts about whether or not he was a 'city queen' who stood on a corner in Queen Street looking for men to take home. The prosecutor drew the court's attention to the accused's panama hat and the red flower he wore in his masher-like jacket, suggesting that he used these to signal his homosexuality to those in the know.[6]

For years before the signal events of the Naughty Nineties, men's fashions had steadily been moving toward greater informality.

Lounge suits were beginning to replace formal evening wear; top hats were giving way to bowlers or Panama hats. Loose-fitting sporting wear was being bought in quantity. In Australia the climate was a spur to these developments. No one who had suffered in a frock-coat through a sweltering Australian summer could regret a light jacket taking its place. A growing emphasis on athleticism was also influential, partly motivated by concerns that urban life was causing men to become less vigorous.[7] Since it amplified these concerns, the new link between effeminate dandyism and homo-sexuality helped to consolidate the movement away from more formal and flamboyant styles of male attire. This was particularly the case among male larrikins, who were even more concerned than most to prove themselves possessed of heterosexual virility through their dress.

In 1905, an article bearing the lurid heading 'Naughty News-boys' appeared in Brisbane's muck-raking paper, *Truth*. It reported the prosecution of two Brisbane youths for sodomising 16-year-old Richard Goeldner. The incident occurred in a disused oyster saloon on Queen Street, Brisbane's main thoroughfare. Goeldner told police that both assailants had held him down and anally pen-etrated him against his will: first 17-year-old Albert McNamara and then 19-year-old newsboy William Guilfoyle. In his defence, McNamara said that Goeldner was a 'puff' – a slang word for an effeminate homosexual obviously related to 'poof'. 'It is not the first time he has done it', McNamara continued. 'I can bring a wit-ness who will swear that he got ten bob from a black fellow that stuffed him . . . [T]here are plenty of others in Brisbane who do it besides us mob, so I am not the first'.[8]

Picturing what Albert McNamara called 'us mob' having sex in disused Brisbane buildings becomes rather startling when one considers that larrikins frequented the same sorts of spaces. They were in and out of street corners, parks, vacant lots and abandoned buildings, and would surely have occasionally come across other young men from the social backgrounds who were interested in same-sex acts there. As a 1907 case also reported in the *Truth* reveals, there were other spaces in which larrikin and emergent homosexual networks would have rubbed up against each other: these being boarding houses around town.

In 1907, 26-year-old Joseph Cavanagh was sharing a room with his 23-year-old mate, Frank Scanlon, at the Woodlands Boarding House in Ann Street, Brisbane. Both men had been up north cutting sugarcane and were back in the city looking for work. Also staying at the Woodlands was James Stuart Marshall, well-dressed manager of the Moreheads Wool Room. Later described by police as a man of the 'coffee-room class' on account of his dapper moustache and dress, Marshall struck up a conversation with Cavanagh on several occasions. On the first of these, he had come into the boarding house parlour to play the piano and found Cavanagh playing cards there. On the second, he had invited Cavanagh into his room, asking him to help undo his collar stud. Marshall had then unsuccessfully propositioned the muscular cane-cutter, putting his hand on his thigh.

Hours after Cavanagh had brushed off Marshall's advances, guests at the Woodlands Boarding House were woken in the night to the sound of the wool manager's screams. When they rushed in to find out what was happening, Cavanagh was discovered beating Marshall with a belt strap in the room he shared with Scanlon, shouting 'you call yourself a man!' Cavanagh later told police that the attack had been provoked by Marshall, who had climbed into his bed and tried to sodomise him while he slept. Hearing this the police promptly overlooked the assault and arrested Marshall for indecency instead.

Upon his arrest Marshall said: 'this is a try-on by the Spring Hill push over that watch affair at Christmas-time'. As a consequence, police questioned both Cavanagh and Scanlon about whether or not they were members of the Spring Hill push. It is tempting to imagine from this that the two men had push connections and that larrikin friends from Spring Hill had induced Cavanagh to pay Marshall back for some earlier grievance. This is simply speculation, however – we will never know what Marshall actually meant when he mentioned the Spring Hill push. Still, Cavanagh gave a curious response when quizzed on this point by police. He denied knowlege of the Spring Hill push by saying he had never heard of Spring Hill, an unlikely circumstance given that the Woodlands Boarding House was not far away.[9]

Even if Cavanagh had nothing to do with members of a Spring Hill push, the circumstances surrounding Marshall's arrest throw the proximity of push and homosexual circles into sharp relief. They show that the distance between these two subcultures needed only to be as far as it took to cross a boarding house corridor, jar of oil in hand. Larrikins would certainly have come across homosexual men in these places. Young men who shared boarding-house rooms also had the opportunity for same-sex activity with each other. Homosexual acts were, after all, a frequently reported occurrence in the prisons and industrial schools in which some larrikins spent time. They would also take place among certain servicemen during the First World War.[10]

A 1901 case involving two young men allegedly belonging to North Melbourne's Crutchy push suggests that young men living and socialising together could be affected by hard-to-explain sexual jealousies and desires. In September that year, James Walsh and George Reginald Hill sub-let a room together from a woman in Hardwicke Street, North Melbourne. They had been living together a few weeks when friends saw them quarrelling outside a pub one Saturday afternoon. One of these friends was Valentine

Keating, fellow member of the Crutchy push. He later told police that he saw George Reginald Hill beating James Walsh, adding that both were in a flushed half-drunk state.

Before their punch-up in the street outside, Hill and Walsh had been sitting with other male friends at the Morning Star Hotel in Abbotsford Street, North Melbourne. At one point, Hill apparently said jokingly to Walsh: 'you are not a bad-looking mate, Jim'. In reply, Walsh said to Hill: 'I wish I had your mo, I would steal your girl'. Inexplicably enraged, Hill had lunged across the table and hit Walsh twice in the face. Walsh jumped up, fists raised, but was again beaten by Hill after they went to settle matters outside. Their friends pulled them apart and enticed them to return to the pub, making futile attempts to reconcile them over drinks. Growing sick of their efforts, a sullen and swollen-faced Walsh finally decided to leave.

According to witnesses, Hill tried to stop him from leaving the Morning Star. 'Come on home', he told him, roughly seizing Walsh's arm. Looking frightened, Walsh brushed him aside. 'I am not going home there no more', he told Hill before striding off up Abbotsford Street alone. Some hours later, someone bashed the aggressive Hill with an iron bar as he lay in his bed in Hardwicke Street. He died of a haemorrhage close to dawn; the bar was found sticky with hair and blood in the fireplace in his room. Though there was never enough evidence to convict Walsh of murder, he was considered the obvious suspect – both on account of his ability to let himself into the room unopposed and the tumultuous relationship that he and Hill had shared.[11]

Though frustratingly scant in their details, the Woodland Boarding House and Hardwicke Street cases allow us to imagine the anxiety that certain larrikins must have felt on account of hard-to-articulate feelings about same-sex acts. They also evoke something of the friction that must have existed between the members of larrikins and homosexual networks, not only sharing the same spaces but possibly overlapping at particular points in time. This friction may well have enticed male larrikins to make trouble for known homosexuals such as James Stuart Marshall. It may also have enticed them to make sartorial efforts to distinguish themselves from 'queens' and 'puffs', anxious to ward off unwelcome advances from homosexual men and disclaim any personal interest in homosexuality.

There are a number of indications that male larrikin dress started to become sharper and leaner around the turn of the century. It was not as if a dramatic shift in style took place. There had long been a preference for tight-fitting clothes in dark materials among disorderly youth with flash inclinations. There are also occasional references from the 1900s to larrikins wearing bob-tail coats or red neckerchiefs. On the whole, however, such colourful items were dropped from male rowdies' sartorial repertory around the start of the century. So were flared pants, high-cut-coats, fingers twinkling with rings, watch-chains trailing trinkets, flowers in the lapel, loud-checked tweed, plush-collared coats, masher hats and perfume.[12]

We get an inkling of larrikins' shift away from showy scarves and fussy tailoring from an 1898 case in Sydney called the 'Newtown affray'. In February that year, six men aged in their late teens to early twenties were arrested after attacking fellow Newtown youth Edward Clothier. The press represented these young men as a push, as did the judge who eventually convicted all but one of them on charges of causing grievous bodily harm. Notably including two brothers, the six prisoners had been among a group of about 10 to 15 similarly aged men who had laid in wait for Clothier outside his Commodore Street home and then brutally kicked him and fractured his skull. Held in remand until it was discovered whether or not Clothier would survive, the prisoners were said to have attacked him as pay-back over a romantic dispute. In their mugshots, each of these Newtown larrikins exuded the hard finish that Sidney Baker later commented upon: oiled-down hair, dark sharp jackets and white shirts with starched or celluloid collars.

Figures 31 and 32. *Thomas Pritchard (18 y.o. labourer) (left) and Walter Gentle (23 y.o. groom) (right), early 1898*
State Records NSW[13]

It is possible that the Newtown push-ites were dressed especially for court in these mugshots, and that they did not otherwise wear such slick suits. Amateur photographs taken by Melbourne's Joseph Bane in 1903, however, suggest that a range of Australian men adopted the sharp-lined Edwardian look that would later inspire London's 'Teddy' boys and the Australian equivalents known as 'bodgies'. The young men in Bane's photographs were not necessarily larrikins, but their dark suits and restrained insouciance indicate an interest in looking streetwise. It is likely that when Louis Stone described the 'height of larrikin fashion' in *Jonah*, he had something of these youths' hard sleekness in mind. The outfit worn to a wedding by his protagonists Jonah and Chook was one of 'surprising neatness', Stone wrote. It consisted of tight dark suits, black felt hats, white shirts with black mufflers and heeled boots studded with perforated toe-caps and brass eyelet holes. Though this outfit bore obvious connections to colonial larrikin dress, it was still neater and less gaudy, more concerned with being tough than flash.[14]

Figure 33. *Melbourne youths, Joseph Bane ca. 1903 State Library of Victoria*[15]

Male rowdies' changing look was not solely influenced by a desire to distance themselves from homosexual effeminacy. Toughness was indeed increasingly prized in their inner-suburban communities, both as a response to material hardship and as a way for manual labourers to exhibit their masculinity. For male larrikins, the greater prominence given to toughness rather than flashness was also affected by the greater regulation of street commerce that took place early in the century. They no longer had the same numbers of self-promotional street sellers or market exhibitors on which to model a cock-a-hoop style. Each of these things was implicated in the male larrikin's movement away from a gaudily tinted leariness towards a more rough-and-ready working-class look.[16]

The new priority placed on tough working-man status was part of the further shift in larrikin dress that took place during the 1910s. Many inner-suburban youths came to view toughness as incompatible with *any* kind of sartorial display in that decade, ditching even the lean suits and metallic-toed shoes. The aim of push larrikins, in particular, was now to dress as if they cared nothing about what they looked like – as if any sign of care in one's appearance was a sign of effeminacy. We can see this attitude at work in the recollections of Sydney man Bert Hickey who was born in 1905. Looking back on his adolescence in Forest Lodge – a suburb he described explicitly as 'working class' – this man Hickey recalled that a group of young bloods called the Hegarty Street mob had walked the streets in plain dress. 'I think they wore clothes as cheaply as they could fit to the occasion', he told an interviewer late in life. The same applied to other streetwise young men. 'We were all tough, we didn't have too many clothes', Hickey said. 'It was mostly a thin singlet and a thin shirt at the most and in winter you were very lucky if you had . . . one of those heavy heavy [sic] braided coats. You had them but you didn't really need them. You were tough'.

In April 1919, five Melbourne larrikins were described wearing cheap clothing similar to that of the Hegarty Street mob. Then in their late teens, these larrikins had stolen guns from a local pawnshop and used them to rob Alexander Byron, a Fitzroy youth around their own age. When questioned by police, they said they had targeted Byron because he belonged to the Checkers push. Each was 'poorly dressed, of the type common in slum areas', a reporter for the *Argus* declared.[17] Photographed by Sydney police in 1921, the unruly thief Charles Berry was dressed the same way. Aged 16, he wore a dirty slop-made jacket and unkempt shirt, a far cry from the light trousers with brown stripe and red silk necktie once worn by the colonial larrikin 'Plucky' Jim.

Figure 34. *Charles James Berry, 10 January 1921*
Historic Houses Trust NSW[18]

There were of course plucky dressers to be found in inner-suburban localities during the 1920s. Though most residents from the larrikin belt earned too little to live it up, this was still the age of jazz and Hollywood, when images of Gatsby-like excess were projected in cinemas and snappily conjured from gramo-phones. Police photographs from the period offer us portraits not just of ramshackle Charles Berrys in crumpled jackets but also of flashly dressed youth such as Roy Walton, a car thief caught in 1929. Young men involved in car-stealing rings frequently exhib-ited Walton's '"flash" quality', dressed in a white suit with a rosette on his lapel and a white scarf swathed high at his neck. Men who aspired to the sinister panache of Melbourne underworld figure 'Squizzy' Taylor also affected flash dress. When managing his race-fixing, debt-collecting and cocaine-vending rackets, Taylor dressed

in suave suits and diamond-studded tie-pins. He was not, in fact, a
'larrikin crook', however, regardless of the fact that his biographer
Hugh Anderson later chose to describe him thus. Taylor might
have mixed in larrikin circles as a would-be jockey in his teens, but
by the time he was dressing in high-gangster fashion he had left
them well and truly behind.[19]

Like Taylor, Sydneysider John Frederick 'Chow' Hayes was a
larrikin who became a career criminal at the end of his teens.
Around the start of the 1930s Hayes swapped his push for a razor
gang. By the time he had established himself as a leading figure
in Sydney's underworld in 1940, no one would have called him a
'larrikin crook'.[20] Other push larrikins almost certainly followed
Hayes' trajectory, moving away from push circles into organised
crime. For the most part, male larrikins became ordinary working
men once they left the push behind. They may have been hard-
drinking, fist-ready working men, but they had no place in the
worlds inhabited by Squizzy Taylor or Sydney's equivalent, Tilly
Devine. For the most part, too, a clear distinction could be drawn
between push members involved in territorial fights and football
skirmishes and criminals associated with cocaine and prostitution
rings. Dress was an obvious way this was drawn. By the 1920s it
was only the career criminals who dressed to look slick or 'fly'. To
put it another way: by that time criminal circles had superseded
larrikin ones as the repository of flash desires.

The vaudeville comedians who played larrikin characters during
and after the war vividly illustrate the flash larrikin's demise. In
1916, Nat Phillips and Roy Rene began performing a double act
on vaudeville stages that catapulted them to instant stardom. Playing the scallywags Stiffy and Mo, their first season at the Princess
Theatre on Sydney's Broadway broke theatrical box office records.
Phillips' unfortunately named Stiffy was explicitly presented as a

Figure 35. *'Chow' Hayes, 19 y.o. (left) standing beside his cousin Ezzie Bollard, 23 y.o. (right), 6 November 1930. This photograph was taken five years after Bollard was sent to the Emu Plains Farm for Boys for actual bodily harm (see chapter six). It was also taken in a period in which Hayes and Bollard were making the transition from push-ites to gangsters. Hayes' dapper suit and slicked hair are a sign of these ambitions.*
Historic Houses Trust NSW[21]

Sydney larrikin of Irish-Australian descent. He was also presented as a fanatic supporter of the Rabbitohs – a canny addition, given how much of the Princess Theatre audience lived in the southern suburbs. In interviews, Phillips talked up Stiffy's authenticity. 'Until I brought Stiffy on the scene', he said in 1919, 'the larrikin . . . was always portrayed as a coster[monger]. This always appeared incongruous to me . . . I decided to try the experiment with the Sydney larrikin'. Stiffy dressed accordingly in a worn South Sydney football guernsey, a well-greased pair of trousers and clod-hopping boots. Said to have been modelled on a Jewish pawnbroker, Rene's character Mo dressed in similarly dilapidated style.[22]

Though Phillips claimed that Stiffy was a new and authentic character, his stage persona had direct links to stage-Irish routines long popular in blackface minstrel and other variety shows. Rene's Mo was also connected to the raggedly dressed Jim Crow and Jewish types appearing on the minstrel stage.[23] By the 1910s there were plenty of other Australian performers who had cut their teeth on Irish or blackface comedy and were specialising in knockabout characters with self-consciously Australian overtones. Though probably not presented as a larrikin *per se* – he was far too fat to play one convincingly – Jack 'Porky' Kearns played a series of happy-go-lucky and poorly dressed Aussie-bloke characters of this kind. 'Don't you call me a loafer or I'll have you up on definition of character', was a line for which one of his creations was renowned. Another introduced himself as 'a scene-shifter by trade and a beer-sinker by birth'.

In the years leading up to the war, Kearns played a range of sites that had become available for vaudeville shows and were easily accessible to residents from Sydney's larrikin belt. These included the Princess Theatre on Broadway, South Sydney Amusement Hall at the Waterloo tram terminus, Redfern Picture Palace and Harry Clay's Bridge Theatre (now the Hub Theatre), across the road from Newtown Station. Other performers presented like characters in these venues and similar ones in Melbourne and Brisbane. Throughout the 1910s, for example, Arthur Tauchert was a knockabout comedian renowned for his somersaults and mischievous buffoonery. Cheeky attempts to shirk work, mock his boss, get drunk and get drunk again were standard fare for his routines. Given that film-maker Raymond Longford picked him to play Bill the larrikin in *The Sentimental Bloke* (1919), some of Tauchert's characters were likely to have been larrikins. In 1917, another low comedian of the day, Harry Blister, played a similar type in the 'Loo-ite Blister', a Woolloomooloo tough, at the Bridge Theatre in Sydney's Newtown.[24]

Stage characters such as Phillips' Stiffy or Tauchert's fall-down drunks existed in a push-me pull-you relationship to low-lifes on the streets. When developing their costumes, the performers would have drawn on clothes worn by actual push-ites and drunks: Souths guernseys, for example, or ill-fitting who-gives-a-damn suits. Audiences would simply not have responded to these characters unless they were sartorially plausible in this way. Once they became known as new-era larrikins, however, Stiffy and his ilk would have in turn influenced the self-presentation of youths such as Charles Berry or the members of the Hegarty Street mob. This same process of art imitating life (and vice versa) may be found among the Australian servicemen who started fashioning themselves as 'diggers' during the First World War.

As anyone who has lived in Australia long enough well knows, the archetypal image of the Anzac digger was of an ordinary working man given to drunkenness, irreverent humour, anti-authoritarianism and nonchalance in the face of adversity. This image first came into being through the self-generated culture of Australian servicemen. It emerged through the stories and jokes they told about themselves as 'diggers', some of which were performed as theatrical skits by night or reproduced in battalion newspapers like *The Dinkum Oil*. It then achieved currency back in Australia, whether through servicemen's letters or war correspondents' reports or other publications and stage acts.[25] Importantly, all of these various forms attributed the digger with carelessness in dress along with his other qualities. Time after time, they portrayed him in dishevelled clothes meant to complement his lack of interest in social niceties.

For servicemen, the digger's unkempt dress was a way to express resentment towards certain military officers. They continually complained that members of the 'top brass' valued spit and polish above courage on the front line. Sung in camps during the hostilities, the song 'Horseferry Road' expressed this resentment in blunt and tellingly homophobic form:

> He was stranded alone in London, and strode
> To Army Headquarters in Horseferry Road,
> And there met a poofter Lance-Corporal, who said:
> 'You've got blood on your tunic, and mud on your head;
> You look so disgraceful that people will laugh',
> So said the cold-footed bastard from the Horseferry staff.
> The digger jumped up with a murderous glance;
> Said 'Fuck you, I just came from the trenches in France,
> Where fighting was plenty and cunt was for few,
> And brave men are dying for mongrels like you'.[26]

Though Australians joined the war out of a feeling of kinship with Britons, most of the AIF emerged from it convinced of their national distinctiveness. The concept of recognisably Australian traits had, of course, been voiced before then: whether by volunteers for the Boer War, in plays and literature vaunting the bushmen's qualities, or via images of the fresh-faced Australian girl. During the First World War, however, servicemen gave the notion of a distinctive Australianness an 'aggressive, even pugnacious edge'. Their belief in their unique identity as Australians came partly from playing up to British expectations of their vulgarity. This practice would have appealed most to industrial workers from the inner suburbs, large numbers of whom had joined the AIF.[27] Already well-versed in ways to maintain self-dignity in the face of social prejudice, one can easily envisage them reclaiming the image of the rough-and-ready colonial as a source of pride instead of shame. In representing themselves as dinkum 'diggers', servicemen also drew on local qualities and traits familiar from Australian popular culture before the war.

We all know now about the extent to which the figure of

the bushmen informed the official Anzac legend: the one that celebrated the AIF's glorious comportment on the battlefield. In the case of the more grassroots digger legend, however, the male larrikin provided the material most immediately at hand. Some of the reasons for this are obvious. A small number of inner-suburban recruits would already have thought of themselves as larrikins before they joined the AIF. After they joined, the fact that two-up, promiscuity and drunkenness became rife within the AIF – all of them practices long associated with larrikinism – would have induced other soldiers to start calling themselves larrikins. In August 1918, for example, a soldier calling himself 'South Digger' sent a letter to the South Melbourne *Record*. It suggested that he and his friends had come to feel an imagined connection to push larrikins. South Digger wrote that he heard news about a new South Melbourne 'mob' from known as the Hungry Seventies. This was probably the push described elsewhere in the *Record* as the 'Hungry Fifteen', *habitués* of South Melbourne's infamous Bloodhouse pub. 'They seem a pretty willing mob when we hear about them in London', South Digger wrote approvingly.[28]

Australian servicemen's perceived affinity with push larrikins was no doubt heightened by the fact that some of those volunteering after 1916 would have seen larrikin routines *à la* Stiffy and Mo. There was indeed an extraordinary similarity between the digger figure and the stage larrikins of the day.[29] This was accentuated by the fact that some of the men who enlisted for the AIF were vaudeville performers. During the war, they may well have offered entertainments to their fellow soldiers in which they played characters modelled on Arthur Tauchert- or Nat Phillips-style acts. When they returned, these performers continued to play low-comic figures now got up as 'diggers' for Australian audiences. They ensured that the stage larrikin and digger became entwined in civilian as well as military consciousness.

Jim Gerald was one of the performers who brought together the raffish larrikin stage comedy of the pre-war years with post-war digger acts. Already well-known in Australia before 1914, he starred in mini-plays such as *The Raw Recruit* upon his return. In this one-act drama, he impersonated a callow would-be digger dressed in ragged dungarees. (Incidentally, this character was juxta-posed with a foppish British army officer played by his wife Essie Jennings. Dressed in pantomime tights and a ludicrously plumed military hat, her character gave a new and nationalist twist to con-nections between dandy dress and effeminacy). Other performers who had entertained fellow soldiers during the war joined vaude-ville troupes with other ex-servicemen on return to civilian life. Chief among these troupes were the All Diggers Company, the Aussie Smart Set Diggers and Pat Hanna's Famous Diggers, each of which toured Australia and New Zealand in the years immedi-ately following the war.[30]

The most obvious example of a connection between diggers and stage larrikins was CJ Dennis' *The Moods of Ginger Mick*. Pub-lished as a sequel to *The Sentimental Bloke* in 1916, this collection of verse retained Bill the Bloke as its narrator, but focused on the exploits of his larrikin friend, Ginger Mick. For readers unfamiliar with *The Sentimental Bloke,* Bill introduced Mick as his hard-drinking 'cobber' from a Melbourne mean-street called Spadgers Lane. Ginger Mick was 'a rorty boy, a naughty boy', he said: a 'leery bloke' who ran with pushes and enjoyed a bet on the track. In the subsequent verse, Ginger Mick was shown heeding 'the Call uv Stoush', enlisting and being sent to Cairo. He was well-suited to serve in the AIF, the Bloke said:

'Is early trainin' down in Spadgers Lane
Done 'im no 'arm fer this-'ere orl-in fight.

Fighting with other larrikin types such as 'little Smith uv Collin'wood', Mick took to the war like a duck to water, eventually dying a hero on the battlefield.

The Moods of Ginger Mick began walking out of bookstores as soon as it hit the shelves in October 1916. Forty-two thousand copies were sold in the following six months in Australia alone. The work was also issued in a 'Pocket Edition for the Trenches', avidly read by servicemen. If the success of this edition is anything to go by, Australian soldiers identified with Ginger Mick and his experiences. They would thus have used him as another source when producing images of the digger type among themselves. This process continued after the armistice when Dennis' characters were kept in the public eye via the silent films *The Sentimental Bloke* (1919) and *Ginger Mick* (1920). Stage productions of these works were also performed during the 1920s.[31]

Yet another influence on the popular merger of the digger and the larrikin after the war was *Smith's Weekly,* formed in Sydney in August 1919. Describing itself as 'the Digger's Paper', *Smith's* had ex-*Bulletin* editor JF Archibald on board in its early days. Under his guidance, the paper ran cartoons of diggers featuring similar traits to those once attributed to larrikins in the *Bulletin*. *Smith's* offerings were nationalist in tone, however: they presented the digger not just as a comic figure, but as a jaunty metaphor for Australian national identity. In the first caricature below, for example, the anti-authoritarian digger was contrasted with both a stuffy British officer as well as a Johnny-come-lately American. In the second caricature, the larrikin traits of irreligiousness and love of drunkenness with 'the boys' were cheerfully attributed to the digger, and thus to Australian men at large.

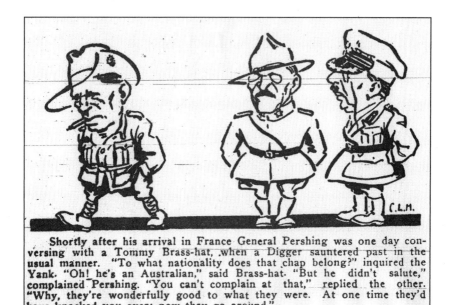

Shortly after his arrival in France General Pershing was one day conversing with a Tommy Brass-hat, when a Digger sauntered past in the usual manner. "To what nationality does that chap belong?" inquired the Yank. "Oh! he's an Australian," said Brass-hat. "But he didn't salute," complained Pershing. "You can't complain at that," replied the other. "Why, they're wonderfully good to what they were. At one time they'd have knocked you over; now they go around."

Figure 36. Smith's Weekly, *15 November 1919, p. 23*

Digger (to popular chaplain): "The boys arst me to invite you to join 'em in a drink."

Padre: "No, Digger, thanks old man; not now, I'm just getting ready to preach a sermon."

Digger "That's nothing, Sir. We're getting ready to listen to you."

Figure 37. Smith's Weekly, *13 December 1919, p. 9*

One of the reasons that diggers were likened to larrikins was that it downplayed the seriousness of the misdemeanours in which AIF soldiers were involved. When soldiers described themselves as 'larrikins', their racist assaults on Egyptian civilians and instances of murder, rape and inveterate brothelising could be passed off as if no more than the actions of mischievous youth. The same applied when soldiers' sympathisers invoked the 'l' word. An outrageously revisionist piece written by serviceman Herbert Nicholls for the *Anzac Memorial* of 1917 makes this clear. Nicholls suggested that colonial larrikins had paved the way for Anzac diggers such as himself on account of their daring and chivalry. 'I have frequently heard ladies say', he wrote, 'that if they needed any bit of courtesy, such as a man can often afford a woman, they would always walk up to a push on the street corner and ask help'.[32]

The concept of larrikinism was often used to make light of hooliganish behaviour among the AIF men during and after the war. It was not until the end of the 1920s, however, that the myth of the knockabout larrikin and his kinship with the happy-go-lucky digger were complete. Before then, these images still had to compete with public awareness of street disorder among returned servicemen and with more traditionally negative attitudes towards larrikins. When an angry group of returned soldiers physically assaulted the Premier and sacked his office during Victorian peace celebrations in July 1919, for example, the Returned Sailors' and Soldiers' Imperial League (now the RSL) was keen to distance its members from the 'larrikin element' among ex-AIF men. The inner-suburban press also frequently expressed the anxiety that disturbed veterans were hooking up with younger 'larrikins' and inciting them to unrest.[33]

The gun-fights and post-football stoushes that continued to take place among pushes were another reason why larrikinism could not be purged of all its connotations of loutish disorder in the

1920s. As long as pushes such as the Wanderers and Checkers were shooting each other in Fitzroy streets, the term larrikin could not be completely divested of notions of criminality and unruliness. It was only once gun ownership and veteran unrest had been brought under control that celebratory views of 'harmless' larrikinism as a trait shared by diggers, if not male Australians more generally, could prevail. It was only at that time that the image of the larrikin could be unloosed from its connections to a street-fighting youth subculture and made to stand for a lovable national type.

The celebration of the larrikin digger had an obvious impact on female rowdies. It highlighted the fact that larrikinism was now imagined as an emphatically masculine affair. No female counterpart to the scruffily mischievous Stiffy type came to prominence during and after the war. Young women who might once have styled themselves as 'brazen larrikinesses' now began toying with a more glamorous flapper persona, buying vivid lipstick and bobbing their hair. Their look was worlds away from the Hegarty Street mob in their knockabout clothes. We can see here the beginnings of the dissonance between the sexes that flowered during the Second World War, when Australian girls made eyes at flash Yank soldiers and disdained plainly dressed local boys. Much like the journalists who excoriated GI Joe-loving girls during that later war, *Smith's Weekly* became obsessed with the flapper during the 1920s. Juxtaposing the flapper's gaudy femininity with the digger's laconic masculinity, the paper's caricaturists drew attention to the gulf that had opened between the sexes when it came to street style.[34]

As larrikinism became detached from its connections to rough youth, push members stopped calling themselves larrikins. The word lingered into the 1930s as a way for others to describe fanatic football barrackers and the members of street gangs, but it was no longer a way for those youths to identify themselves. If a man called himself a larrikin in the 1930s, it usually meant he was laying claim to the qualities of the ideal digger: rough-and-readiness, waggish humour and a determined heterosexuality. By the 1930s, a man no longer needed to be young in order to call himself a larrikin. Nor did he need to live in the inner suburbs, work as a badly paid 'fact'ry 'and', or 'kick the living daylights' out of other pushes by night. What had been said prematurely in 1910 was thus finally true: 'larrikinism as we used to understand it is dead'.

Afterword

Larrikinism since 1930

Figure 38. *Undated photo of actor Paul Hogan (right) with John 'Strop'
Cornell (left) from the TV program,* The Paul Hogan Show
Newspix/News Ltd

When I told men of a certain age that I was writing a history
of larrikinism, I was surprised by the number who winked
and said jovially: 'well, you'll know all about me then!' These men
included an uncle who was a builder wearing Paul Hogan-esque
cut-off shirts in the 1970s and now runs a small joinery business.

The others, however, were for the most part baby-boomer professionals more likely to order expensive home renovations than labour on a building site. That such men should present themselves as cheekily irreverent and down-to-earth makes it evident that we still live in the grip of a larrikin myth. By this, I mean the myth that real Australians, especially real Australian men, are practical-joking plain-talking fellows regardless of their class or income. It was this myth that Kevin Rudd tried valiantly but ineffectually to exude when he spoke of the 'fair shake of the sauce bottle' as prime minister in 2009.[1] The same applies to any politician or company executive who talks of being 'fair dinkum' or says 'mate' in a public forum today. The larrikin myth is all about engaging in a performance of egalitarian Australianness, usually via the exhibition of ocker vernacular and the anti-intellectualism this implies. In its roguish informality, it is also a way to portray oneself as non-conformist, whether or not this bears any relation to everyday realities.

The first stirrings of the larrikin myth may arguably be found in the 1890s, when *Bulletin* contributors and theatrical performers first presented depictions of 'push society'. In most of these cases, however, no attempt was made to identify with larrikins. The term had far too much loutish notoriety for that to be desirable at the time. Though the *Bulletin* caricaturists and writers claimed a familiarity with a lower-class city *milieu*, they were still at pains to demonstrate their superiority over their larrikin subjects by making them the butt of their jokes. It was only in the second decade of the 1900s – most obviously among self-proclaimed diggers towards the end of the First World War – that claiming to be a larrikin or possessing a 'larrikin streak' became acceptable outside adolescent street circles. This practice had become more widespread by the early 1930s, chiefly as a result of the growing connection between diggers and larrikinism in Australian popular culture.[2]

In 1930, the publication of *Here's Luck,* a novel by comic journalist, Lennie Lower, helped to develop Australia's larrikin myth.
Though Lower is hardly a household name these days, the man
once described as a 'Chaplin of words' had a much larger profile
in his own day. Depression-era readers paid hard-to-come-by cash
first for *Here's Luck* (1930), then for Lower's second book, *Here's
Another* (1932), and his assorted adventures in prose comedy in
the press. Though Lower never explicitly described the protagonist
of *Here's Luck* as a larrikin, the book was understood as larrikin-
esque by its contemporaries, covering similar terrain to Louis
Stone's *Jonah* and film versions of *The Sentimental Bloke.* Set in
inner-Sydney, it featured a cheerfully debauched forty-something,
Jack Gudgeon and his gormless son, Stanley, wending a ruinous
path through Darlinghurst pubs, the Randwick races, flirtations
with two-up and dates with 'gimme girls'. It ended with the pair
burning down their rented terrace during a massive party involving boxers, barmen, two-up school doormen, dance-hall boys and
the said gimme girls.

Like the baby-boomer professionals who now call themselves
larrikins, neither Lower nor his alter ego, Gudgeon, were working class. In *Here's Luck*, Gudgeon was a bludging office worker,
although in what capacity and at what manner of establishment
was left unclear. In reality, Lower's father Sydney was a pharmacist
and his mother Edith had grown up in a middle-class Adelaide
family. Lower himself was of course a professional writer, part of
a boozy fraternity that included pressmen, ad-men, graphic artists, theatrical agents, sporting buffs and their friends. These fellows
were more frankly commercial in bent than the turn-of-the-
century bohemians. They were happy enough to admit that they
wore white collars to an office by day. They still energetically disclaimed respectability, however – some of the funniest potshots
in *Here's Luck* were directed at mortgage-paying suburbanites on

Sydney's North Shore. Keeping up a grinning raffishness and mak-ing digs at wives and lawyers, these inter-war cads were classic early adopters of the larrikin myth.[3]

In their insistence on happy-go-lucky disreputability, Lower and his colleagues paved the way for the cultural mavericks associated with the Sydney Push and the Melbourne Drift, both bohemian scenes of the late 1950s and early 1960s. In Sydney, these mid-century bohemians invoked the memory of colonial larrikin pushes in choosing to call themselves 'the Push'. That memory was highly selective and romanticised, however: one in which the early push-ites were re-packaged as attractive renegades, exhibiting what one member later called a 'cheerful contempt for authority'. It is telling that the likes of Bruce Beresford, Lilian Roxon, Robert Hughes and Germaine Greer were uninterested in the so-called bodgies and widgies whooping it up to rock'n'roll and holding street fights in their own day. As wild young things with flash clothes and uncouth manners, the bodgies and widgies were far more obvious inheritors of the first push-ites' raw precocity than the university-educated journalists and *poet manqués* who belonged to the Push. It was only because colonial larrikins were viewed through the flattering lens of nostalgia that the Push could regard them so approvingly.[4]

In Melbourne, something of the Push's conscious brashness could be found not just in the Drift but in Ray Lawler's play, *Summer of the Seventeenth Doll*. Set in Carlton in the summer of 1953 and debuting two years later, it starred the muscular, emotionally-stunted cane-cutters, Barney and Roo, memorably described as 'flamin' larrikins'. Much was made at the time of the fact that Lawler had started out as a working-class boy in 1920s Footscray, labouring in a factory at age thirteen. As the Next Big Thing in Australian theatre, however, he had become a *déclassé* figure by the 1950s. He was to be hailed as the founding father of any number of plays featuring working-class protagonists and Australian accents over the following years. In this period of assertive cultural nationalism, television also began to experiment with the portrayal of male larrikin types. The best early example of this was *In Melbourne Tonight,* a post-vaudevillian variety program hosted by Graham Kennedy from 1957. It was followed in the 1960s by the *Mavis Bramston Show,* featuring a singlet-wearing knockabout called Ocker played by Gordon Chater – and, of course, in the 1970s, by *The Paul Hogan Show.*[5]

In 1968, the comedian Barry Humphries produced a comic book called *The Wonderful World of Barry McKenzie,* starring an Aussie *naïf* let loose on swinging London. It was made into a film, *The Adventures of Barry McKenzie,* directed by Bruce Beresford and starring Barry Crocker in 1972. Though he was already a foppish expatriate with plummy vowels by then, Humphries would later say that McKenzie (actually played by Crocker in the film) provided 'a good outlet for my Australianness'. He expressed this imagined Australianness through the invention of a spectacularly crass vernacular for McKenzie, some of which is still in use today. Among other things, the beer-guzzling, lamington-scoffing protagonist of *The Adventures of Barry McKenzie* called a penis a 'donger', an erection 'cracking the fat', sex 'sinking the sausage', and vomit a 'technicolour yawn'. The musician Colin Hay of Men At Work allegedly wrote his band's 1981 hit, 'Down Under', as a paean to Bazza McKenzie's as-low-as-it-gets comic charm.[6]

Both the original film and its sequel, *Barry McKenzie Holds His Own* (1974) belonged to what historian Kath Leahy has called a 'larrikin revolution' in Australian popular culture in the late 1960s and early 1970s. It was in this period that folk musician Warren Fahey created Larrikin Records, now infamous for its infringement of copyright suit against Men at Work over the 'Down Under' song. At the same time, a cavalcade of waggish jokers were wisecracking or (in Bazza's case) farting and chundering their way across Australian stages and screens. An obvious example of these in-your-face fellows was the self-confessed larrikin, Graeme Blundell, playing the eponymous hero in the pube-flashing sex comedy, *Alvin Purple* (1973). So were the protagonists of films such as *Stork* (1971) and *Don's Party* (1976), both based on David Williamson plays. Recalling her experiences of the era, Leahy described the 1970s as a time of 'almost compulsory downward mobility', when even high fliers and future prime ministers showed off their beer-drinking prowess and capacity for Strine. To have any credibility during this period, Leahy observed, 'one had to keep one's "bourgeois" connections to oneself'.[7]

Figure 39. *Bob Hawke at the height of his larrikin days in 1975, eight years before he became prime minister.*
Fairfax Syndication

While it is easy to characterise the larrikin myth as a way for professionals to conceal their bourgeois connections, playing with a rakishly *déclassé* or working-class modality when it suited them, this is by no means the whole story. Middle-class men are not the only Australians who have enjoyed calling themselves larrikins. Given the origins of the concept, it is hardly surprising that consciously working-class Australians have also styled themselves thus. By the time the word had lost the worst of its street-gang stigma in the late 1920s, a range of people from working-class communities were indeed embracing a 'lovable larrikin' identity. Lennie Lower's combination of ironic wit and ratbag humour certainly appealed to working-class readers as well as those from more privileged backgrounds. The roisterous supporter at Fitzroy football games known as Ginger Mick in 1930s Melbourne is also testament to the appeal of CJ Dennis' attractive larrikins within largely blue-collar inner-suburban communities. Though Roy Rene and Nat Phillips no longer appeared on vaudeville stages as Stiffy and Mo in the 1930s, Rene's Mo character continued to be popular with a diverse audience into the 1940s, both in theatrical revues and in radio plays.[8]

Figure 40. *The 'AC/DC larrikin', Bon Scott 1976*
Ton Linsen/Fairfax Syndication

Born in 1937 in the Sydney suburb of Balmain, the Olympic swimming champion Dawn Fraser provided a model of emphatically working-class larrikinism throughout her career. One of the few women to expressly present herself as a larrikin in public life, Fraser reminisced in her autobiography about acting as a runner for a local SP bookie, scoffing beer and barracking at the football in the 'very working-class' streets of her youth. A similar though more squarely masculine larrikinism was attributed to the Australian rules great, EJ 'Ted' Whitten, a star for solidly working-class Footscray. Before he died in London amid Bazza McKenzie-like debauchery in 1980, AC/DC frontman Bon Scott provided another example of a working-class larrikin identity. Who could forget those iconic photographs of him from the mid-1970s, Tooheys KB in hand or flashing his groin tattoo? In the 1980s, too, Rodney Rude and Kevin Bloody Wilson both enjoyed cult followings for their ludicrously bawdy style of stand-up comedy. Wilson still sells tickets to shows in rural and working-class suburban locations, having first become famous as the 'Kalgoorlie Larrikin' in his Western Australian mining home town.[9]

Since it appears to hold a special appeal for white men in their fifties or older, it is a real question whether or not the larrikin myth will remain relevant in the future. Certainly the numbers of Anglo men born in the 1940s who later became famous as larrikins seems out of touch with a multicultural Australia where American hip-hop, Latin pop and Indian bhangra can be heard alongside nostalgic playings of Men at Work and AC/DC. It is interesting, however, that we now sometimes find non Anglo-Australian men claiming to be larrikins or being publicly described as such. The Greek-Australian comedian Nick Giannopoulos of *Wog Boy* fame, the Indigenous actor, Ernie Dingo, artist Larrikin Sturt and a group of Indigenous performers recently celebrated for their 'larrikin humour' during a tour of China all fit this category.

In spite of the flagrant heterosexuality long associated with larrikinism, we also occasionally find homosexual men such as the actor John Hargreaves being called larrikins. On the other hand, such things as advertisements for Bundaberg Rum make it clear that old-style versions of the larrikin myth still hold an appeal. Described ungrammatically as 'having a bit of larrikin' by a former company executive, Bundaberg Rum's 'Bundy Bear' mascot is frequently depicted on television helping his friends win women's attention through slyly comic stunts. Winking and nudging with his white mates, the Bear's larrikinism represents Bundy's aspirations to be considered a quintessentially Australian drink.[10]

In December 2010, the *Sydney Morning Herald* music writer, Bernard Zuel, ruminated on why Australia has produced so few rock stars. Australia has had successful rock musicians aplenty, of course. Bar the pop-rock singer Michael Hutchence, however, it has had scant examples of strutting rock gods. Most Australian musicians seem to have refrained from on-stage swagger out of a concern that they might be considered ridiculous. As Bernard Fanning, frontman for the former Brisbane band, Powderfinger, once put it: 'I've [always] had that great Australian fear that my mates are going to give me shit'.[11] With its insistence on being able to laugh at one's own and others' pretensions, the larrikin myth is largely responsible for this. Ironically, however, the first larrikins were all about swagger and big-noting themselves. The male adolescents who once proclaimed themselves 'King of the Larrikins' or the young women who boasted they could 'fight any man' were in each case experts in showy one-upmanship. They adopted nicknames such as 'Cocky' and 'Rorty' to underline this point. Mouthy boasters such as Indigenous boxer Anthony Mundine or lippy 'bogan' girls getting into fights are thus perhaps more true to the original larrikin sensibility than laconic humorists with the common touch.

Though plenty about the larrikin image has altered over time, it still enjoys a close relationship with masculine sports, most notably boxing and football. The very fact that Mundine might be considered a bearer of the original larrikin spirit is indicative of this. The number of times that 'larrikin' is still used to describe Australian rules or rugby league players is also telling. It would be impossible to count the times that the waggish humour of *The Footy Show* has been described as larrikin in bent. The bad behaviour of football stars involved in sex scandals and drunken assaults has also frequently been downplayed through their description as larrikins. Underlining this, Bundy Bear ads or their beery equivalents routinely appear during football games. Since the popularity of these sports is not set to decline, we have every reason to expect that the larrikin myth will remain relevant in spite of its origins in White Australia days.

The fact that the word 'larrikin' turns up so frequently at moments of high sentiment is another reason to expect that it will retain currency. Steve Irwin is not the only Australian man to have been eulogised as a 'true-blue Aussie larrikin' upon his death in recent years. Among others are Queensland's George Creed, mayor of Gladstone, mourned as 'a prankster and a jokester' in December 2010; 22-year-old Victorian electrician, Brendan Hopcraft, killed when his motorcycle hit a tree the preceding April; Corporal Mathew Hopkins, a Newcastle soldier killed in Afghanistan, and the Geelong policeman, Andrew Hines, both farewelled in 2009. Don Chipp, the founder of the Democrats who vowed to 'keep the bastards honest', was similarly extolled as a larrikin at his funeral in 2006.[12] This widespread use of 'larrikin' by ordinary people to describe their loved ones makes it clear that larrikinism is not just something that exists at the level of public commentary or popular culture. There is still a rich interrelationship between the ways in which larrikinism is publically represented and people's intimate circumstances, just as there was between the late 1860s and 1920s when the first larrikins were alive.

The role played by larrikinism in Australia today in many ways sits uneasily against what we know of the larrikin subculture in earlier decades. Those who use 'larrikin' to eulogise departed friends may dislike knowing that it was once a term of abuse. The individuals who took part in anti-Chinese riots or gang rapes are also better remembered in shame rather than pride. There is no claiming them now as heart-of-gold larrikin heroes. These aspects of Australia's larrikin history are important to face honestly rather than gloss over with romantic anecdotage, however – and at any rate, not everything about the first larrikins' efforts to assert themselves is a cause for shame.

The fact that Australians have turned an identity born in hardscrabble conditions into a source of national mythology ultimately tells us a great deal about their sensibilities. England had hooligans in abundance in the late nineteenth century, after all. Other Western nations also had adolescent 'hoodlums' or their equivalents at that time. At no point during the early 1900s, however, did the citizens of those countries start praising their nation's 'hooligan spirit' or 'hoodlum streak', as if that were an exultant fact. That so many Australians should choose to adopt a version of larrikinism as a badge of national identity thus reveals a great deal about Australian culture and history in spite of the obviously mythic character of the 'true blue Aussie larrikin'.

Acknowledgments

Immense thanks first to Graeme Turner, Director of the Centre for Critical and Cultural Studies at the University of Queensland, where this book was researched and written. He read every draft and was ever-ready with incisive critique and encouragement. I challenge anyone to find a more supportive director of a research centre anywhere.

Thanks too to the Australian Academy of Humanities, who awarded a much-needed subsidy for the publication of images in this book.

Appreciation to my editors Kabita Dhara and John Hunter; to Clay Djubal, ace research assistant and font of knowledge on the history of Australian variety theatre; and to Helen Harris OAM for extraordinary research in the Public Records of Victoria.

Gratitude to colleagues who read chapter drafts or related pieces, sharing ideas and critique: Yorick Smaal, Graeme Davison, Mark Finnane, Jill Matthews, Richard White, Martin Crotty, Margaret Maynard, Richard Fotheringham, Andrew Davies, Kath Leahy, Veronica Kelly, Peter Spearritt, Marian Quartly, Jon Stratton,

Murray Phillips and Simon Sleight. Simon, in particular, went well beyond the call of collegiality, carefully reading drafts, generously sharing primary sources and offering invaluable insights along the way.

To Fergus Grealy, Jillian Keetley, Trish Brown and Garry Brown: many regards for proofreading and encouragement. And finally, as always, to Luke Morey: for your sure eye, and everything else besides.

Endnotes

Introduction

1. For examples of people calling Steve Irwin a larrikin, see the entry on the Made In Oz website (madeinoz.com/famous.html); and a comment by 'Nathan' to an article on Steve Irwin on the TMZ website, written 5 September 2006 (tmz.com/2006/09/04/crocodile-hunter-irwin-killed-by-stingray/15). See also: 'Beaconsfield miners' book launched by PM', National Nine News, 6 November 2006 (news.ninemsn.com.au/article.aspx?id=105624); Emma Chamberlain, 'Beers, cheers and tears at Beaconsfield', National Nine News, 9 May 2006 (news.ninemsn.com.au/article.aspx?id=99319).

2. Clem Gordon, *The Larrikin streak: Australian writers look at the legend*, Pan Books, Sydney, 1990; Peter Goldsworthy, 'The Australian temperament', in his *True blue? On being Australian*, Allen & Unwin, Sydney, 2008, p. 13; Catriona Elder, *Being Australian: narratives of Australian identity*, Allen & Unwin, Sydney, 2007, pp. 33–4, 43, 47; & Jessica Milner Davis, '"Aussie" humour and laughter: joking as an acculturating ritual', in Fran de Groen & Peter Kirkpatrick (eds), *Serious frolic: essays on Australian humour*, University of Queensland Press, Brisbane, 2009, pp. 31–47. Examples of biographies with 'larrikin' in the title: Kathleen Jordan, *Larrikin angel: a biography of Veronica Brady*, Round House Press, Fremantle, 2009; Michael Crouch, *The literary larrikin: a critical biography of TAG Hungerford*, University of Western Australia Press, Perth, 2004; Helen Elward, *Larrikin and saint: Graeme 'Changa' Langlands*, Legenz, Sydney, 2001; Hector VJ Hanson & Petronella E Wilson, *Memoirs of a larrikin: a Red Hill lad remembers*, Hanson, Rosebud Vic., 1984; Ron Casey with Richard Sleeman, *Ron Casey, confessions of a larrikin*, Lester-Townsend, Paddington NSW, 1989; Tony Stephens, *Larrikin days: 100 years of growing up in an Australian suburb*,

Nicholson St Public School P&C Association, Balmain NSW, 1983; Hugh Anderson, *Larrikin crook: the rise and fall of Squizzy Taylor,* Jacaranda, Brisbane, 1971. On Gorton: *Time,* 22 March 1971; *Sydney Morning Herald (SMH),* 20 May 2002.

3. *SMH,* 13 July 2009.

4. CJ Dennis, *The songs of a sentimental bloke* (published in later editions as *The sentimental bloke),* Angus & Robertson, Sydney, 1915, pp. 15, 22; & *The moods of Ginger Mick,* Angus & Robertson, Sydney, 1916; Margaret Herron, *Down the years,* Hallcraft, Melbourne, 1953, pp. 63-4. On 'Ginger Mick' as a moniker, see: June Senyard, '1944 and all that', in Fitzroy Historical Society (ed), *Fitzroy: Melbourne's first suburb,* Melbourne University Press, Melbourne, 1991, p. 244. Barry Andrews, 'Ginger Meggs: his story', in Susan Dermody et al (eds), Nellie Melba, *Ginger Meggs and friends: essays in Australian cultural history,* Kibble Books, Malmesbury Vic., 1982, pp. 211–33.

5. My understanding of the term 'subculture' is informed by critiques which warn against defining it as a bounded social group. Like other more recent youth subcultures, larrikinism was a collection of dress styles, leisure pursuits, cultural practices and social networks based in certain localities in which young people took part. The amount of time that an individual spent participating in the larrikin subculture could differ, however, as could the degree to which they chose to identify with the term 'larrikin'. For some, larrikinism effectively operated more as a 'scene' than a 'subculture': something that they occasionally dabbled in at a sporting match or dance hall, but with which they did not closely identify. It is for this reason that I speak variously of the larrikin *subculture* and *scene* in this book: what it was depended on the extent of an individual's involvement and desire. For the best critique of subculture as a bounded social group, see: Peter J Martin, 'Culture, subculture and social organisation', in Andy Bennett & Keith Kahn-Harris (eds), *After subculture: critical studies in contemporary youth culture,* Palgrave Macmillan, New York, 2004. For a discussion of the term 'scene', see Geoff Stahl's chapter in the same work.

6. Ruth Park, *The companion guide to Sydney,* Collins, Sydney, 1973, pp. 36–7. Though I have no proof that Park made up the interview, some of what she claims was told to her by her informant sounds suspiciously like sections of Bill Beatty's article, 'They wore photos on their feet', *SMH,* 17 January 1953, p. 9. Her informant also tells her that his father was a member of 'Griffo's mob', even though doubt has been cast on whether or not the boxer Albert 'Griffo' Griffiths was ever a member of the larrikin push scene. On this and Pratt's hoax, see chapter 3 following. On Foley: Kenneth

Roberts, *Captain of the push: when a larrikin chief ruled the Rocks,* Lansdowne Press, Melbourne, 1963.

7. John Hirst, 'Convicts and national identity: an oddity from the start', *The Monthly,* July 2008, pp. 39–40.

8. DIY etymology: Edgar Waters, 'Some aspects of the popular arts in Australia, 1880–1915', PhD Thesis, Australian National University, 1962, pp. 188–99. The 'lar-ra-kin, Your Worship' story: 'Garryowen', *The chronicles of early Melbourne, 1835 to 1852,* vol 2, Fergusson & Mitchell, Melbourne, 1888, p. 768; *Brisbane Courier,* 7 October 1885, p. 7; Letters to the editor, *Argus,* 4 August 1896, p. 7; Edward Morris, *Austral English: a dictionary of Australasian words, phrases and usages,* Sydney University Press, Sydney, 1972, p. 260; *Lone Hand,* 2 December 1908, p. 115; Susan Priestley, 'Larrikins and the law 1849–1874', *Victorian Historical Journal* 74.2, 2003, pp. 243–50. The word's English origins: GA Wilkes, *Stunned mullets and two-pot screamers: a dictionary of Australian colloquialisms,* Oxford University Press, Oxford, 2008, p. 221; Bruce Moore, *Speaking our language: the story of Australian English,* Oxford University Press, Oxford, 2008, pp. 97–98.

9. There is a whole body of sociological theory concerning youths being labelled as troublemakers and its effects on their treatment and perception in the broader society. On this, see: Stanley Cohen, *Folk devils and moral panics: the creation of the mods and rockers,* 3rd edn, London, 2002. While this book draws on labelling and moral panic theories, it also seeks to explore the way such youths act and portray themselves and its relationship to the way they are represented and treated in the broader society – something about which such theories have little to say.

10. *Guardian,* 5 September 2006. 'Scepticism in the face of bombast' is a phrase of Inge Clendinnen's cited in Goldsworthy, 'The Australian temperament', p. 12. Mun Mun Larrikin is an artist from the Kutjungka region of northeast Western Australia listed on the Warlayirti Culture Centre website: balgoart. org.au/art_centre/full_list_of_artists.htm. Larrikin Sturt (b. 1944) is listed as having sold work in John Furphy's *Australian Art Sales Digest,* aasd.com. au/subscribers/list_all_works.cfm?concat=SturtLarri.

Chapter 1

1. Complaints re Granites: *Argus,* 1 May 1871, p. 7; 2 May 1871, p. 6. Singing rooms: *Argus,* 3 July 1869. Fitzroy Boy's recollections: *Argus,* 4 August 1896, 7.

2. Origins of 'larrikin': Bruce Moore, *Speaking our language: the story of Australian English,* Oxford University Press, Oxford, 2008, pp. 97–98. Meaning of 'leary': James Hardy Vaux, 'Vocabulary of the flash language' in *The memoirs*

of James Hardy Vaux, ed. Noel McLachlan, Heinemann, London, 1964, pp. 250, 242. Pronunciation of 'larrikin': *Argus,* 18 January 1882, p. 6. 'Leary kinchin': Edgar Waters, 'Some aspects of the popular arts in Australia, 1880–1915', PhD Thesis, Australian National University, 1962, p. 189.

3. *Age,* 7 February 1870, p. 3.

4. *Argus,* 1 May 1871, p. 7.

5. Marcus Clarke, 'Melbourne's larrikins', in *A colonial city: high and low life. Selected journalism of Marcus Clarke,* ed. LT Hergenhan, University of Queensland Press, Brisbane, 1972, pp. 78–9; *Argus,* 21 March 1870, p. 4; 28 April 1870, p. 6; 29 April 1870, p. 4; 7 June 1870, p. 5; 2 September 1870, p. 6; 2 May 1871, p. 6; 1 December 1870, p. 5; 1 May 1871, p. 7.

6. *SMH,* 15 December 1870, p. 5; *Brisbane Courier (BC),* 1 August 1871, p. 2; 28 December 1891, p. 5; *Argus,* 20 May 1876, p. 4.

7. Lynette Finch, 'On the streets: working-class youth culture in the nineteenth century', in Rob White (ed), *Youth subcultures: theory, history and the Australian experience,* NCYS, Hobart, 1993, pp. 75–9; see also Rob White, 'Taking it to the streets: the larrikins and the Lebanese', in Scott Poynting & George Morgan (eds), *Outrageous! Moral panics in Australia,* NCYS, Hobart, 2007, pp. 40–52.

8. Cabbage-tree mob: *SMH,* 14 May 1850, p. 3; 6 July 1841, p. 4; 29 May 1850, p. 3; 10 October 1850, p. 2; 15 January 1851, p. 3; GC Mundy in Paul McGuire et al, *The Australian Theatre,* Oxford University Press, London, 1948, p. 103. Commentators comparing larrikins to the cabbage-tree mob: Sidney Baker, *The Australian language,* 2nd edn, Currawong Publishing, Sydney, 1966, p. 119; Graham Seal, *The lingo: listening to Australian English,* University of New South Wales Press, Sydney, 1999, p. 39. Bonneting: *Argus,* 23 March 1874, p. 6; & 5 June 1879, p. 8.

9. Deposition of Frances Danby, Documents for coronial inquiry, 10 October 1883, p. 101, in *R v Williams,* Clerk of the Peace, Supreme Court Darlinghurst, 9/6703, State Records New South Wales (SRNSW). Turvey: *Argus,* 17 February 1871, p. 5. Howe: *Argus* 10 December 1875, p. 7. Ned Kelly, 'The Jerilderie letter', Alex McDermott, (ed) Text Publishing, Melbourne, 2001, p. 69.

10. Hall, in Charles Fahey, Patricia Grimshaw & Melanie Raymond, 'The other side of "Marvellous Melbourne"', in Jane Beer et al (eds), *Colonial frontiers and family fortunes,* History Department, University of Melbourne, 1989, p. 87. I am grateful to Graeme Davison for this insight.

11. JW McCarty, 'Australian capital cities in the nineteenth century', in CB Schedvin & JW McCarty (eds), *Urbanisation in Australia: the nineteenth*

century, Nelson, Sydney, 1970, p. 21; Graeme Davison, *The rise and fall of marvellous Melbourne,* 2nd edn, Melbourne University Press, Melbourne, 2004, pp. 47–84.

12. Davison, *The rise and fall*; Chris McConville, 'Outcast Melbourne: social deviance in the city, 1870–1914', MA Thesis, University of Melbourne, 1974, pp. 200–58; Shirley Fitzgerald, *Rising damp: Sydney 1870–1890,* Oxford University Press, Melbourne, 1987, pp. 18–28; Ronald Lawson, *Brisbane in the 1890s: a study of an urban society,* University of Queensland Press, Brisbane, 1973, pp. 99–100.

13. Bernard Barrett, *The inner suburbs: the evolution of an industrial area,* Melbourne University Press, Melbourne, 1971; Susan Priestley, *South Melbourne: a history,* Melbourne University Press, Melbourne, 1995, pp. 122–3, 219.

14. Grace Karskens & Melita Rogowsky (eds), *Histories of Green Square,* School of History, University of New South Wales, 2004; Christopher Keating, *Surry Hills: the city's backyard,* Hale & Iremonger, Sydney, 1991; Shirley Fitzgerald & Christopher Keating, *Millers Point: the urban village,* Hale & Iremonger, Sydney, 1991; Shirley Fitzgerald, *Chippendale: beneath the factory wall,* Hale & Iremonger, Sydney, 1990; Bradley Bowden, 'Transience, community and class: a study of Brisbane's east ward, 1879–91', *Labour History* 79, 1977, pp. 160–89; Rod Fisher, 'Old Frog's Hollow: devoid of interest, or a den of iniquity', in Brisbane History Group (ed), *Brisbane in 1888: the historical perspective,* Brisbane History Group Papers 8, Brisbane, 1988, pp. 43–44.

15. Examples of contemporaries talking about 'high class' larrikins are quoted by Noel McLachlan, a Melbourne historian, in his impressive 1950 thesis. McLachlan rightly dismisses this notion of affluent larrikins, agreeing that almost all were from the 'lower classes': McLachlan, 'Larrikinism: an interpretation', MA Thesis, University of Melbourne, 1950, pp. 36–9. Livers and red blacks (sometimes also called 'black reds'): X.O. (pseud.), 'Australian pushes', Hayes Collection, Fryer Library, University of Queensland; *SMH,* 17 March 1886, p. 5. Larrikin boot-factory hands: *BC,* 18 October 1884, p. 3; *Collingwood Mercury,* 4 December 1880, p. 3; 11 December 1880, p. 2.

16. Davison, *The rise and fall,* pp. 69–71; McLachlan, 'Larrikinism', pp. 85–109. I use the term 'de-skilling' in inverted commas because it is a culturally loaded term concealing the amount of aptitude involved in the work it describes. The same applies to 'unskilled', but since I use it so often I have left off the inverted commas. For a critique of these terms see: Raelene Frances, *The politics of work: gender and labour in Victoria, 1880–1939,* Cambridge University Press, Cambridge, 1993.

17. Street enterprise: Andrew Brown-May, *Melbourne street life: the Itinerary of our days*, Australian Scholarly Publishing, Melbourne, 1998, pp. 142–52: Fitzroy: Helen Harris, *Helen Hart: founder of woman's suffrage in Australasia*, Harriland Press, Melbourne, 2009, p. 116. Brisbane paper-sellers: *BC*, 15 October 1885, p. 4; Mr Hughes, Folder 4 no. 17 in Ronald Lawson, 'Notes for a PhD thesis', 1970, F407, Fryer Library.

18. Simon Sleight, 'The territories of youth: young people and public space in Melbourne, c. 1870–1901', PhD Thesis, Monash University, 2008, p. 87; Yorick Smaal, 'More than mates? Masculinity, homosexuality and the formation of an embryonic subculture in Queensland, 1890–1914', MPhil Thesis, University of Queensland, 2004, pp. 97–8.

19. Evidence of Henry Keogh, 'Report of select committee into Infant and Children's Protection Bill ('Children's bill report'), New South Wales, Legislative Council, *Parl Papers* 1891–2, vol. 49, Part 2, app. C, p. 43.

20. Jack Read, *Griffo: his life story and record*, Fine Arts Publishers, Sydney, 1926; *SMH*, 19 September 1936, p. 13; Wobbegong, 'Young criminals. "Pushes" and killers', *NSW Police News*, 7 August 1925, pp. 25–6.

21. Mangan, Douglas and Oscroft: A & M Tuffley, *Five days to justice: the Mount Rennie gang*, AMJ Productions, Ernest Qld, 1989, p. 66, 127–29. Statement of William Newman, in 'Report of His Honor Mr Justice Windeyer on the case of William Hill & ors', in Papers of Sir William Charles Windeyer, Windeyer Family Papers, MLMSS 186 Box 21 Item 7, State Library NSW.

22. *SMH*, 8 October 1890, p. 6; Deposition of Valentine Keating in *Re the death of George Hill*, 5 September 1901, Police Records, VPRS 30/P/O Unit 1265 File 455, Public Records Office Victoria AB Paterson, 'The bottle-oh man', available on Wikisource at http://en.wikisource.org/wiki/The_%22Bottle-oh%22_Man, accessed 20 January 2011.

23. John Benson, *The penny capitalists: a study of nineteenth-century working-class entrepreneurs*, Gillan Macmillan, Dublin, 1983. For a discussion of the significance of penny capitalism, job-hopping and trade-shifting in London's East End as a way to pursue independence in this period, see Donna Loftus, 'Investigating work in late nineteenth century London', *History Workshop Journal*, forthcoming. Finnegan: McConville, 'Outcast Melbourne', p. 239. Howard: *BC*, 22 May 1888, p. 7; 2 December 1892, p. 3; 10 June 1893, p. 3; 10 November 1887, p. 7; 7 January 1888, p. 4; 1 October 1888, p. 3; 15 August 1891, p. 5; 17 May 1892, p. 3.

24. George Howard, Prison Record, QSA Item 662645 (id0098 1889), Queensland State Archives.

25. *SMH,* 10 January 1882, p. 6; X.O., 'Australian pushes'. Consider also the larrikins who disrupted strike pickets organised by Melbourne's Tramways Employees Union in 1888 and those who ruined a friendly society picnic raising money for the Maritime Strike on Eight Hours Day 1890: *Argus,* 16 February 1888, p. 8; *SMH,* 7 October 1890, p. 5.

26. Ross Thorne, *Theatre buildings in Australia to 1905: from the time of the first settlement to the arrival of cinema,* vol. 1, University of Sydney, Sydney, 1971, pp. 183–209; John West, *Theatre in Australia,* Cassell, Sydney, 1978, pp. 47–8, 62–5.

27. Pamela Heckenberg & Philip Parsons, 'Pictorial documents', in Harold Love (ed), *The Australian stage: a documentary history,* University of New South Wales Press, Sydney, 1984, p. 295; Kath Leahy, *Lords and larrikins: the actor's role in making Australia,* Currency, Sydney, 2009, pp. 46–7.

28. Evelyn Ballantyne, 'Some impressions of the Australian stage', *Theatre* (London) 19, 1892, p. 186; John Freeman, *Lights and shadows of Melbourne life,* Sampson Low, Marston, Searle & Rivington, London, 1888, p. 77; Sleight, 'The territories of youth', p. 137 n. 68; Leahy, *Lords and larrikins,* p. 47.

29. Mr Hughes, Folder 4 no. 17; Mr Richardson, Folder 4 no. 10 and Mr Downie, Folder 2 no. 14, in Lawson, 'Notes'.

30. Charles Frederickson, *Bourke Street on Saturday night: the memories of Charlie Fredricksen – 'the man outside Hoyts',* Frank van Straten, (ed.) Melbourne, n.d., no pagination; Harris St dance saloon: 'Children's bill report', p. 33. Sixpenny Hop: *Bird O'Freedom,* 4 June 1892, p.3.

31. Bourke St & Eastern Market: Frederickson, *Bourke Street;* McConville, 'From "criminal class"', p. 74. Flying Angel: *Argus,* 13 September 1901, p. 7. Public toilets: Sleight, 'The territories of youth', p. 51 n. 26.

32. Bummers: *SMH,* 17 March 1886, p. 5; 8 January 1885, p. 5. Waterloo girl: Deposition of Mary Ann M. in *Depositions for trial of Ewan Alfred Cameron et al,* Central Criminal Court, February 1887, 9/6746, SRNSW. Paddy's entertainments: Carol Henty & Tony Schmeaehling, *Paddy's Market,* Tempo Books, Sydney, 1973. Brisbane markets: *BC,* 27 July 1877, p. 2.

33. Haymarket Music Hall: *BC,* 9 June 1890, p. 5. Variety/Oxford Music Hall: *Boomerang,* 24 December 1887, p. 14; 18 February 1888, p. 7; 14 March 1888, 12; 24 March 1888, p. 7; *BC,* 6 May 1889, p. 4. Vagabond: *Argus,* 20 May 1876, p. 4. Singing rooms: *Argus,* 3 July 1869, p. 4. Star-*comiques:* 'A pupil of the late Prof. John Woolley', *Vice and its victims in Sydney, the cause and cure,* Sydney, 1873, pp. 41–2.

34. O'Neil: *Argus,* 23 June 1869, p. 8. Vance: JS Bratton, *The Victorian popular ballad,* Macmillan, London, 1975, pp. 98–99; Gareth Stedman Jones, 'The "cockney"

and the nation, 1780–1988', in D Feldman & GS Jones (eds), *Metropolis, London: histories and representations since 1800,* Routledge, London, 1989, p. 294. The 'Vic' was a well-known music hall in Hoxton, East London.

35. Chickaleary at Café Chantant: *SMH,* 27 December 1871, p. 8. Public ear: *SMH,* 25 July 1888, p. 6.

36. Jones, 'The "cockney"', pp. 294–6. On other leary 'coster' acts: *SMH,* 9 September 1872, p. 8 (School of Arts); 12 December 1872, p. 10 ('Theatre Royal', York Street); 18 and 21 February 1873, p. 8 (Scandinavian Hall); *BC,* 6 December 1873, p. 1 (School of Arts); *Argus,* 26 November 1874; 12 March 1875, p. 8; 8 October 1877, p. 6 (Apollo Hall; Theatre Royal; St George's Hall).

37. *Argus,* 23 June 1884, p. 6.

38. Peter Bailey, *Popular culture and performance in the Victorian city,* Cambridge University Press, Cambridge, 1998, p. 59; 'Costermonger Joe', in Martha Vicinus, *The industrial muse: a study of nineteenth-century British working-class literature,* Croom Helm, London, 1974, pp. 270–1.

39. Lonnen: Waters, 'Some aspects of the popular arts', pp. 213–4. Whitburn: *Australian Melodist 20,* Melbourne, n.d., p. 53.

40. RW Connell & Terry Irving, *Class structure in Australian history: poverty and progress,* 2nd edn, Longman Cheshire, Melbourne, 1992, p. 129.

Chapter 2

1. *Collingwood Mercury (CM),* 20 March 1890, p. 3.

2. *BC,* 8 June 1893, p. 3; 4 July 1893, p. 7; 12 July 1893, p. 4; 15 July 1893, p. 3. Depositions re Rebecca Lacey, 14 July 1893, *Deposition and Minute Book,* Brisbane Police Court, Item 971002, Queensland State Archives (QSA).

3. Vane Lindesay, *The inked-in image: a survey of Australian comic art,* Heinemann, Melbourne, 1970, pp. 13, 16–17, 94, 101; Marion Mahood, *The loaded line: Australian political caricature, 1788-1901* (Melbourne University Press, 1973), p. 239.

4. *Bird O'Freedom (BOF),* 16 July 1892, p. 1; *Bulletin,* 16 December 1899, p. 12. Other examples are: *Bulletin,* 19 February 1898, p. 12; 17 January 1899, p. 14; 27 May 1899, p. 11; 24 March 1900, p. 14; 18 August 1900, p. 14.

5. McMullin, *Will Dyson,* pp. 4–6.

6. On Cockney 'donah' songs: Martha Vicinus, *The industrial muse: a study of nineteenth-century working-class literature,* Croom Helm, London: 1974, pp. 271–4, 318–9.

7. *Argus,* 12 December 1892, p. 6; 7 July 1893, p. 4; *Bulletin,* 22 October 1892, p. 6; 17 December 1892, p. 8; 18 May 1895, p. 8; *Argus,* 12 December 1892, p. 6; *Lorgnette,* April 1893, 4th series no. 117; *BC,* 23 March 1893, p. 4.

8. AB (Banjo) Paterson, *An outback marriage: a story of Australian life,* Angus & Robertson, Sydney, 1906, ch. 3. Music for *Sentimental Bloke*: *Smith's Weekly,* 17 January 1920, p. 20.

9. Louis Stone, *Jonah,* Methuen, London, 1911, p. 12.

10. Barbara Garlick, 'Australian travelling theatre: a study in popular entertainment and national ideology', PhD Thesis, University of Queensland, 1994, pp. 102–55; *Illustrated Sporting Dramatic News* (Melb.), 3 January 1907, p. 15.

11. Clay Djubal, 'What oh tonight: the methodology factor and pre-1930s variety theatre', PhD Thesis, University of Queensland, 2005, pp. 26, 157. An example of an Australian 'donah' song is 'My donah', *Australian Melodist* 20, Melbourne, n.d., p. 44. This was sung by Johnny Gilmore, a regular in Harry Rickards' vaudeville shows (the precursor of the Tivoli). See also 'My little leary', *Australian Melodist* 20, p. 61; 'Chowder on a holiday': Tivoli Programmes (1893–1900), 2 December 1893, Mitchell Library, Sydney.

12. James Murray, *Larrikins: 19th century outrage,* Landsowne Press, Melbourne, 1973, p. 114; see also Sidney Baker, *The Australian Language,* 2nd edn, Currawong Publishing, Sydney, 1966, p. 128, n.13. Baker suggests that 'clinah' was another male-larrikin word for girlfriend on the basis that it appeared in poems published in the *Bulletin.* I have not come across this word in other primary material.

13. *BC,* 18 January 1886, 5; *BOF,* 23 July 1892, p. 1; Murray, *Larrikins,* p. 115; Chris McConville, 'Outcast Melbourne: social deviance in the city, 1870–1914', MA Thesis, University of Melbourne, 1974, p. 225; see also Raelene Frances, *Selling sex: a hidden history of prostitution,* University of New South Wales Press, Sydney, 2007, pp. 170–1.

14. Evidence of Sergeant J Dalton, 'Report of the select committee re Crimes and Offences Prevention Bill' ('Crimes bill report'), Victoria, Parliament, Legislative Council, *Votes and Proceedings* (*V&P*) 1874, p. 26; McConville, 'Outcast Melbourne', p. 196; Rod Fisher, 'Old Frogs Hollow: devoid of interest, or a den of iniquity?', in Brisbane History Group (ed), *Brisbane in 1888: the historical perspective,* Brisbane History Group Papers 8, Brisbane, 1988, pp. 43–44.

15. Margaret M Pawsey, 'Annie Wilkins: life on the margins in nineteenth-century Collingwood', *Victorian Historical Journal* 66.1, 1995, p. 7; Statement of Mary Ann McDonald, 25 May 1887, *Police correspondence,* Series 937 Unit 321 Bundle 3, Public Records Office of Victoria (PROV).

16. *CM*, 29 April 1882, p. 2.
17. Mixed-sex larrikin groups: *CM*, 26 June 1878, p. 2; 'Disorderly state of Bourke Street', 8 June 1882, *Police correspondence*, Series 937 Unit 306 Bundle 5, PROV; *Record*, cited in Susan Priestley, *South Melbourne: a history*, Melbourne University Press, Melbourne, 1995, p. 205. Larrikins at prison gates: Dalton, 'Crimes bill report', p. 26; Noel McLachlan, 'Larrikinism: an interpretation', MA Thesis, University of Melbourne, 1950, p. 64; *BOF*, 21 February 1891, p. 1.
18. *CM*, 28 October 1882, p. 4.
19. Elizabeth Pollock, Prisoner No. 4691, VPRS 516-PO, Unit 8, p. 191, PROV.
20. *CM*, 11 March 1882, p. 2; Maria Clements, Victorian Birth Certificate, 1867, No. 22619. Studley Park rape: *Argus*, 24 January 1889, p. 8.
21. *Collingwood Observer*, 18 and 28 November 1880, p. 4.
22. *BC*, 29 September 1884, p. 6; 26 November 1886, p. 6; *Argus*, 16 April 1879, p. 5.
23. *SMH*, 7 October 1890, p. 5.
24. Chowder Bay riot: *SMH*, 8 October 1890, p. 6. The married women arrested were Florence J Stewart nee Fletcher, Amy Walburn nee Reynolds, and Mary Moore nee Fegan. (See NSW Marriage Certificates for William Stewart & Florence Fletcher, 70/1889; Stephen W Moore & Mary Fegan, 859/1889; & Walter Walburn & Amy E Reynolds, 424/1889. Also see NSW Birth Certificates, Florence J Fletcher, 2193/1868; & Amy E Reynolds, 2495/1869). Botany disturbance: *SMH*, 29 December 1890, p. 7.
25. *CM*, 29 April 1882, p. 2; see also 6 March 1890, p. 2. On similar policing in late-Victorian Manchester: Andrew Davies, 'Those viragoes are no less cruel than the lads": young women, gangs and violence in late-Victorian Manchester and Salford', *British Journal of Criminology* 39.1, 1999, pp. 72–88.
26. E.g. *BC*, 8 August 1884, p. 6; 9 October 1884, p. 6; see also Judith Allen, *Sex and secrets: crimes against Australian women, 1880–1930*, Oxford University Press, Melbourne, 1990, pp. 54–6; Jill Bavin-Mizzi, *Ravished: sexual violence in Victorian Australia*, University of New South Wales Press, Sydney, 1995, pp. 157–70.
27. *BC*, 26 June 1885, p. 6; Depositions of Swan, Schultries, Hayes & Bowden, 25 June 1885, pp. 476–79, *Deposition and Minute Book*, Item 970966, QSA.
28. My thoughts on the significance of female friendship here are informed by Kerry Carrington, 'Cultural studies, youth culture and delinquency', in Rob White (ed), *Youth subcultures: theory, history and the Australian experience*, National Clearinghouse for Youth Studies, Hobart, 1993, pp. 27–32.

29. Judith Walkowitz, *Prostitution and Victorian society: woman, class and the state*, Cambridge University Press, Cambridge, 1980, pp. 200–1; Frances, *Selling sex*, p. 138.

30. *BC*, 3 January 1888, p. 7; 23 August 1894, p. 3; 5 March 1895, p. 2; *NSW Police Gazette*, 24 August 1893, p. 286.

31. Evidence of Charles Cowper, 'Report of the select committee into public charities, no. 2' ('Public charities report'), New South Wales, Parliament, Legislative Assembly, *V&P* 1873–4. Statements of inmates, 8 November 1873: Administration and Investigations into Biloela Industrial School (Biloela investigation), Colonial Secretary, 4/798.3, State Records NSW (SRNSW).

32. Evidence of Brackenregg, Rowland, & Dunn, 'Public charities report', pp. 106, 108, 111, 126.

33. *BC,* 8 June 1893, p. 3; 25 December 1885, p. 5; *CM*, 8 April 1882, p. 2; 29 April 1882, p. 2; 10 June 1882, p. 2.

34. E.g.: *NSW Police Gazette* (NSW PG), 9 March 1887, p. 80 (15 y.o. Annie Bennet, St Leonards, with girl named Drury); 28 July 1886, p. 229 (15 y.o. Eliza Daniels, Waterloo); 29 April 1891, p. 153 (15 y.o. Annie Ward, Newtown, with girl named Rowswell); 19 August 1896, p. 295 (15 y.o. Margaret Davies, Balmain).

35. Deposition of Mary Ann M., in *Depositions for trial of Ewan Alfred Cameron et al*, Central Criminal Court, February 1887, 9/6746, SRNSW; see also Statement of McDonald, PROV.

36. *Argus,* 28 May 1876, p. 4; *BC*, 9 December 1882, p. 5; 2 August 1887, p. 2.

37. Robert C Allen, *Horrible prettiness: burlesque and American culture*, University of North Carolina Press, Chapel Hill, 1991; Djubal, 'What oh', pp. 153–4; *Bulletin*, 8 October 1892, p. 6.

38. *BC*, 22 January 1898, p. 2; *SMH*, 9 April 1895, p. 2; *Bulletin*, 13 April 1895, p. 8. On 'Botany Bay', see entry on Mark Gregory's *Australian folk songs* website, http://folkstream.com/010.html, accessed 29 March 2011.

39. DF Cheshire, *The music hall in Britain,* Fairleigh Dickinson University Press, Rutherford, 1974, p. 68; *Bulletin,* 17 & 24 September 1892, pp. 6, 8; *Age,* cited in Djubal, 'What oh', p. 138.

40. Ronald Lawson, *Brisbane in the 1890s: a study of an urban society,* University of Queensland Press, Brisbane, 1973, p. 65; Beverly Kingston, *My wife my daughter and poor Mary Ann: women and work in Australia,* Nelson, Melbourne, 1975, pp. 29–73.

41. Mrs Dobson, Folder 4 no. 19; Mrs Mullen, Folder 4 no. 21, in Ronald Lawson, 'Notes for a PhD Thesis', 1970, F407, Fryer Library, University of

Queensland; John Freeman, *Lights and shadows of Melbourne life,* Sampson Low, Marston, Searle & Rivington, London, 1888, p. 77.

42. Frances, *Selling sex,* p. 123.

43. WH Delihanty, 'Love among the roses', Melbourne, n.d.; Evidence of Austin, 'Public charities report', p. 134; on brothel piano rooms, see Frances, *Selling Sex,* p. 131.

44. Reports re Catherine Frederickson, 19 July 1895 and 12 August 1896, *Police correspondence,* Series 807/P/O Unit 25 File B6212, PROV; Vanessa Toulmin, *A fair fight: an illustrated review of boxing on British fairgrounds,* World's Fair, Oldham, 1999.

45. *CM,* 20 November 1880, p. 2; *BOF,* 13 August 1892, p. 1; *Argus,* 29 December 1903, p. 3.

46. Lucy Chesser, *Parting with my sex: cross-dressing, inversion and sexuality in Australian cultural life,* University of Sydney Press, Sydney, 2008, Part 2; Yorick Smaal, 'Coding desire: the emergence of a homosexual subculture in Queensland, 1890–1914', *Queensland Review* 14.2, 2007, pp. 13–28.

47. *Bulletin,* 14 January 1882, p. 1; 'A pupil of the late Prof. John Woolley', *Vice and its victims in Sydney: the cause and cure,* Sydney, 1873, p. 48; see also Chesser, *Parting with my sex,* Part 1.

48. For an example of a Left scholar championing the punks, see: Dick Hebdige, *Subculture: the meaning of style,* Methuen, London, 1979. For feminist critiques of 1960–70s accounts of street subcultures, see: Angela McRobbie & Jenny Garber, 'Girls and subcultures: an exploration', in Stuart Hall & Tony Jefferson (eds), *Resistance through rituals: youth subcultures in post-war Britain,* Hutchison, London, 1975, pp. 209–22; Carrington, 'Cultural studies'. For examples of Australian scholars championing male larrikins in broadly similar terms see: McConville, 'Outcast Melbourne', p. 235; RW Connell & Terry Irving, *Class structure in Australian history: poverty and progress,* Longman Cheshire, Melbourne, 1992, p. 129; Jon Stratton, *The young ones: working-class culture, consumption and the category of youth,* Black Swan Press, Perth, 1992, pp. 33–58.

49. Statement of schoolmaster of *SS Vernon,* 17 October 1871, Biloela investigation; Evidence of Agnes King, 'Report and minutes of proceedings of select committee into Infant and Children's Protection Bill', New South Wales, Parliament, Legislative Council, *V&P* 1892, XLIX, p. 30.

Chapter 3

1. Ambrose Pratt, '"Push" larrikinism in Australia', *Blackwood's magazine* 170, July 1901, pp. 27–40.

2. *Sydney Morning Herald* (*SMH*), 12 July 1901, p. 5; 10 August 1901, p. 8; *Argus*, 2 August 1901, p. 4; Rod Howard, *The fabulist: the incredible story of Louis de Rougemont,* Random House, Sydney, 2006; Diane Langmore, 'Pratt, Ambrose Goddard Hesketh (1874–1944)', *Australian Dictionary of Biography* 11, Melbourne University Press, Melbourne, 1988, pp. 274–5.

3. Ambrose Pratt, *The great "push" experiment*, Grant Richards, London, 1902, Preface.

4. *Adelaide Advertiser,* 8 December 1904, p. 8; 9 December 1904, p. 4; *Australian Star,* 8 December 1904, p. 4.

5. *Argus,* 18 February 1908, p. 4; 10 March 1908, p. 6; 6 October 1908, p. 7; *SMH,* 18 February 1908, p. 7; *BC,* 22 February 1908, p. 6; *Adelaide Advertiser*, 6 October 1908, p. 7. Thanks to Simon Sleight for these references.

6. Manning Clark, *A history of Australia*, vol. 3, Melbourne University Press, Melbourne, 1987, pp. 361–2; Isadore Brodsky, *Heart of the Rocks of old Sydney,* Old Sydney Free Press, Sydney, 1965, pp. 90-1; James Murray, *Larrikins: nineteenth century outrage*, Lansdowne Press, Melbourne, 1973, pp. 127–30. See also Noel McLachlan, 'Larrikinism: an interpretation', MA Thesis, University of Melbourne, 1950, pp. 64–6; Sidney Baker, *The Australian language,* 2nd edn, Currawong Publishing, Sydney, 1966, p. 119. Accounts using racialised language are: Kenneth Roberts, *Captain of the push: when a larrikin chief ruled the Rocks*, Lansdowne Press, Melbourne, 1963; Ruth Park, *Ruth Park's Sydney*, 2nd edn, Duffy & Snellgrove, Sydney, 2003, p. 34; Geoffrey Moorhouse, *Sydney*, Allen & Unwin, Sydney, 1999, p. 180.

7. One or other of the pushes in this list are mentioned in association with the 19th century in the following: Clark, *A history of Australia*, p. 361; Murray, *Larrikins*, p. 31; Moorhouse, *Sydney*, p. 180; John Ramsland, *With just but relentless discipline: a social history of corrective services in New South Wales,* Kangaroo Press, Sydney, 1996, p. 55.

8. This overview is informed by Chris McConville, 'From "criminal class" to "underworld"', in Graeme Davison, David Dunstan & Chris McConville (eds), *The outcasts of Melbourne: essays in social history,* Allen & Unwin, Sydney, 1985, pp. 74–6.

9. Rob White & Santina Perrone, 'Young people and gangs', *Trends and Issues in Crime and Criminal Justice* 167, Australian Institute of Criminology, Canberra, 2000, Foreword; *Sydney Herald,* 31 December 1840, p. 2; *Sydney Gazette & NSW Advertiser,* 26 May 1842, p. 2; *SMH,* 14 May 1850, p. 3; 10 October 1850, p. 2; 15 January 1851, p. 3. The term 'cabbage-tree mob' was also used for certain radicals: Terry Irving & Rowan Cahill, *Radical Sydney:*

places, portraits and unruly episodes, University of New South Wales Press, Sydney, 2010, p. 59.

10. E.g. *Collingwood Observer,* 18 November 1880; *BC,* 5 December 1873, p. 2; *Argus,* 17 January 1871, p. 4; 1 May 1871, p. 7; 21 June 1872, p.3; 4 December 1874, p. 4; 9 April 1876, p. 7; *Record,* 23 April 1874; 28 December 1871, p. 4.

11. Blair Ussher, 'The salvation war', in *The outcasts of Melbourne,* pp. 124–39; *Argus,* 12 November 1881, p. 9; 'Salvation Army annoyed at Richmond', *Police correspondence,* Series 937 Unit 306 Bundle 3, Public Records Office of Victoria (PROV); *BC,* 15 August 1885, p. 5; 6 April 1886, p. 4.

12. *Bulletin,* 8 January 1881, p. 1.

13. *SMH,* 12 September 1876, p. 4; 15 February 1874, p. 5; Simon Sleight, 'The territories of youth: young people and public space in Melbourne, c.1870–1901', PhD Thesis, Monash University, 2008, p. 133; *Argus,* 16 November 1874, p. 7.

14. JH Vaux, 'A vocabulary of flash language' in *The memoirs of James Hardy Vaux,* Noel McLachlan, (ed) Heinemann, London, 1964, p. 260; Michael Davitt, *Leaves from a prison diary,* Chapman & Hall, London, 1885, p. 11; EE Morris, *Austral English: a dictionary of Australasian words, phrase and usages,* Macmillan, London, 1892, pp. 372–3; *Collingwood Mercury (CM),* 29 April 1882, p. 2; *SMH,* 17 March 1886, p. 5. The word 'push' was also used to mean 'gang' in some American cities in the same period, eg. the Lake Shore Push of Cleveland: McLachlan, 'Larrikinism', p. 29.

15. *Argus,* 16 July 1886, p. 6; and *Age,* 20 January 1891, p. 6.

16. *SMH,* 23 October 1895, p. 6 (Harris-street); 14 June 1892, p. 3 (Abercrombie-street & Waterloo); 7 October 1890, p. 5 (Woolloomooloo); 6 November 1891, p. 3; 31 December 1898, p. 4 (Paddington); 12 February 1892, p. 7; 6 August 1892, p. 13 (Rocks); 26 June 1893, p. 6 (Miller's Point); 7 October 1890, p. 5; 6 October 1891, p. 6; 20 June 1893, p. 3; 3 October 1893, p. 5; (Gipps-st). On the re-naming of Gipps Street: Isadore Brodsky, *Sydney looks back,* Allen & Unwin, Sydney, 1957, p. 153.

17. Rob White & Ron Mason, 'Youth gangs and youth violence: charting the key dimensions', *Australian and New Zealand Journal of Criminology* 39.1, 2000, p. 56.

18. Deposition of Thomas Smith, 13 September 1886, in *R v William Hill & eight ors,* Clerk of the Peace (CP), Central Criminal Court Sydney (CCCS), 9/6379, State Records New South Wales (SRNSW).

19. Deposition of William Smith, 31 January 1884, in *R v Edward Williams & ors,* CP, CCCS, 9/6702, SRNSW.

20. McConville, 'From "criminal class"', p. 75; *Depositions for trial of John Woods,* CP, Sydney Gaol Delivery, 9/6771, SRNSW.

21. *Maitland Mercury,* 4 April 1885, Supplement p. 12; *SMH,* 30 January 1926, p. 14; 'Police report respecting disturbances between the military and a certain section of the public known as "pushes"', New South Wales, Parliament, Legislative Assembly, *Votes & Proceedings* 1900, vol. 3, pp. 807–12.

22. Roberts, *Captain of the push*; Jack Read, *Griffo: his life story and record,* Fine Arts Publishers, Sydney, 1926; *SMH,* 19 September 1936, p. 13; Peter Corris, *Lords of the ring,* Cassell, Sydney, 1980, pp. 53–4.

23. On larrikin 'knuckle fights': *Argus,* 22 September 1874, p. 4; 4 February 1879, 5; *Collingwood Mercury,* 10 June 1880, p. 2; *Daily Telegraph* (Sydney), 14 December 1886, p. 5; Wobbegong, 'Young criminals. "Pushes" and killers', *New South Wales Police News,* 7 August 1925, pp. 25–6. For background: Richard Waterhouse, 'Bare-knuckle prize fighting, masculinity and nineteenth-century Australian culture', *Journal of Australian Studies* 73, 2002, pp. 101–10.

24. *CM,* 11 March 1882, p. 2; see also the young women arrested for fighting each other at the Chowder Bay riot: *SMH,* 29 December 1890, p. 7.

25. *Argus,* 4 October 1904, p. 8.

26. Harriet Adderley, Prison Record, VPRS 516-PO, Unit 13, p. 18, PROV.

27. *Age,* 20 January 1891, p. 6; *Collingwood Observer,* 28 March 1901, p. 5; *Truth* (Syd.), 18 January 1903, p. 3.

28. *Argus,* 28 February 1882, p. 9; Jill Bavin-Mizzi, *Ravished: sexual violence in Victorian Australia,* University of New South Wales Press, Sydney, 1995, p. 150.

29. Depositions of Robert Pert & George Pearson, in *R v Henry Doohan & ors,* CP, CCCS, 9/6846, SRNSW.

30. Deposition of James Dever, *R v Doohan.*

31. *SMH,* 11 February 1892, p. 4; 12 February 1892, p. 7.

32. Henry Lawson, 'The captain of the push', *Bulletin,* 26 March 1892, p. 19.

33. On youth gangs today: White & Mason, 'Youth violence', p. 57; Kerry Carrington, *Offending youth: sex, crime and justice,* Federation Press, Sydney, 2009, pp. 121-36; see also Jon Stratton, *The young ones: working-class culture, consumption and the category of youth,* Black Swan Press, Perth, 1992, pp. 45–54.

34. Deposition of John Kyneur, *R v Doohan.*

35. Ned Kelly, *The Jerilderie letter,* Alex McDermott, (ed) Text Publishing, Melbourne, 2001, p. 69.

36. *SMH,* 6 January 1885, p. 7; 8 January 1885, p. 5; 9 January 1885, p. 5. For other larrikins resisting arrest see: *Argus,* 7 March 1874, p. 9; 19 May 1876, p. 2; 2 April 1879, p. 6; *BC,* 11 March 1884, p. 6; *Daily Telegraph* (Sydney),

14 December 1886, p. 5; *Collingwood Observer,* 9 January 1890, p. 8; *SMH,* 26 June 1890, p. 6; 7 May 1892, p. 6; 7 November 1894, p. 3.

37. Jeremiah Sullivan, Prison record, 7 April 1888, NRS 2138 Item 3/6049 (Reel 5102 Photo 4168) & 14 January 1885, NRS 2138 Item 3/6047 (Reel 5101, Photo 3462), SRNSW; *Echo* (Sydney), 6 April 1888, p. 6.

38. Stephen Garton, 'Pursuing incorrigible rogues: patterns of policing in New South Wales 1870–1920', *Journal of the Royal Australian Historical Society* 77.3, 1991, pp. 16-29; Mark Finnane, 'Larrikins, delinquents and cops: police and young people in Australian history', in Rob White & Christine Alder (eds), *The police and young people in Australia,* Cambridge University Press, Cambridge, 1994, pp. 16–17.

39. Grabosky, *Sydney in ferment,* pp. 82–4. Since these statistics are not age-specific, they do not indicate the rate at which adolescent youth were arrested. They still show, however, that police were more generally cavalier about issuing arrests in the 1880-90s than they were in later decades.

40. Ramsland, *With just but relentless discipline,* p. 141.

41. Michael Davitt, *Life and progress in Australasia,* Methuen, London, 1898, p. 429; *SMH,* 10 April 1886, p. 13.

42. *SMH,* 2 September 1895; p. 5; 5 November 1888, p. 8; 7 October 1890, p. 5. Other cases of civilians helping police: *BC,* 11 March 1884, p. 6 (civilians aiding larrikin arrest); *Echo* (Sydney), 6 April 1888, p. 6 (civilian saving constable from Redfern larrikins); *SMH,* 28 May 1890, p. 4 (civilians aiding arrest of Sussex St larrikins); see also Mark Finnane & Stephen Garton, 'The work of policing: social relations and the criminal justice system in Queensland, 1880–1914. Pt 1', *Labour History* 62, 1992, pp. 53–5.

43. Russell Hogg & Hilary Golder, 'Policing Sydney in the late nineteenth century', in Mark Finnane (ed), *Policing in Australia: historical perspectives,* University of New South Wales Press, Sydney, 1987, pp. 66–70; *Balmain Observer,* 10 February 1888, p. 2.

44. X.O. (pseud.), 'Australian pushes', Hayes Collection, Fryer Library, University of Queensland, p. 6.

45. Chowder fence: *SMH,* 8 October 1898, p. 6. Botany: *SMH,* 29 December 1890, p. 7; 6 October 1891, p. 6.

46. Middle Eastern and Chinese Australian residents in South Sydney: Melita Rogoswky, 'Exodus and retreat: the Chinese of Alexandria and Waterloo', & Susan O'Reilly, 'From German streets to Russian libraries: immigrant histories of Green Square', both in Grace Karskens & Melita Rogowsky (eds), *Histories of Green Square,* School of History, University of New South Wales, 2004, pp. 97–108; 110–11. For a comparative discussion of Chinese in inner

Melbourne: Sophie Couchman, "'Oh, I would like to see Maggie Moore again!'": selected women of Melbourne's Chinatown', in Sophie Couchman, John Fitzgerald, and Paul McGregor (eds), *After the rush: regulation, participation, and Chinese communities in Australia, 1860–1940,* Special edition of *Overland* 9, 2004, pp. 171–90.

47. My ideas here are informed by the approach to delinquency developed by Clifford Shaw and Henry McKay at the University of Chicago's School of Sociology in the 1920–30s. I have not adopted their so-called 'social dis-organisation' theory wholesale, however: firstly, because it is not possible to provide a one-size-fits-all explanation for delinquency and secondly because their ideas must be read alongside work on the impact of over-policing on particular groups of youth. Having said this, Shaw and McKay's emphasis on the need to recognise delinquency as a social and cultural phenomenon occurring in neighbourhoods marked by transience and heterogeneity has been useful in my thinking about the late-colonial push. For a discussion of social disorganisation theory and other approaches to juvenile delinquency, see Donald Shoemaker, *Theories of delinquency: an examination of explanations of delinquent behaviour,* 5th ed., Oxford University Press, New York, 2005, pp. 82–96; Carrington, *Offending youth,* ch. 1.

Chapter 4

1. Marcus Clarke, 'Melbourne's larrikins', in *A colonial city: high and low life. Selected journalism of Marcus Clarke,* ed. LT Hergenhan, University of Queensland Press, Brisbane, 1972, pp. 78–9. On 'Sam Hall': JS Bratton, *The Victorian popular ballad,* Macmillan, London, 1975, pp. 97–8.

2. Ned Kelly, *The Jerilderie letter,* Alex McDermott, (ed) Text Publishing, Melbourne, 2001, p. 40; Ian Jones, *Ned Kelly: a short life,* Lothian, South Melbourne, 2003, p. 200.

3. Raymond Evans, *Fighting words: writing about race,* University of Queensland Press, Brisbane, 1999, p. 89 (Brisbane riot); *Argus,* 9 December 1878, p. 6 (Rocks cabinet-makers); *Collingwood Mercury,* 12 May 1879, p. 7 (larrikins chase 'negro boys'); *SMH,* 25 November 1880, p. 7 (East Melbourne attack); see also *CM,* 11 December 1880, p. 2.

4. Judith Allen, *Sex and secrets: crimes against Australian women, 1880–1930,* Oxford University Press, Melbourne, 1990, pp. 54–6; Deposition of James Douglas in *R v Edward Williams & five others,* Clerk of the Peace (CP), Supreme Court, 1884, 9/6702, State Records NSW (SRNSW).

5. The best discussions of the Mount Rennie scandal are: Amanda Kaladelfos,

'Crime and outrage: sexual villains and sexual violence in NSW, 1870–1930', PhD Thesis, University of Sydney, 2010, ch. 2; Juliet Peers, *What no man had ever done before,* Dawn Revival Press, Sydney, 1992; & David Walker, 'Youth on trial: the Mount Rennie case', *Labour History* 50, 1986, pp. 27–41. On other larrikin gang rapes, see: Simon Sleight, 'The territories of youth: young people and public space in Melbourne, c. 1870–1901', PhD Thesis, Monash University, 2008, pp. 153–55; Jill Bavin-Mizzi, *Ravished: sexual violence in Victorian Australia,* University of New South Wales Press, Sydney, 1995, pp. 157–70; Murray Johnson, 'Larrikin "push", 1902', in Raymond Evans & Carole Ferrier (eds), *Radical Brisbane: an unruly history,* Vulgar Press, Melbourne, 2004, p. 123–7. On Hines, see Maitland Gaol's website: maitlandgaol.com.au/history/historyinfo, accessed 5 February 2010. A Joseph Campbell was also executed at Darlinghurst for carnal knowledge of a girl under ten in 1901. Thanks to Amanda Kaladelfos for this information.

6. On the Skaf gang-rapes, see: Kate Gleeson, 'White natives and gang rape at the time of centenary', in Scott Poynting & George Morgan (eds), *Outrageous! Moral panics in Australia,* National Clearinghouse for Youth Studies, Hobart, 2007, p. 171. On Cobby and Leigh, see: Julia Sheppard, *Someone else's daughter: the life and death of Anita Cobby,* Ironbark Press, Sydney, 1991; Kerry Carrington, *Who killed Leigh Leigh? A story of shame and mateship in an Australian town,* Federation Press, Sydney, 1998. The Bali Nine are nine young Australians arrested for heroin trafficking and sentenced to death in Bali on 17 April 2005. At the time of writing, they are still on death row.

7. Peers, *What no man . . .,* pp. 85, 97; *Daily Telegraph* (Sydney) (*DT*), 11 September 1886, p. 5; 2 October 1886, p. 9.

8. TJ Curtis, Letter to the Editor, *DT*, 4 December 1886, p. 5; Peers, *What no man . . .,* p. 82.

9. Peter Bailey, *Popular culture and performance in the Victorian city,* Cambridge University Press, Cambridge, 1998, pp. 30–46.

10. Murray Lee, 'The blame game: struggles over the representation of the "Macquarie Fields riots"', in *Outrageous!,* pp. 53–6; *SMH,* 5 March 2005.

11. Stanley first went to Redfern police station, but since no officers available there to investigate the crime, they telephoned their colleagues in Darlinghurst. Officers from Darlinghurst thus discovered Hicks around 5pm: Frank Clune, *Scandals of Sydney Town,* Angus & Robertson, Sydney, 1957, pp. 6–10. Details of the 'Waterloo push' come from Walker, 'Youth on trial'; transcripts of the committal hearing for Hicks' rape (*R v William Hill & eight others,* 24 September 1886, pp. 71–87 &177–80, CP, Central Criminal

Court, 9/6379, SRNSW); & 'Report of His Honour Mr Justice Windeyer on the case of William Hill & ors', in Papers of Sir William Charles Windeyer, Windeyer Family Papers, MLMSS 186 Box 21 Item 7, State Library NSW. On Keegan's riotous behaviour: *NSW Police Gazette*, 17 March 1886, p. 83. Details of the rape come from Justice Windeyer's report; Peers, *What no man . . .*; Mary Jane Hicks' evidence in *R v William Hill*; & 'Minute for the Governor from the Executive Council, 4 January 1887', in *Confidential papers re Mt Rennie case*, Colonial Secretary, 1886–7, 2/8095B.2, SRNSW.

12. George Keegan & Michael Donnellan, 14 September 1886, Darlinghurst Gaol, NRS 2138 Photos 3751 and 3754, SRNSW.

13. Statements of George Keenan & Michael Donnellon [sic], found in *Confidential papers re Mt Rennie case* & Windeyer's report. On Donnellan's address & his mother's birthplace: M & A Tuffley, *Five days to justice: the Mount Rennie gang*, AMJ Publications, Ernest Qld, 1989, pp. 136, 435.

14. Clune, *Scandals*, p. ix; Deborah Beck, *Hope in hell: a history of Darlinghurst Gaol and the National Art School*, Allen & Unwin, Sydney, 2005, pp. 138–44.

15. Evidence of Constable Joseph Meyer, William Stanley & William Brown, *R v William Hill*, pp. 32, 131–56; 197–204. Another of Clune's errors is his claim that Donnellan presented medical evidence at the trial which proved he was 'suffering from a disease which could have prevented him from participating in the alleged crime'. In fact, the medical evidence he adduced only proved that he did not have gonorrhoea. It was aimed far more narrowly at disproving the prosecution's claim that Donnellan had given Hicks this disease: Clune, *Scandals*, p. 22; Peers, *What no man . . .*, pp. 74, 195. Clune further attempts to suggest that the jury should have relied on the alibi evidence adduced by Donnellan's mother, aunt, and several other friends and associates who testified that they saw him during the crucial period. Justice Windeyer later gave detailed reasons why these witnesses' evidence was unreliable; the jury evidently came to the same view: Windeyer's report, p. 17.

16. Tuffley, *Five days*, pp. 381, 358–60.

17. Windeyer's report, p.23.

18. Janet McCalman, *Struggletown: public and private life in Richmond, 1900–1965*, Hyland House, Melbourne, 1998; Grace Karskens, 'Small things, big pictures: new perspectives on the Rocks' in Alan Mayne & Tim Murray (eds), *The archaeology of urban landscapes: explorations in slumland*, Cambridge University Press, Cambridge, 2001, pp. 69–85.

19. Depositions for *R v Henry Doohan & ors*, CP, CCC, SRNSW; 9/6846, especially pp. 35–6.

20. The term 'humdrum immediacy' was used by Alan Mayne & Tim Murray to characterise daily life in most so-called 'slum' districts in the introduction to their edited collection, *The archaeology of urban landscapes*. Mayne and Murray have published revisionist accounts of Melbourne's Little Lonsdale Street in the 1870s, talking up both its ordinariness and 'vibrant cosmopolitanism' as a way of counteracting its slum stereotype. Though sharing their criticism of such stereotypes, I still think their work glosses over the degree of violence and criminality in the district – a characteristic move by revisionists in this field. Mayne & Murray, 'Imaginary landscapes: reading Melbourne's "Little Lon"', in *The archaeology of urban landscapes,* pp. 89–105.

21. Donnellan's statement, Windeyer Papers; *Balmain Observer,* 8 January 1887.

22. Bailey, *Popular culture,* pp. 30–46.

23. Mr Grigson, Folder 3 no. 6 & Mr Richardson, Folder 4 no. 10, both in Ronald Lawson, 'Notes for a PhD thesis', 1970, F407, Fryer Library, University of Queensland.

24. Letter from unidentified Waterloo resident, extracted in Clune, *Scandals,* p. 225; see also Tuffley, *Five days,* pp. 384–9.

Chapter 5

1. 'How mee fadir beet the push', *Bird O'Freedom (BOF)*, 10 December 1892, p. 5; 'A push picnic', *BOF,* 27 January 1894, p. 1; 'Bill Brisket: the romance of a butchers' picnic', BOF, 27 May 1893, p. 6; 'How Sally fell out with her bloke', *BOF,* 4 June 1892, p. 3; 'Throwing stones', *BOF,* 15 April 1895, p. 6. Whitburn: 'The Larrikins' Hop' and 'Woolloomooloo', *Australian Melodist* 19, pp. 15, 25–6; 'I'm One of the South Melbourne', *Australian Melodist* 20, p. 53; 'Parody of Molly Riley-O', *Joe Slater's imperial songster* 15, Sydney, n.d., p. 33; see also Charles Norman, *When vaudeville was king: a soft shoe stroll down forget-me-not lane,* Spectrum, Melbourne, 1984, p. 58. For a discussion of why Whitburn played a larrikin with a blacked face: Melissa Bellanta, 'Leary kin: the Australian larrikin and the blackface minstrel dandy', *Journal of Social History* 42.3, 2009, pp. 677-695. For an English travel writer mocking larrikin style: Edward Kinglake, *The Australian at home: notes and anecdotes of life at the Antipodes,* Leadenhall Press, London, 1892, p. 107.

2. *Victorian Police Gazette (VPG),* 29 October 1872, p. 281 ('shabby appearance'); John Freeman, *Lights and shadows of Melbourne life,* Sampson Low, Marston, Searle & Rivington, London, 1888, p. 77; 30 September 1875, p. 285 ('larrikin named Kennedy ... wore dirty light tweed suit'); 13 August 1890, 250 ('dirty black suit'); 14 July 1874, p. 150 ('slovenly appearance').

3. *SMH*, 9 October 1891, p. 7. See also an image of a barefoot larrikin in Nicholas Caire, 'Swanston Street Looking South' (albumen silver print, c. 1880), held at State Library of Victoria. Thanks to Simon Sleight for these references.

4. *New South Wales Police Gazette* (*NSWPG*), 3 July 1889, p. 213.

5. Both mugshots come from Central Register of Male Prisoners, VA 1464, VPRS 515/P0, Public Records Office Victoria. George Jenkins: Unit 15 (1872), p. 351, prisoner no. 10024; John Kenworthy: Unit 13 (1871), p. 398, prisoner no. 9084. See these and other larrikin mugshots in Sleight, 'Interstitial acts', p. 240.

6. Norman Lindsay, 'The question of Ned Kelly's perfume', *Bulletin*, 18 March 1967, pp. 36–7; JS Allan, 'The larrikin', in his *Colonials Black and White*, published by the *Wellington Times*, Wellington NZ, 1895.

7. For contemporary quotes or images re larrikin dress, see: *Melbourne Punch*, 30 October 1873, p. 141; Nat Gould, *Town and bush: stray notes on Australia*, Routledge, London, 1896, p. 105; Henry A White, *Tales of crimes and criminals in Australia*, Ward & Downey, London, 1894, p. 283; see also those quoted in Margaret Maynard, *Fashioned from penury: dress as cultural practice in colonial Australia*, Cambridge University Press, Cambridge, 1994, pp. 92–4; Murray, *Larrikins*, 1973, pp. 32–5; Simon Sleight, 'Interstitial acts: urban space and the larrikin repertoire in late-Victorian Melbourne', *Australian Historical Studies* 40.2, 2009, pp 238–9; & Noel McLachlan, 'Larrikinism: an interpretation', MA Thesis, University of Melbourne, 1950, Appendix C, p. 161. Girls in police gazettes: *NSWPG*, 13 January 1886, p. 13 (Mary Powell); 28 July 1886, p. 229 (Emma McGrath); 9 March 1887, p. 80 (Annie Bennet); 27 April 1887, p. 131 (Sarah Ivison); 8 June 1887, p. 177 (Ada Croft); 19 August 1896, p. 295 (Margaret Davies); *VPG*, 23 September 1885, 264 (Edith Blackburn); *Queensland Police Gazette*, 23 May 1891, p. 222 (Deasy McWhor [sic]); *Newtown Chronicle* (Sydney), 13 May 1899, p. 6; *Collingwood Observer*, 18 July 1895, p. 3.

8. Evidence of Caroline Brackenregg, 'Report of the select committee into public charities, no. 2' ('Public charities report'), New South Wales, Parliament, Legislative Assembly, *Votes and Proceedings* 1873–4, p. 106; *BC,* 25 December 1885, p. 5. Bone ornaments: *Argus*, 31 January 1882, p. 4. Thanks to Simon Sleight for this reference.

9. William Lane, *The workingman's paradise: an Australian labour novel*, Edwards Dunlop, London, 1892, p. 35; Statement of Hugh Miller, in Papers of Sir William Charles Windeyer, Windeyer Family Papers, MLMSS 186 Box 21 Item 7, State Library NSW.

10. 'I Owe Ten Shillings to O'Grady', *Coggill Brothers Song Book*, Melbourne, n.d., p. 15. For a Brisbane woman paying off a jacket by instalments see *BC*, 7 June 1887, p. 6.

11. *NSWPG*, 4 March 1882, p. 69; Sleight, 'Interstitial acts', p. 241. On female shopping sprees: look out for Alana Piper's PhD on female criminals in Queensland and Victoria: forthcoming, University of Queensland.

12. *CM*, 2 October 1890, p. 2; *Newtown Chronicle* (Sydney), 13 May 1899, p. 6.

13. Daniel Miller, *Stuff*, Polity, Cambridge, 2010, p. 15; *BC*, 21 May 1880, p. 2 ('jaunty air'); *NSWPG*, 21 January 1885, p. 16 (Lippy Sam); *VPG*, 8 December 1874, p. 259 (Plucky Jim); *SMH*, 8 January 1885, p. 5 (Rorty Grey); Deposition of Frances Danby, Documents for coronial inquiry, 10 October 1883, p. 101, in *R v Williams*, Clerk of the Peace (CP), Supreme Court Darlinghurst, 9/6703, State Records New South Wales (SRNSW).

14. CM Gee, 'A larrikin hop', *The Ant* (Melbourne), 3 March 1892, p. 5. I am grateful to Simon Sleight for this article. Men dancing together: Lindsay, 'The question of Ned Kelly's perfume', p. 37. Examples of larrikins step dancing: *CM*, 26 June 1878, p. 2; *BC*, 7 October 1885, p. 9; *Argus*, 31 January 1882, p. 4; Sleight, 'Interstitial acts', p. 234. Link between boots and step-dancing: Marcus Clarke, 'Arcades Ambo' in *A colonial city: high and low life. Selected journalism of Marcus Clarke*, LT Hergenhan, (ed) University of Queensland Press, Brisbane, 1972, p. 70.

15. Frederick William Neitenstein Papers, Pictorial Material ca. 1883-1911, Pic. Acc. 1710, State Library NSW.

16. *VPG*, 8 April 1874, p. 77; 8 December 1874, p. 259; Deposition of Tom Smith, 13 September 1886, pp. 3–4, in *R v William Hill & eight ors*, Clerk of the Peace (CP), Central Criminal Court Sydney (CCCS), 9/6379, SRNSW.

17. Edward E Morris, *Austral English: a dictionary of Australasian words, phrases and usages*, London, Macmillan, 1898, p. 262; William Boyce, Prison record, Series NRS2138, Item 19/9835, SRNSW; Deposition of James Dever, in *R v Henry Doohan & ors*, CP, CCC, SRNSW; 9/6846, pp. 42–3; *SMH*, 5 July 1893, p. 7; James Dever, Prison record, Darlinghurst Gaol, Series NRS 2138, Item 3/6050, SRNSW. On Moran, see Sleight, 'Interstitial acts', p. 242. Partially-shaved London youth: Geoffrey Pearson, *Hooligans: a history of respectable fears*, Macmillan, London, 1983, p. 94.

18. Hamish Maxwell-Stuart, 'The search for the convict voice', *Tasmanian Historical Studies* 6.1, 1998, pp. 80–4; Hamish Maxwell-Stuart & James Bradley, 'Behold the man: power, observation and the tattooed convict', *Australian Studies* 12.1, 1997, pp. 71–97. George Howard, Prison record, 1889, Item

662645, Queensland State Archives; Norah Swan: *Queensland Police Gazette*, 3 September 1892, p. 316.

19. James Hardy Vaux, 'Vocabulary of the flash language' in *The memoirs of James Hardy Vaux,* ed. Noel McLachlan, Heinemann, London, 1964, pp. 140–1; Kay Daniels, 'The flash mob: rebellion, rough culture and sexuality in the female factories of Van Diemen's Land', *Australian Feminist Studies* 18, 1993, pp. 133–50; Thomas Livingstone Mitchell, *Journal of an expedition into the interior of tropical Australia,* Longman, Brown, Green & Longmans, London, 1848, p. 419–20; William Augustus Miles, *Registry of flash men*, NRS3406, SRNSW, digital copy available at srwww.records.nsw.gov.au/ebook/flashmen.asp, accessed 11 January 2011.

20. Jane Elliot, 'Was there a convict dandy? Convict consumer interests in Sydney, 1788–1815', *Australian Historical Studies* 26.104, 1995, p. 391; Charles Dickens, *Oliver Twist,* Lea & Blanchard, Philadelphia, 1839, p. 89; Tracy C Davis, *The economics of the British stage, 1800–1914,* Cambridge University Press, Cambridge, 2000, pp. 141–2.

21. Ian Jones, *Ned Kelly: a short life,* Lothian, South Melbourne, 2003, pp. 43–4 (Kelly called 'flash'); Alex McDermott, 'Who said the Kelly letters? The question of authorship and the nature of wild language', *Australian Historical Studies* 33.118, 2002, p. 267 (Kelly's rhetorical style); Keith McMenomy (ed), *Ned Kelly: the authentic illustrated story,* Curry O'Neil Ross, Melbourne, 1984, p. 83, 143 (clothes worn by Ned Kelly and Greta Mob); *Argus,* 12 December 1878, p. 5 (bush dandies); *SMH,* 26 November 1880, p. 3 (Kate Kelly on Oliver Twist).

22. Mary the Larrikin: Jones, *Ned Kelly,* p. 181; John Meredith & Bill Scott, *Ned Kelly: after a century of acrimony,* Lansdowne Press, Melbourne, 1980, p. 101. Retinue: *Argus,* 9 November 1880, p. 6. 'Lairies': *Daily Telegraph* (Melbourne), 27 November 1880, p. 6.

23. John Rickard, 'Lovable larrikins and awful ockers', *Journal of Australian Studies* 56, 1998, p. 79; see also Joan Fox, 'Designing differences', in Verity Burgmann & Jenny Lee (eds), *Making a life: a people's history of Australian since 1788,* vol. 2, McPhee Gribble, Melbourne, 1988, pp. 26–28.

24. Maynard, *Fashioned from penury,* especially p. 160; Clarke, 'Nasturtium villas', in *A colonial city,* pp. 327–31.

25. Peter Bailey, *Popular culture and performance in the Victorian city,* Cambridge University Press, Cambridge, 1998, pp. 113, 115–6; Shane White & Graeme White, *Stylin': African American expressive culture from its beginnings to the zoot suit,* Cornell University Press, Ithaca & London, 1999, pp 85–124. Mashers & dudes: Brent Shannon, *The cut of his coat: men, dress and consumer*

culture in Britain, 1860–1914, University of Ohio Press, Athens OH, 2006, pp. 137–54; 'The butterfly dude' and 'The jolly dude' in *Australian Melodist* 18, Melbourne, n. d.

26. Gareth Stedman Jones, 'The "cockney" and the nation, 1780–1988', in D Feldman & GS Jones (eds), *Metropolis, London: histories and representations since 1800,* Routledge, London, 1989, pp. 294–5; Christopher Breward, *The hidden consumer: masculinities, fashion and city life* 1860–1914, Manchester University Press, Manchester, 1999, p. 232.

27. Richard Waterhouse, *From minstrel show to vaudeville: the Australian popular stage 1788–1914,* University of New South Wales Press, Sydney, 1990, pp. 89–91; 147–9; see also Bellanta, 'Leary kin'.

28. John Stanley James, *The Vagabond papers,* Michael Cannon (ed), Melbourne University Press, Melbourne, 1969, pp. 211, 231. Boxing photographs: Tom Fatts vs Hock Keys, Golden Gate Club, Sydney, 29 November 1898, nla. pic-vn3639168, & Jack McGowan vs Bob Turner, Gaiety Hall, Sydney, 24 November 1902, nla.pic-vn3260519, both in Thomas Arnold Boxing Collection, National Library of Australia, Canberra. Larrikin in masher hat: Deposition of Tom Smith, 13 September 1886.

Chapter 6

1. *Argus,* 25 October 1899, p. 11; 19 March 1910, p. 21; *Adelaide Advertiser,* 22 December 1924, p. 13.

2. Graeme Davison, 'The city-bred child and urban reform in Melbourne, 1900–1940', in Peter Williams (ed), *Social process and the city,* George Allen & Unwin, Sydney, 1983, pp. 143–8.

3. As in chapter 3, my arguments here are informed by Chris McConville's insightful discussion in 'From "criminal class" to "underworld"', in Graeme Davison, David Dunstan & Chris McConville (eds), *The outcasts of Melbourne: essays in social history,* Allen & Unwin, Sydney, 1985, pp. 69–90.

4. *Argus,* 18 March 1910, p. 8 (multiple police preparing for fight); 13 April 1910, p 10 (Lincoln Sq.); 29 March 1910, p. 6 (concealed weapon); 1 October 1910, p. 18 (football clubs).

5. *Record* (South Melbourne), 5 May 1905, p. 2; 22 July 1905, p. 4; *Richmond Guardian (RG),* 1 June 1907, p. 2; 6 November 1909, p. 2; 2 July 1910, p. 2; 8 June 1912, p. 2 (street football). Janet McCalman, *Struggletown: public and private life in Richmond, 1900–1965,* Hyland House, Melbourne, 1998, p. 26. Richard Stremski, *Kill for Collingwood,* Allen & Unwin, 1986, p. 74; Telephone conversation between Melissa Bellanta and Richard Stremski,

7 December 2010. Unfortunately, the taped interview that Stremski conducted with Harold Rumney has been lost.

6. *Record*, 26 January 1918, p. 2.

7. *Record,* 16 March 1918, p. 3; 27 April 1918, p. 2; 29 June 1918, p. 2; 23 November 1918, p. 2 (Wayside Inn). *Argus,* 10 June 1901, p. 6 (White Rose Football Club). *Argus,* 5 August 1901, p. 3; 9 March 1903, p. 5; 18 April 1904, p. 6; 21 January 1905, p. 3; Brief for prosecution, *R v Denis Tobin,* VPRS 30/P/O Unit 1398, File 371, Public Records Office Victoria (PROV) (White Roses).

8. Jack Dyer, as told to Brian Hansen, *Captain Blood,* Stanley Paul, London, 1965, p. 22; *RG,* cited in McCalman, *Struggletown,* p. 132.

9. The VFL was formed at the end of the season in 1896 after the VFA's strongest teams broke away to form their own competition. The VFL's eight founding clubs were Carlton, Collingwood, Essendon, Fitzroy, Geelong, Melbourne, St Kilda and South Melbourne. The teams that continued to play for the VFA were Richmond, North Melbourne, Port Melbourne, Footscray and Williamstown (joined in the early 1900s by Northcote and Brighton and in the next decade by Hawthorn). Richmond ended up defecting to the VFL in 1908, while North Melbourne, Footscray and Hawthorn came on board in 1925. On the relationship between the VFA and VFL, see Leonie Sandercock & Ian Turner, *Up where, Cazaly? The great Australian game,* Granada, St Albans, 1981, pp 38–53.

10. Marc Fiddian, *Forever Fitzroy: a history of the Brunswick Street Oval,* Galaxy Print & Design, Hastings Vic., 2000, p. 7; Rob Hess, 'The Victorian Football League takes over, 1897–1914', in Rob Hess & Bob Stewart (eds), *More than a game: an unauthorised history of Australian Rules football,* Melbourne University Press, Melbourne, 1998, pp. 86–7.

11. *Argus,* 28 August 1899, p. 6; *Illustrated Sporting & Dramatic News,* 23 June 1907, p. 11; see also Ted Dyson, *Benno and some of the push,* NSW Bookstall, Sydney, 1911, ch. 11. On more general rowdyism at games: June Senyard, 'Marvellous Melbourne, consumerism and the rise of sports spectating', in Matthew Nicholson (ed), *Fanfare: spectator culture and Australian Rules football,* Australian Society for Sports History, Melbourne, 2005, pp. 25–40; Sandercock & Turner, *Up where, Cazaly?,* pp. 36–7; 85–6; June Senyard, '1944 and all that', in Fitzroy Historical Society (ed), *Fitzroy: Melbourne's first suburb,* Melbourne University Press, Melbourne, 1991, pp. 214–32.

12. Chris McConville, 'Football, liquor and gambling in the 1920s', *Sporting Traditions* 1.1, 1984, pp. 34–55; *Argus,* 11 August 1919, p. 8; 22 August 1923, p. 9.

13. Richard Cashman, *Sport in the national imagination: Australian sport in the*

Federation decade, Walla Walla Press, Sydney, 2002, pp. 53–4; *Referee,* cited in Chris Cunneen, 'Men, money, market, match', in David Headon & Lex Marinos (eds), *League of a nation,* ABC Books, Sydney, 1996, p. 23; George Parsons, 'Capitalism, class and community: "civilising" and sanitising the people's game', also in *League of a nation,* pp. 8–15.

14. Murray Phillips, 'Football, class and war: the rugby codes in New South Wales, 1907–1918' in John Nauright & Timothy JL Chandler (eds), *Making men: rugby and masculine identity,* Frank Cass, London, 1996, pp. 158–63; Chris Cunneen, 'The rugby war: the early history of rugby league in New South Wales', in David Headon, (ed), *The best ever Australian sports writing: a 200 year collection,* Black Inc, Melbourne, 2001, pp. 313–25; Max & Reet Howell, *The greatest game under the sun: the history of rugby league in Queensland,* Queensland Rugby Football League, Brisbane, n.d.; Richard Waterhouse, *Private pleasures, public leisure: a history of Australian popular culture since 1788,* Longman, Melbourne, 1995, p. 78.

15. Andrew Moore, *The mighty Bears: a social history of North Sydney rugby league,* Macmillan, Sydney, 1996, pp. 35–6; Chris Cunneen, 'Messenger, Herbert Henry (Dally) (1883–1959)', *Australian Dictionary of Biography* 10, Melbourne University Press, Melbourne, 1986, pp. 488–9; Phillips, 'Football, class and war', p. 162; Tony Stephens, *Larrikin days: 100 years of growing up in an Australian suburb,* Nicholson Street Public School P&C Association, Sydney, 1983, pp. 31–2.

16. Interview with Haynes, Collingwood Oral History Project (COHP), Transcript held at Collingwood Library. Interviews with Hickey and Drummond, NSW Bicentennial Oral History Project (NSW BOHP), MLMSS 5163, State Library of NSW, Sydney.

17. Interview with Maybery, COHP. For other examples of residents dismissing mobs/pushes as non-serious, see: Interviews with Arthur Towers & Jim Hocking, COHP; Millie Weston, NSW BOHP; Reminiscences of Bill Monagle of Montague, cited in Susan Priestley, *South Melbourne: a history,* Melbourne University Press, Melbourne, 1995, p. 318; Surveys by Miss Sheldon (Folder 1 no. 8); Mrs Krone (Folder 4 no. 22); & Mr Smith (Folder 2 no. 17), in Ronald Lawson, 'Notes for a PhD thesis', 1970, F408, Fryer Library, University of Queensland.

18. Murray Johnson, 'Larrikin "push", 1902', in Raymond Evans & Carole Ferrier (eds), *Radical Brisbane: an unruly history,* Vulgar Press, Melbourne, 2004, p. 125; *Argus,* 2 April 1906, p. 4; *SMH,* 5 September 1904, p. 6.

19. Hayes, cited in David Hickie, *Chow Hayes: gunman,* Allen & Unwin, Sydney, 1990, p. 79.

20. On Cranshaw: *Argus,* 18 April 1904, p. 6; 12 May 1904, p. 7; 19 May 1904, p. 7; 6 February 1905, p. 6. On Hill: *Adelaide Advertiser,* 21 September 1901, p. 7; 16 October 1901, p. 5; *Re the Death of George Hill,* 5 September 1901, Police Records, VPRS 30/P/O, Unit 1265 File 455, PROV.

21. On young people in the 'transition state': Charles Fahey, Patricia Griffiths & Melanie Raymond, 'The other side of "Marvellous Melbourne"', in Jane Beer et al, *Colonial frontiers and family fortunes: two studies of rural and urban Victoria,* History Department, University of Melbourne, 1989, p. 144. On debates about the female age of consent and its links to notions of feminine adolescence, see: Catherine Driscoll, *Girls: feminine adolescence in popular culture and cultural theory,* Columbia University Press, New York, 1992, ch. 1. On adolescence more generally, see: Christine Griffin, *Representations of youth: the study of youth and adolescence in Britain and America,* Polity Press, Cambridge, 1993, pp. 1–26; Simon Sleight, 'The territory of youth: young people & public space in Melbourne, c. 1870–1901', PhD Thesis, Monash University, 2008, p. 84; Ann Larson, *Growing up in Melbourne: family life in the late nineteenth century,* Australian National University, Canberra, 1994, pp. 146–7.

22. John Springhall, *Coming of age: adolescence in Britain 1860-1960,* Gill and Macmillan, Dublin, 1986, p. 28; Jan Kociumbas, *Australian childhood: a history,* Allen & Unwin, Sydney, 1997, pp. 132–42.

23. Davison, 'The city-bred child', pp. 143–74; Bryan Jamieson, 'Brisbane Institute of Social Science' in *Radical Brisbane,* pp. 130–1; Sleight, 'Territory of youth', pp 107–8; John Ramsland, 'Onians, Edith Charlotte (1866–1955)', *Australian Dictionary of Biography* 11, Melbourne University Press, Melbourne, 1988, pp. 88–89.

24. E.g. the claims of Reverend William George Taylor of Sydney's Central Methodist Mission: WG Taylor, *The life story of an Australian evangelist,* Epsworth Press, London, 1921, pp. 224–32.

25. Stephen Garton, 'Frederick William Neitenstein: juvenile reformatory and prison reform in New South Wales, 1878–1909; *Journal of the Royal Australian Historical Society* 75.1, 1989, pp. 51–64; Chris Cunneen & Rob White, *Juvenile justice: youth and crime in Australia,* 3rd edn, Oxford University Press, Melbourne, 2007, pp. 13–5. On advocacy of the lash as a larrikin cure: Gregory D Woods, *A history of criminal law in New South Wales: the colonial period, 1788–1900,* Federation Press, Sydney, n.d., pp. 324–6; JB Castieau, *The difficulties of my position: the diaries of prison governor John Buckley Castieau, 1855–1884,* ed. Mark Finnane, National Library of Australia, Canberra, 2004, pp. 1012.

26. Robert van Krieken, *Children and the state: social control and the formation of*

Australian child welfare, Allen & Unwin, Sydney, 1992, pp. 84–110; Kerry Carrington, *Offending youth: sex, crime and justice,* Federation Press, Sydney, 2009, pp. 26–8.

27. I make this very general summation of trends in policing juveniles on the basis of: Mark Finnane & Stephen Garton, 'The work of policing: social relations and the criminal justice system in Queensland, 1880–1914. Part 2', *Labour History* 63, 1992, p. 57; & Mark Finnane, 'Larrikins, delinquents and cops: police and young people in Australia', in Christine Alder & Rob White (eds), *Police and young people in Australia,* Cambridge University Press, Cambridge, 1994, pp. 7–26. On the use of the 'kick up the backside' as a form of discretionary policing, see: Interview with William Sarnich, born 1904, NSW BOHP; Interview with George Cairns, born 1914, in City West Development Corporation, *Interviews with residents of Pyrmont and Ultimo,* 1996, MLOH 224, State Library NSW; Interview with Elizabeth Haynes, COHP.

28. *RG,* 21 May 1910, p. 2.

29. McCalman, *Struggletown,* ch. 1.

30. Ian Turner & Leonie Sandercock, *In union is strength: a history of trade unions in Australia 1788–1983,* 3rd edn, Thomas Nelson, Melbourne, 1983, pp. 55–9; Charles Fahey, 'Unskilled male labour and the beginnings of labour market regulation, Victoria 1901–1914', *Australian Historical Studies* 119, 2002, pp. 157–60.

31. Andrew Brown-May, *Melbourne street life: the itinerary of our days,* Australian Scholarly/Arcadia & Museum Victoria, Melbourne, 1998, p. xvii.

32. Interview with Sarnich.

33. *RG,* 21 May 1910, p. 2; McCalman, *Struggletown,* p. 132.

34. Wendy Lowenstein & Tom Hills, *Under the hook: Melbourne waterside workers remember working lives and class war, 1900–1980,* Melbourne, Melbourne Bookworkers, 1982, pp. 27–8.

35. Billy Pascoe, cited in Sue Rosen, *We never had a hotbed of crime! Life in twentieth-century South Sydney,* Hale & Iremonger, Sydney, 2000, p. 179.

36. McCalman, *Struggletown,* pp. 28–33.

37. Bert Hope, cited in Senyard, '1944 and all that', p. 223; see also Rob Hess, '"Ladies are specially Invited": women in the culture of Australian rules football', in J A Mangan & John Nauright (eds), *Sport in Australasian society: past and present,* Frank Cass, London, 2000, pp. 111–141; Hess, 'The VFL takes over'.

38. *Record,* 30 December 1911, p. 2; Matt Florence in Dawn Buckberry (ed), *An oral and visual history of early Paddington. Living memories from the heart of*

Brisbane, Red Hill Paddington Community Centre & the Paddington History Group, Red Hill, 1999, p. 98.

39. *RG,* 24 June 1911, p. 4; 1 June 1912, p. 2; Herbert Moran, *Viewless winds: being the recollections and digressions of an Australian surgeon,* London, 1939, p. 92.

40. *Collingwood Mercury,* 26 June 1878, p. 2; Gail Bederman, *Manliness and civilisation: a cultural history of gender and race in the United States, 1880–1917,* University of Chicago Press, Chicago & London, 1995, pp. 16-7; John Tosh, *A man's place: masculinity and the middle-class home in Victorian England,* St Edmundsbury Press, Bury St Edmonds, 2007, ch. 8.

41. Interviews with Hickey and Cairns. 19th-century push fights: Chris McConville, 'Outcast Melbourne: social deviance in the city, 1880–1914', MA Thesis, University of Melbourne, 1974, pp. 76–7; *SMH,* 14 June 1893, p. 3; *Argus,* 19 March 1910, p. 21; X.O. (pseud.), 'Australian pushes', Hayes Collection, Fryer Library, University of Queensland, p. 19.

42. Hickie, *Chow Hayes,* pp. 14, 23, 79. According to Chow (b. 1911), the youth attacked by his cousin died. Contrary to this, newspaper reports indicate that the youth was still alive, though slurred in speech, at the time of Bollard's trial: *SMH,* 25 May 1925, p. 4; 26 May 1925, p. 6; 8 May 1925, p. 5.

43. Harold James Patrick Smith, Prisoner No. 35351, & William Joseph Flynn, Prisoner No. 35352, both in Central Register of Male Prisoners, VPRS 515/P0, Unit 69, pp. 312-3, PROV; *Argus,* 12 December 1919, p. 9.

44. Cinema shooting: *Argus,* 22 November 1920, p. 6; 7 December 1920, p. 8. Drive-by: *SMH,* 5 December 1925, p. 16. Other push gun-fights: McConville, 'From "criminal class"', p. 75; *Argus,* 21 February 1920, p. 21 (Checkers fire at member of Woolpacks); 28 June 1920, p. 8 (Northcote Imps).

45. Peter Doyle, interviewed for 'Cops, crims and consorting' on Radio National's *Hindsight,* 6 September 2009. (The transcript for this program is available at http://www.abc.net.au/rn/hindsight/stories/2009/2661854. htm); Martin Crotty, *Making the Australian male: middle-class masculinity 1870–1920,* Melbourne University Press, Melbourne, 2000, pp. 27–8.

46. Ramón Spaaij, 'Men like us, boys like them: violence, masculinity, and collective identity in football hooliganism', *Journal of Sport and Social Issues* 32, 2008, pp. 381–2.

Chapter 7

1. Sidney Baker, *The Australian language,* 2nd edn, Currawong Publishing, Sydney, 1966, pp. 120, 94; Norman Lindsay, 'The question of Ned Kelly's

perfume', *Bulletin,* 18 March 1967, pp. 36–7. On rumours about Steve Hart cross-dressing, see: Lucy Chesser, *Parting with my sex: cross-dressing, inversion and sexuality in Australian cultural life,* Sydney University Press, Sydney, 2008, pp. 71–2.

2. Lindsay, 'The question of Ned Kelly's perfume'.

3. Matt Cook, *London and the culture of homosexuality, 1885–1914,* Cambridge University Press, Cambridge, 2003; Brent Shannon, *The cut of his coat: men, dress, and consumer culture in Britain, 1860-1914,* Ohio University Press, Athens OH, 2006, pp. 174–90. On Prince Albert Victor: Christopher Breward, *The hidden consumer: masculinities, fashion and city life 1860–1914,* Manchester University Press, Manchester, 1999, pp. 246–53.

4. Chesser, *Parting with my sex,* pp. 172–88.

5. Clive Moore, *Sunshine and rainbows: the development of gay and lesbian culture in Queensland,* University of Queensland Press, Brisbane, 2001, pp. 60-73; Yorick Smaal, 'Coding desire: the emergence of a homosexual subculture in Queensland, 1890–1914', *Queensland Review* 14.2, 2007, pp. 13–28. For a comparative discussion focused on Sydney, see: Walter Fogarty, '"Certain habits": the development of the concept of the homosexual in New South Wales law', in Robert Aldrich & Garry Wotherspoon (eds), *Gay perspectives: essays in Australian gay culture,* Department of Economic History, University of Sydney, 1992, pp. 59–76.

6. Robert French, *Camping by a billabong: gay and lesbian stories from Australian history,* Blackwattle Press, Sydney, 1993, pp. 43–6; Moore, *Sunshine and rainbows,* pp. 85–6.

7. Margaret Maynard, *Fashioned from penury: dress as cultural practice in colonial Australia,* Cambridge University Press, Cambridge, 1994, p. 153; Marion Fletcher, *Costume in Australia, 1788–1901,* Oxford University Press, Melbourne, 1984, pp. 186–7.

8. Yorick Smaal, 'More than mates? Masculinity, homosexuality, and the formation of an embryonic subculture in Queensland, 1890–1914', MPhil Thesis, University of Queensland, 2004, pp. 97–8.

9. I am grateful to Yorick Smaal for supplying me with a transcript of the police documents in this case (Depositions, John Stuart Marshall, *Briefs, depositions and associated papers in criminal cases heard,* 1 May 1907 to 30 May 1907, SCT/CC184, Queensland State Archives). I am also grateful to him for many of the ideas developed in this chapter concerning the interrelationship between male larrikins and homosexual men.

10. Chesser, *Parting with my sex,* pp. 185–6. For an earlier example of same-sex activity among the Hobart Female Factory's 'flash mob', see Daniels, 'The

flash mob'. On homosexuality within the AIF, see: Peter Stanley, *Bad characters: sex, crime, mutiny, murder and the Australian Imperial Force,* Pier 9, Sydney, 2010, pp. 141–4.

11. Depositions, *Re the death of George Hill,* 5 September 1901, Police Records, VPRS 30/P/O Unit 1265 File 455, Public Records Office Victoria.

12. Edward Dyson, *Fact'ry 'ands,* Robertson, Melbourne, 1906, p. 160 (Chiller Green in bob-tail jacket and red tie); *Richmond Guardian,* 15 January 1910, p. 2 (Rowena Parade Rats push in red neckerchiefs).

13. Walter Gentle and Thomas Pritchard, Darlinghurst Gaol Photographic Description Book 1897–1898 (3/6062), NRS 2138, Reel 5107 p179–80, State Records NSW.

14. Stone, *Jonah,* Methuen, London, 1911, pp. 67–8.

15. Although this photographs is undated, it features the same style of clothes as other photographs taken by Joseph Bane dated 1903. The majority of his photographs given to the State Library of Victoria (SLV) by later family members seem to have been taken on a single day. SLV Accession no. H93.385/38. I am grateful to Simon Sleight for this.

16. Andrew Brown-May, *Melbourne street life: the itinerary of our days,* Australian Scholarly/Arcadia & Museum Victoria, Melbourne, 1998, p. xvii.

17. Interview with Bert Hickey, NSW Bicentennial Oral History Project (NSW BOHP), MLMSS 5163, State Library NSW; *Argus,* 29 April 1919, p. 4.

18. Keith Stanley Maxwell and Charles James Berry, Special Photograph number 284, 10 January 1921, Parramatta Police Station, Sydney, photographer unknown, New South Wales Police Forensic Photography Archive, Justic & Police Museum, Historic Houses Trust DES_FP07_0037_005.

19. Doyle, *Crooks like us,* p. 185; Hugh Anderson, *Larrikin crook: the rise and fall of Squizzy Taylor,* Jacaranda Press, Brisbane, 1971, p. 123.

20. David Hickie, *Chow Hayes: gunman,* Angus & Robertson, Sydney, 1990; Doyle, *Crooks like us,* pp. 233–4.

21. Eddie McMillan, John Frederick 'Chow' Hayes, Thomas Esmond Bollard, Special Photograph number 2957, 6 November 1930, Central Police Station Sydney, photographer unknown, New South Wales Police Forensic Photography Archive, Justice & Police Museum, Historic Houses Trust DES_FP07_0141_004.

22. *Theatre* (Sydney), 1 January 1919, pp. 1–2; Clay Djubal, 'What oh tonight: the methodology factor and pre-1930s variety theatre', PhD Thesis, University of Queensland, 2005, pp. 259–96.

23. Kath Leahy, *Lords and larrikins: the actor's place in the making of Australia,* Currency Press, Sydney, 2010, p. 98.

24. Clay Djubal, 'Jack Kearns', 'Arthur Tauchert' & '*Dockum Street Woolloomooloo*', all entries on the AUSTLIT database's Australian Popular Theatre subset, austlit.edu.au.ezproxy1.library.uq.edu.au/specialist/Datasets/AustPopTheatre.

25. Graeme Seal, *Inventing ANZAC: the digger and national mythology*, University of Queensland Press, Brisbane, 2004, p. 13 & throughout.

26. 'Horseferry Road', in Stanley, *Bad characters*, p. 145.

27. Seal, *Inventing Anzac*, p. 17; LL Robson, 'The Australian soldier: formation of a stereotype', in M McKiernan & M Browne (eds), *Australia two centuries of war and peace*, Australian War Memorial in association with Allen & Unwin, Sydney, 1988, pp. 313–38. Industrial workers from New South Wales were the highest single occupational/state group in the AIF: LL Robson, 'The origin and character of the first AIF, 1914–18', *Historical Studies* 15.61, 1973, p. 745.

28. *Record,* 10 August 1918, p. 2.

29. Clay Djubal, '"For the duration": the fashioning of an imagined Australian national identity on the variety stage between 1914–1918', unpublished manuscript, available online on Clay Djubal's Australian Variety Theatre Archive: http://ozvta.com/publications-3-mixed-bag/.

30. Clay Djubal, 'Jim Gerald', on the AUSTLIT database's Australian Popular Theatre subset; Richard Fotheringham, 'Laughing it off: Australian stage comedy after World War I', *History Australia* 7.1, 2010, pp. 3.1–3.20.

31. CJ Dennis, *The moods of Ginger Mick,* Angus & Robertson, Sydney, 1916, pp. ix, 30, 31; Seal, *Inventing Anzac,* pp. 75–77.

32. Stanley, *Bad characters,* pp. 214–6; Herbert Nicholls, 'The Anzac's forebears', in *Anzac memorial,* 2nd edn, Returned Soldiers' Association, Sydney, 1917, p. 282.

33. In November 1918, for example, a returned soldier called Patrick O'Hehir was arrested after inciting a crowd to assault a police officer outside the Wayside Inn in South Melbourne. After deliberating on whether or not it was right to imprison a 'young man who had done his duty', the local magistrate decided that the 'larrikins of Montague' had to be taught a lesson in how to behave: *Record,* 23 November 1918, p. 2. See also *Argus,* 22 July 1919, p. 5, 23 July 1919, p. 9; Marilyn Lake, 'The power of Anzac', in *Australia two centuries of war and peace,* pp. 210–22; Stanley, *Bad characters,* pp. 230–4.

34. Marilyn Lake, 'The desire for a Yank: sexual relations between Australian women and American servicemen during World War II', *Journal of the History of Sexuality* 2.4, 1992, pp. 621–33. For select examples of *Smith's Weekly* flapper cartoons, see: *Smith's Weekly,* 7 February 1925, p. 14; 21 November

1925, p. 26; George Blaikie, *Remember Smith's Weekly?*, Rigby, Adelaide, 1975, p. 22.

Afterword

1. Amy Simmons, 'Canberra chameleon: Rudd gets saucy', *ABC news online,* 10 June 2009, abc.net.au/news/stories/2009/06/10/2594427.htm.

2. The fact that Australian bohemians began claiming a familiarity with a larrikin-like milieu in the 1890s, adopting a rough vernacular and hanging out in pubs, has been discussed by Tony Moore in his history of Australian bohemianism. He calls this distinctively Australian bohemian style the 'larrikin carnivalesque'. Moore, 'Australia's bohemian tradition', PhD Thesis, University of Sydney, 2007; Tony Moore, *The Barry McKenzie movies,* Currency Press, Sydney, 2005, ch. 4.

3. Lennie Lower, *Here's Luck,* Angus & Robertson, Sydney, 1930; Bill Hornadge, *Lennie Lower: he made a nation laugh,* Angus & Robertson, Sydney, 1993; Cyril Pearl, 'Lennie Lower: a memoir', in Lennie Lower, *Here's Lower,* ed. Tom Thompson, Hale & Iremonger, Sydney, 1983, pp. 8–11; Peter Kirkpatrick, *The sea coast of Bohemia: literary life in Sydney's Roaring Twenties,* University of Queensland Press, Brisbane, 1992, p. 150. Thanks to Peter Spearritt for introducing me to *Here's Luck.*

4. The Push: Judy Ogilvie, *The Push: an impressionist memoir,* Primavera, Sydney, 1995, front matter; see also Anne Coombs, *Sex and anarchy: the life and death of the Sydney Push,* Viking, Melbourne, 1996. The term *poet manqués* was used by Barry Humphries to describe the Sydney Push: cited in Elizabeth Farrelly, 'When the Push came to shove', *SMH,* 4 April 2009. The Drift: Barry Humphries, 'Arthur Boyd: a life', in David Marr (ed), *The best Australian essays 2008,* Black Inc., Melbourne, 2008, p. 164. On bodgies and widgies as descendants of early larrikinism: Jon Stratton, *The young ones: working-class culture, consumption and the category of youth,* Black Swan Press, Perth, 1992.

5. Katharine Brisbane, 'From Williamson to Williamson: Australia's larrikin theatre', *Theatre Quarterly* 7.26, 1977, pp. 56–60; Jonathan Bollen, Adrian Kiernander & Bruce Parr, *Men at play: masculinities in Australian theatre since the 1950s,* Rodopi, Amsterdam, 2008, pp. 40–1; Alan McKee, *Australian television: a genealogy of great moments,* Oxford University Press, Melbourne, 2001, chapters 1, 4 & 7; Moore, *The Barry McKenzie movies,* p. 80, n. 52.

6. Moore, *The Barry McKenzie movies,* pp. 57, 73–76. Entry for 'Down Under' on the *Songfacts* website, songfacts.com/detail.php?id=2962.

7. 'Larrikin Records and Larrikin Music founder speaks out', Undated media release available on Warren Fahey's *Australian folklore unit* website: warren-fahey.com/larrikin-5.htm. Kath Leahy, *Lords and larrikins: the actor's role in the making of Australia,* Currency House, Sydney, 2009, p. 155; Catherine Lumby, *Alvin Purple,* Currency Press, Sydney, 2008.

8. Pearl, 'Lennie Lower', p. 8; Pat Sheil, 'Twang! That's my side splitting', *SMH,* 20 September 2003. Mo: Leahy, *Lords and larrikins,* pp. 97–118.

9. Dawn Fraser, *Dawn: one hell of a life,* rev. ed., Hodder Headline, Sydney, 2002, p. 3; Murray Phillips & Gary Osmond, 'Filmic sports history: Dawn Fraser, swimming and Australian national identity', *International Journal of the History of Sport* 26.14, 2009, pp. 2129–37. Whitten: John Rickard, 'Lovable larrikins and awful ockers', *Journal of Australian Studies,* 56, 1998, pp. 83–4. Hogan: Leahy, *Lords and larrikins,* pp. 156–8; McKee, *Australian television,* pp. 118–35. Clinton Walker, *Highway to hell: the life and death of Bon Scott,* Picador, Sydney, 2007, pp. xii, 18, 20, 34. On Rude: see his website, rude. com.au/index.php, accessed 10 May 2011. On Wilson: Kevin Bloody Wilson and Gavin Miller, *Dilligaf: The life and rhymes of Kevin Bloody Wilson,* Allen & Unwin, Sydney, 2010. On the appeal of larrikinism in other mining towns, including coal-mining towns in New South Wales's Hunter Valley: Andrew Metcalfe, *For freedom and dignity: historical agency and class structures in the coalfields of NSW,* Allen & Unwin, Sydney & London, 1988, pp. 73–88.

10. Synopsis of *The Wog Boy* on *Urban cinefile: the world of film in Australia,* urbancinefile.com.au/home/view.asp?a=3293&s=reviews; Interview with Ernie Dingo on *George Negus Tonight,* 8 September 2003, abc.net.au/gnt/ history/Transcripts/s941430.htm. Larrikin Sturt: see ch. 1 n. 10. 'Chooky dancers take larrikin act to China', ABC News, 8 February 2011, abc.net. au/news/video/2011/02/08/3133102.htm. Hargreaves: Rickard, 'Lovable larrikins', pp. 78, 84. Bundy Bear: Mark Dapin, 'Triumph of the spirit', *Good Weekend, SMH* supplement, 28 August 2010, p. 50.

11. Bernard Zuel, 'Let there be rock stars, *SMH, Spectrum* supplement, 2–3 October 2010, p. 10.

12. Hopcraft: 'Family, friends mourn "lovable larrikin"', *Knox Leader,* 9 April 2010. Creed: Ren Lanzon, 'George was a larrikin', *Gladstone News,* 3 December 2010. 'Hines funeral a tribute to a hero, larrikin and father', *Geelong Advertiser,* 4 September 2009. Hopkins: Tyron Butson, 'Farewell to "a soldier, a friend, a larrikin"', *Age,* 28 March 2009. 'Larrikin Chipp remembered at funeral', *SMH,* 2 September 2006; see also Rickard, 'Lovable larrikins', pp. 78–9.

Index